Technology and the City

The interplay between smart urban technologies and city development is a relatively uncharted territory. *Technology and the City* aims to fill that gap, exploring the growing importance of smart technologies and systems in contemporary cities, and providing an in-depth understanding of both theoretical and practical aspects of smart urban technology adoption and its implications for our cities.

Beginning with an elaboration of the historical significance of technologies in economic growth, social progress and urban development, Yigitcanlar introduces the most prominent smart urban information technologies. The book showcases significant smart city practices from across the globe that use smart urban technologies and systems most effectively. It explores the role of these technologies and asks how they can be adopted into the planning, development and management processes of cities for sustainable urban futures. This pioneering volume contributes to the conceptualisation and practice of smart technology and system adoption in our cities by disseminating both conceptual and empirical research findings with real-world best practice applications.

With a multidisciplinary approach to themes of technology and urban development, this book is a key reference source for scholars, practitioners, consultants, city officials, policymakers and urban technology enthusiasts.

Tan Yigitcanlar is an Associate Professor at the School of Civil Engineering and Built Environment, Queensland University of Technology, Brisbane, Australia.

T0384232

'This book is an important and exciting addition to the growing literature of interrelations between technology and cities. It is a detailed account on the history, present and future of societal developments caused by technological advancements. This book will be a most welcome addition to all students, researchers and practitioners working with topics of urban planning, economic geography and civil engineering.' — *Tommi Inkinen, Professor of Economic Geography, University of Helsinki, Finland*

'For those who want to know more about the evolution of urban technologies, this well-written book offers a comprehensive overview over the state-of-the art in smart city development. Arguing that smart city development processes need to be more open, participatory and collaborative, Yigitcanlar calls for more technologically and economically balanced approaches by responsible city governments. The author's detailed insights into the numerous applications of smart technologies in urban development are another impressive outcome of his sedulous explorations into the evolution of knowledge development in cities.' — *Klaus R. Kunzmann, Professor Emeritus, Technical University of Dortmund, Germany*

'With *Technology and the City*, Tan Yigitcanlar delivers a comprehensive account of smart cities that translates the buzz of the term into a rigorous treatment of the topic. On the basis of discussing smart city systems and applications, it is the resulting implications that pose new and exciting questions for the reader to ponder.' — *Professor Marcus Foth, Director, Urban Informatics Research Lab, Queensland University of Technology, Australia*

'The term "smart cities" has become as ubiquitous as the technology that makes smart cities possible. In this ambitious book, Tan Yigitcanlar offers a vast panorama of urban development ranging from the Stone Age to an urban future infused with, and disrupted by, the information and communication technologies first developed in the late twentieth century. The author not only describes the emergence of smart cities and details how they work, he also gives a detailed description of the operation of smart cities in urban centers around the world and the implications of smart cites for urban economies, environments and quality of life. In the final chapter, Yigitcanlar speculates on the future of smart technologies and smart cities and the effects they will have on the planet itself. This chapter will, I believe, prove prescient and will provide ways for scholars and practitioners to conceive of and use smart technologies to confront the myriad of issues facing an increasingly urbanised world.' — *Richard E. Hanley, Editor, Journal of Urban Technology, The City University of New York, USA*

'*Technology and the City* is a timely and thoughtful analysis of the complex relationships between urban life and the technologies that shape cities. There have always been smart cities, and this volume shows how technology has affected urban life from ancient times to the present. Of note is the detailed analysis of the technological systems that form urban infrastructures, and are used to manage modern cities. It is a valuable text for scholars and students interested in how cities evolve and function.' — *Mark Wilson, Associate Director of School of Planning, Design and Construction, and Professor of Urban & Regional Planning/Geography, Michigan State University, USA*

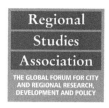

Regions and Cities
Series Editor in Chief
Susan M. Christopherson, *Cornell University, USA*

Editors
Maryann Feldman, *University of Georgia, USA*
Gernot Grabher, *HafenCity University Hamburg, Germany*
Ron Martin, *University of Cambridge, UK*
Martin Perry, *Massey University, New Zealand*
Kieran P. Donaghy, *Cornell University, USA*

In today's globalised, knowledge-driven and networked world, regions and cities have assumed heightened significance as the interconnected nodes of economic, social and cultural production, and as sites of new modes of economic and territorial governance and policy experimentation. This book series brings together incisive and critically engaged international and interdisciplinary research on this resurgence of regions and cities, and should be of interest to geographers, economists, sociologists, political scientists and cultural scholars, as well as to policy-makers involved in regional and urban development.

For more information on the Regional Studies Association visit www.regional studies.org

There is a **30% discount** available to RSA members on books in the *Regions and Cities* series, and other subject related Taylor and Francis books and e-books including Routledge titles. To order just e-mail alex.robinson@tandf.co.uk, or phone on +44 (0) 20 7017 6924 and declare your RSA membership. You can also visit www.routledge.com and use the discount code: **RSA0901**

Technology and the City

Systems, applications and implications

Tan Yigitcanlar

Routledge
Taylor & Francis Group

LONDON AND NEW YORK

First published 2016
by Routledge

2 Park Square, Milton Park, Abingdon, Oxfordshire OX14 4RN
52 Vanderbilt Avenue, New York, NY 10017

Routledge is an imprint of the Taylor & Francis Group, an informa business

First issued in paperback 2019

British Library Cataloguing in Publication Data
A catalogue record for this book is available from the British Library

Library of Congress Cataloging in Publication Data
Names: Yigitcanlar, Tan, author.
Title: Technology and the city : systems, applications and implications /
   Tan Yigitcanlar.
Description: Abingdon, Oxon ; New York, NY : Routledge, 2016.
Identifiers: LCCN 2015046211| ISBN 9781138826700 (hardback) |
   ISBN 9781315739090 (ebook)
Subjects: LCSH: City planning. | Information technology. | Cities and
   towns—Technological innovations.
Classification: LCC HT166 .Y54 2016 | DDC 307.1/216—dc23
LC record available at http://lccn.loc.gov/2015046211

ISBN: 978-1-138-82670-0 (hbk)
ISBN: 978-0-367-87142-0 (pbk)

Typeset in Times New Roman
by Swales & Willis Ltd, Exeter, Devon, UK

This book is dedicated to my life-long friend and wife Susan Yigitcanlar, and my beloved daughter Ela Yigitcanlar, the two most important women in my life.

Contents

Figures

Tables

About the author

Tan Yigitcanlar has a multidisciplinary background and 25 years of work experience in private consulting, government and academia. Throughout his academic career, he has been responsible for research, teaching, training and capacity building programs in the fields of urban and regional planning, development and management in esteemed Turkish, Japanese, Finnish and Australian universities.

Tan Yigitcanlar graduated from the Dokuz Eylul University, Izmir, Turkey with a Bachelor of City and Regional Planning (Honours) in 1992. During his studies, he worked as an intern planner in several Turkish local government organisations. Upon graduating, he commenced his professional career as a practising urban and regional planner working in his urban and regional planning consultancy firm. In 1996, he completed a Master of Urban Design (by thesis) study at the Dokuz Eylul University and extended his consultancy work to the design area as an urban design consultant. During his PhD studies at the Izmir Institute of Technology, he worked as an assistant professor at the same institution. After completing his PhD in 2001, he first moved to Japan and worked at the United Nations University as a post-doctoral Fellow, and at the University of Tokyo as a Research Fellow. He then moved to Brisbane, Australia, where he worked at the University of Queensland and Griffith University as a Research Fellow and Lecturer, respectively.

Since 2007, he has been continuing his academic career at the School of Civil Engineering and Built Environment, Science and Engineering Faculty, Queensland University of Technology, Brisbane, Australia. At the Queensland University of Technology, he managed the Master of Urban Development program (2008–2014) and directed the Research Cluster on Sustainable Built Environment (2009–2011). Currently, as an Associate Professor, he undertakes research, teaches two undergraduate-level courses and has seats on several committees at the Faculty. In addition to his academic position, since 2009, he has also held an executive director role at the World Capital Institute, an international think-tank established for the purpose of furthering the understanding and application of knowledge capital as the most powerful leverage for development. At the World Capital Institute, he oversees the organisation of annual international events to promote and advocate knowledge-based urban development at the global scale, i.e. Knowledge Cities World Summit. In 2012, he spent a seven-month sabbatical in Finland as a Visiting Professor to collaborate with his colleagues at the University of Helsinki and Tampere University of Technology. He has been invited to spend a year-long sabbatical as a Visiting Professor at the University of Toronto, Canada in 2017.

The main foci of Tan Yigitcanlar's research are clustered around the following three interrelated themes:

i   The first research theme is 'knowledge-based urban development and knowledge cities'. In this research area, he scrutinises the impacts of globalisation, knowledge economy and urban competitiveness on metropolitan urban locations. He significantly contributes to the theorisation and assessment model development of knowledge-based urban development. His research projects in this theme focus on planning and development of urban knowledge and innovation spaces, along with knowledge city transformation policies.

ii   The second theme is 'sustainable urban development and sustainable cities'. In this theme, he investigates urban sustainability by focusing on land use and transport integration, transport accessibility and modelling, water sensitive urban design, urban ecosystems sustainability and infrastructure resilience through various methods including indicator-based assessment and policy analysis and development.

iii   The third research theme is 'urban technologies and smart cities'. In this research area, he examines the impacts of innovative urban technologies on smart, sustainable and knowledge-based development of contemporary cities. His investigation in the field includes planning, development and management of smart/ubiquitous/eco-cities, web-based participatory planning support systems, online health information and decision support systems and the impacts of urban technologies on cities and societies.

Tan is the Founding Editor-in-Chief of the *International Journal of Knowledge Based Development* and the Editor-in-Chief of *Sustainability, Sustainable Urban and Rural Development Section*. He is an Associate Editor of *International Journal of Environmental Science and Technology*, *Global Journal of Environmental Science and Management*, *Journal of Open Innovation: Technology, Market, and Complexity* and *Asia Pacific Journal of Innovation and Entrepreneurship*. He also has editorial board member roles for four other academic journals, *Journal of Urban Technology*, *Urban Science*, *Measuring Business Excellence* and *International Journal of Knowledge-Based Organizations*.

He has extensively published in the field, including over 100 refereed journal articles and the following key reference books:

i   *Technology and the City: Systems, Applications and Implications* (Routledge 2016);

ii   *Knowledge and the City: Concepts, Applications and Trends of Knowledge-Based Urban Development* (Routledge 2014);

iii   *Sustainable Urban Water Environment: Climate, Pollution and Adaptation* (Edward Elgar 2014);

iv *Building Prosperous Knowledge Cites: Policies, Plans and Metrics* (Edward Elgar 2012);
v *Knowledge-Based Development for Cities and Societies: An Integrated Multi-Level Approach* (IGI Global 2010);
vi *Sustainable Urban and Regional Infrastructure Development: Technologies, Applications and Management* (IGI Global 2010);
vii *Rethinking Sustainable Development: Urban Management, Engineering and Design* (IGI Global 2010);
viii *Knowledge-Based Urban Development: Planning and Applications in the Information Era* (IGI Global 2008);
ix *Creative Urban Regions: Harnessing Urban Technologies to Support Knowledge City Initiatives* (IGI Global 2008).

About the author of the foreword

Mark Deakin is Professor of Built Environment and the Head of Centre of Sustainable Communities at Edinburgh Napier University, UK. He has published extensively on sustainable urban development, sustainable community development, smart cities and place-based transformations. He is also editor of the books *Sustainable Urban Development* (Routledge, volumes 1–3, 2005–2009), *Transition from Intelligent to Smart Cities, Creating Smart-er Cities* and *Smart Cities: Governing, Modelling and Analysing the Transition* (Routledge 2011–2013). His most recent book, *The Mass Retrofitting of an Energy Efficient-Low Carbon Zone* examines how the embedded intelligence of smart cities helps sustain the development of built environments (Springer 2014). He previously directed several research projects on sustainable community development and smart cities for the European Commission, Economic and Social Research Council and Engineering and Physical Sciences Research Council in the UK.

About the author of the afterword

Nicos Komninos is a Professor of Urban Development and Innovation Policy at the Aristotle University of Thessaloniki, Greece and teaches courses on Innovation Systems and Strategies and Intelligent Cities. He is founder and director of URENIO Research and has coordinated more than 100 research projects under the European Competitiveness and Innovation Programme (CIP), Framework Programmes (FP, H2020) and Territorial Cooperation Programmes. He has been honoured with the Award for Excellence and Innovation of Aristotle University for achievements in competitive research. He has published extensively on urban and regional development, innovation territories, and smart and intelligent cities, including the trilogy *Intelligent Cities: Innovation, Knowledge Systems and Digital Spaces* (Routledge 2002), *Intelligent Cities and Globalisation of Innovation Networks* (Routledge 2008), and *The Age of Intelligent Cities: Smart Environments and Innovation-for-all Strategies* (Routledge 2014). He is a member of the editorial board or associate editor on nine academic journals.

Foreword

Innovation distinguishes between a leader and a follower.
Steve Jobs, Co-founder of Apple Inc.

Capturing the state-of-the-art on smart cities

The state-of-the-art on smart cities, the marriage of technology and the city, has been captured by Deakin (2010a, 2011a, 2012a, 2013, 2014a) as a retrospective on the research undertaken, reported on and disseminated as part of the SmartCities project (see http://www.smartcities.info). These studies identify three emerging accounts of smart cities: (i) smart city rankings; (ii) future internet developments; and (iii) the triple helix model. All claim to capture something significant about smart cities and offer a critically insightful account of their development. This Foreword offers a synopsis of these accounts and goes on to outline the version of the triple helix that advances as a critical synthesis of the material drawn attention to. This critical synthesis shall absorb much of the material, which is currently accounted for by the smart city ranking and future internet accounts of smart cities, by outlining a version of the triple helix that offers a minimal theory of smart cities. This minimal theory of smart cities is offered in the interests of forcing a constructive alignment between all three abovementioned accounts of smart cities and developing a platform for the types of applications this calls for. As a minimal theory, it draws heavily upon the critical synthesis of the material previously reported on by Deakin (2014b, 2015). In particular, that version of the triple helix underlies this constructive alignment and, as a result, surfaces as a platform for the types of applications, which are able to overcome the rhetoric that currently surrounds smart city development (Deakin and Cruickshank 2013).

Smart city rankings

The first emerging account of smart cities is the smart city rankings. For Giffinger *et al.* (2008) smart cities offer the means to use these rankings as a method to 'outsmart' each other in marketing their attributes. In this examination of smart cities, standard city ranking procedures are recast by prefixing terms like economy, people, governance, mobility, environment and living, with the word 'smart' and assembling a set of indicators to approximate their respective factor performances. Such factor performances include hard and soft attributes, such as innovative spirit, entrepreneurialism, economic image and trademarks, creativity, cosmopolitism and open mindedness; hard and soft attributes that Giffinger *et al.* (2008: 4) suggest offer cities a measure of 'smartness' in the sense that they 'imply the implicit or explicit ambition/intention to improve performance'.

Future internet developments

The second emerging account of smart cities is the future internet development. The future internet thesis is advanced by Schaffers *et al.* (2011) and Komninos *et al.* (2013). As Schaffers *et al.* (2011) state, the first task cities must address in becoming smart is to create a rich environment of infrastructures able to support digital applications. This includes the following: (i) the development of broadband infrastructure combining cable, optical fibre and wireless networks, offering high connectivity and bandwidth to citizens and organisations located in the city; and (ii) the enrichment of the physical space and infrastructures of cities with embedded systems, smart devices, sensors and actuators, offering real-time data management, alerts and information processing. As Schaffers *et al.* (2011) note, the creation of applications enabling data collection and processing, web-based collaboration and collective intelligence in cloud computing (and compatible with the emerging internet-of-things) is the first task to consider. This is because for Schaffers *et al.* (2011) these are the only technologies that can assure economies of scale in infrastructure provision, standardisation of applications and turnkey solutions. The second task they identify consists of initiating large-scale participatory innovation processes for the creation of applications able to run with and improve every sector of activity, city cluster and infrastructure. Here, all city activities and utilities are characterised as innovation ecosystems, where citizens and businesses participate in the development, supply and consumption of resources (Cruickshank 2011). As Schaffers *et al.* (2011) point out, in creating the infrastructures of this rich environment and initiating large-scale participatory innovation, two different layers of collaboration come into play. The first layer relates to collaboration within the innovation process, which generates interaction between research, technology and application development. Here issues, such as how different research and innovation resources can be accessible and adaptable to specific communities, are clarified. The second layer concerns collaboration at the territorial level, driven by urban and regional development policies aimed at strengthening the innovation systems.

The triple helix of smart cities

The basis for the third account (the triple helix of smart cities) is Leydesdorff and Deakin's (2011) paper on the triple helix of smart cities. This brings to light how the triple helix model of smart cities provides the opportunity to study the knowledge base of an urban economy in terms of civil society's support for the evolution of infrastructures able to underpin their regional innovation systems (see Deakin *et al*. 2011, 2014; Deakin 2012b; Deakin and Leydesdorff 2013; Kourtit *et al*. 2014).

Here cities are densities in networks among at least three relevant dynamics; that is, in the intellectual capital of universities, industry of wealth creation and the participatory governance of the democratic system, which forms the rule of law in civil society. The effects of these interactions are in turn understood to generate spaces, where information and communication technologies (ICTs) are leveraged to bootstrap the notion of smart cities and exploit the opportunities future internet developments offer to not only generate intellectual capital but also to create wealth. That is to say, generate intellectual capital and create wealth, as much from the cultural and environmental attributes of knowledge production, as economic transactions, which in turn relate all of this to the evolving infrastructures of their regional innovation systems.

While the specific combination of knowledge products that are required for these sub-dynamics to align with one another is not known, it is the reflexive instability of the intellectual capital and wealth creation wrapped up in the social capital, culture and environments of these evolving infrastructures, which is of particular interest. This is because what such a co-evolutionary mechanism offers is the prospect of cities being smart in turning this reflexive instability to their advantage and exploiting the opportunity. These evolving infrastructures offer to reflect on how to best participate in such developments. In particular, they offer on how to participate in a way that allows cities to be smart in governing the knowledge, which the economy's globalisation of their 'next-order' dynamics ushers in.

This captures what is one of the most defining features of the ranking, future internet and triple helix accounts of smart cities. In the sense that, while the need for some form of smart city ranking is accepted by each of them, the future internet account is content to merely participate in such developments, whereas the triple helix model sees the governance of smart city developments as something more than either an environmental factor or infrastructure, which is integral to their regional innovation system (Caragliu *et al*. 2013). It instead puts store in the statement of what it means for cities to be smart, as offered by Caragliu *et al*. (2011: 70). That statement, which suggests a city may only claim to be smart, not when it ranks as a high performer, or a particularly good example of a broadband development, but 'when investments in human and social capital and traditional (transport) and modern (ICT) communication infrastructure fuel sustainable economic growth and a high quality of life, with a wise management of natural resources, through participatory government' (Komninos *et al*. 2013: 120).

While still performance-based, this account is particularly valuable for the simple reason that its holistic nature nicely balances the different social, cultural and economic components of smart city developments, without pre-judging either the weight or significance of any specific component. Perhaps more significantly, it also serves to emphasise the role ICT-related developments play in sustaining economic recovery, underpinning social welfare and supporting cultural health and well-being, by highlighting the internet as an enabler of participatory government.

This captures what perhaps best distinguishes future internet accounts of smart cities from triple helix models of their development. In the sense that, while future internet accounts are content to account for the economic attributes and capacities of ICT-related developments, advocates of the triple helix model seek to involve the cultural and environmental in any explanation of smart city development. This is not to suggest advocates of the triple helix model currently offer a particularly insightful account of what cultural and environmental attributes contribute to the governance of such ICT-related developments. For while the triple helix is the only model, which is explicit about the incorporation of governance-related issues into any such system of knowledge production, accounts of the schema offered by Etzkowitz (2002, 2008) tend to restrict such accounts to the rule of law and standards this lays down for the regulation of intellectual property rights.

It is in the interests of loosening the tight grip, which the rule of law currently has over the triple helix, and switching attention towards policy, corporate strategy and leadership. This issue leads to the whole question of governance in the model's dynamics, which are discussed in studies by Deakin (2010a, 2010b, 2012c). The outcomes of this reflection, along with the governance issues surrounding their neo-evolutionary model of smart cities, are captured in a study by Leydesdorff and Deakin (2011). That is in terms of the policies, corporate strategies and academic leadership surrounding the governance of cities, and whose intellectual capital is founded on a process of wealth creation, which is smart because it rests on participatory governance (Deakin 2014b).

It is the construction of these policies, academic leadership qualities and corporate strategies that Lombardi *et al.* (2011, 2012) explore with regards to the four visions of smart cities drawn from the 'Urban Europe' Joint Programme Initiatives (Nijkamp and Kourtit 2011). As Lombardi and Giordano (2012) state, these policy visions are of the: (i) connected city (smart logistic and sustainable mobility); (ii) entrepreneurial city (economic vitality); (iii) liveable city (ecological sustainability); and (iv) pioneer city (social capital and participatory governance). Deakin (2011a) and Deakin and Leydesdorff (2013) take these policy visions further. This is achieved by developing an operational model of smart cities, whose triple helix is based on the social capital of the pioneer city, networking of the intelligence this generates, wealth this creates and ecology it in turn cultivates as an environment for participatory governance.

The new version of the triple helix

Unlike earlier versions of the triple helix, the pioneering version of the model does not rest on the configurative logic of any 'overlapping' interests between university, industry and government. This new version of the triple helix is instead based on the informational basis of the communication system emerging from the reflexivity of smart cities and the stabilisation their development offers. For unlike existing representations of the triple helix, the trans-national regime of knowledge production, intellectual capital and wealth creation this model is founded on, does not rest with the distinction between either the fundamental or strategic research of scientific and technical development, but instead with the informational basis and communication systems of the so-called 'third mission' agenda. That third mission agenda is government-led and, like university and industry, targets the generation of intellectual capital and creation of wealth, but not in this instance from either scientific or technical innovations, but rather from the social networks, cultural attributes and environmental capacities that have tended to fall out with the fundamental and strategic concerns, which pre-occupy their counterparts. Together, such findings suggest that in their current state, cities, which claim to be smart, fail the primary and secondary tests traditionally applied to measure the intensity of knowledge production; namely underlying scientific and technical publications and supporting patent registrations. The absence of such measures in turn tends to suggest that any explanation for the development of smart cities is not to be found in either fundamental or strategic accounts of their innovation systems, but elsewhere.

Towards a minimal theory

In the interest of searching out this 'elsewhere', the following turns attention away from scientific and technological-based accounts of such ICT-related developments and instead towards the intellectual capital of social networks, whose underlying cultural attributes and environmental capacities surface as the third mission agenda of this government-led process venture into wealth creation. That agenda has up until now been of little interest to either university or industry, because the prevailing academic wisdom has considered the cultural and environmental value of this third mission (into networks, attributes and capacities) to be a venture neither fundamental enough, nor sufficiently strategic to warrant particular attention (Deakin 2010a, 2010b).

This challenges the prevailing academic wisdom, which states that such networks, attributes and capacities do not warrant attention from either university or industry. It suggests that what makes the innovation systems of certain cities smart, defines them in this way and allows them to stand out, is the growing tendency for a certain type of academic leadership to consider the embedded intelligence of these networks, attributes and capacities as something of strategic value for the following reasons: (i) they open up the opportunity for communities (academic-led, business orientated and citizen-centred alike) to learn about how their participation in the governance of scientific and technical innovations in the telecommunications sector can leverage a process of wealth creation mutually advantageous to both university and industry alike (Deakin and Al Waer 2011; Deakin 2012a, 2012b); and (ii) that in leveraging such a mutually advantageous process of wealth creation, government involves itself with and participates in a 'third mission' agenda, which is not exclusively proprietary, but communal. In that sense the agenda is wrapped up with policies, corporate strategies and academic leadership of ICT-related developments, which are purposefully designed to be socially inclusive by 'reaching out', 'working alongside and in partnership' with their counterparts (Deakin 2013, 2014a, 2014b, 2015).

This is how the triple helix represented in this model of smart cities neither over-relies on the reflexivity of knowledge production under the political economy of the nation-state (statesman and corporatist), nor on the intuition of cultural creativity within the on-going internationalisation of neo-liberal agendas (laissez faire), but instead localises the contemporary breakdown of the former and territorial expansion of the latter in the wealth created from the ICT-related developments reported on.

This process of wealth creation manifests itself in the development of electronically enhanced services, whose customisation of the networks, cultural attributes and environmental capacities is smart, because it leads cities to co-design these ICT-related developments as a set of business-to-citizen applications. This set of business-to-citizen applications, whose multichannel access and user profiles have the attributes and capacities that communities need to participate in the governance of these developments and for cities to be smart in opening up the spaces, are required for the intellectual capital embedded in this process of wealth creation to act as an exercise in direct democracy.

Such a triple helix model of smart cities not only allows participation to serve as a means to re-integrate government back into the contemporary state of knowledge production but also gets beyond the corporate marketing campaigns of 'smart city ranking' and the more anthropocentric line of reasoning associated with the European Network of Living Labs' (ENoLL) 'living lab' account of ICT-related developments. For rather than following the line of reasoning, which projects the knowledge economy into the vitality of the 'innovation ecosystems' surrounding these emergent spaces, this triple helix inspired model does something else It 'overlays' the communication system onto cities that pioneer such ICT-related developments and which in turn present them as a mirror image of everything which has come to symbolise 'being smart'.

Getting beyond the rhetoric

In order to assemble such an infrastructure and get beyond the rhetoric of cities that claim to be smart, it is necessary to not only survey the status of the cities that proclaim to be smart but assemble the instruments by which to measure any such performance. These instruments include the models, networks, analytical frameworks and metrics, which make it possible to measure the smartness of cities. These models, networks, analytical frameworks and performance measurements in this instance do not present themselves as readily available, off-the-shelf, user-ready knowledge products, but as instruments which need to be assembled, constructed and built before they can meet the governance challenge in hand.

Having presented this in the form of the critical synthesis, which this Foreword advances as a triple helix inspired account of smart city development, the lingering concerns that are associated with such a construction lie with whether the cultural and environmental significance of the emerging innovation systems shall merely reproduce the status quo, or if the participatory governance of direct democracy will only serve to punctuate the divisions underlying civil society and inequalities surfacing in the knowledge economy. Here, concerns linger over the adverse effects that any such fault line within the constitution of smart cities, their regional innovation systems, trans-national manifestation and global extension, has on communities already caught in the digital divide, which their reconstruction as the urban neighbourhoods of city districts aim to bridge.

Based on this, it is evident that while the contributions from the future internet development thesis and triple helix model do much to allay many of the fears surrounding the logic of leading corporate marketing campaigns, anxieties about the social capital, cultural attributes and environmental capacities of the technological possibilities smart cities offer still remain. For it appears the degree to which the accumulation of social capital and deployment of intelligence their networks embed and in turn draw upon to cultivate future internet developments, are seen as being sufficient to undercut the market economics of entrepreneurial-driven business models, is a matter that many still consider to be left 'in the balance'. Given the absence of any methodology supporting the future internet's call for smart cities to be based on citizen-led co-creation, statements about the value of what the business models underlying such reconstructions contribute to 'welfare and well-being' of regional innovation systems probably work best to highlight the true nature of the governance challenge this poses.

This is because such statements still illustrate a tendency to be overloaded with normative intent, unable to reveal where the integration of any such innovations can systematically open up the spaces needed for the urban neighbourhoods of city districts to be smart. For despite all of their groundbreaking features, such accounts of smart cities do not currently cultivate the attributes that are needed for them to participate in the governance of this reconstruction as an exercise in direct democracy, let alone the environmental capacities to sustain any such process of wealth creation.

In the absence of such evidence, the accounts of such reconstructions currently take on the status of meta-narratives, which lack not only the principles but the intermediate concepts that are needed for the intelligence they currently possess to systematically evolve as innovations capable of being scaled up to the size, weight and extent required. In particular, and in this instance, these innovations should not only be able to create wealth on the standard called for but should be a measure of the cultural attributes and environmental capacities that communities need for cities to be smart when escalating their ICT-related developments in a manner which reflects the type of citizen-led change pioneers of this kind expect. For in order to demonstrate such an escalation and do so as a standard measure of wealth creation, it is not so much agendas that are needed, but models that are required. Models that are in turn able to systematically capture the true significance of such future internet developments (i.e. in terms of both the extent, weight and size they amass) and represent this as a standard measure of the value these technologies offer communities to be smart.

The reason for the slack we currently witness can perhaps best be explained by the tendency for future internet developments to undercut the value of social networks, the intelligence they embed, cultural attributes this underpins, and environmental capacities they in turn support as a standard measure of wealth creation; the tendency, that is, which they display to undercut all of this and instead represent smart city developments as the ecology of a predominately technological experience that offers the means by which to shore up the vitality of the knowledge economy.

The representation of the triple helix advanced here does not succumb to this tendency. It instead does not play on the idea of an ecosystem as something that naturally aligns with the economic, but instead represents it as social phenomena. These phenomena serve to underpin the networking of the intelligence smart cities embed, the cultural attributes and environmental capacities that these in turn support, for the simple reason they serve as a means to 'offer up' the 'wealth of creative powers' that communities need in order to cultivate the type of future internet developments cities embark on to be smart. These environmentally sustainable future internet developments not only serve the ecology of urban communities as city districts but are also the very means by which this regional innovation system can hold up such transformations as a vital sign of the knowledge economy.

Professor Mark Deakin
Edinburgh Napier University, UK

References

Caragliu, A, Del Bo, C, Nijkamp, P 2011, 'Smart cities in Europe', *Journal of Urban Technology*, vol. 16, no. 2, pp. 65–82.

Caragliu, A, Del Bo, C, Nijkamp, P 2013, 'Smart cities in Europe', in Deakin, M (ed.) *Smart Cities: Governing, Modelling and Analysing the Transition*, Routledge, Oxford, UK.

Cruickshank, P 2011, 'SCRAN: The network', *Journal of Urban Technology*, vol. 18, no. 2, pp. 83–97.

Deakin, M 2010a, 'A review of city portals: The transformation of service provision under the democratization of the fourth phase', in Reddick, C (ed.) *Politics, Democracy and E-Government: Participation and Service Delivery*, IGI Global, Hershey, PA.

Deakin, M 2010b, 'SCRAN's development of a trans-national comparator for the standardisation of e-government services', in Reddick, C (ed.) *Comparative E-Government: An Examination of E-Government Across Countries*, Springer, Berlin, Germany.

Deakin, M 2011a, 'The embedded intelligence of smart cities', *International Journal of Intelligent Buildings*, vol. 3, no. 2, pp. 189–187.

Deakin, M 2011b, 'From the city of bits to eTopia: Space, citizenship and community as global strategy in the governance of the digitally-inclusive regeneration strategy', in Piaggesi, D, Sund, K and Castelnovo, W (eds) *Global Strategy and Practice of E-Governance: Examples From Around the World*, IGI Global, Hershey, PA.

Deakin, M 2012a, 'Intelligent cities as smart providers: CoPs as organizations for developing integrated models of e-government services', *Innovation: The Journal of Social Research*, vol. 23, no. 2, pp. 115–135.

Deakin, M 2012b, 'SCRAN: Assembling a community of practice for standardizing the transformation of e-government services', in Aikins, S (ed.) *Managing E-Government Projects: Concepts, Issues and Best Practices*, IGI Global, Hershey, PA.

Deakin, M (ed.) 2012c, *Creating Smart-er Cities*, Routledge, Oxon, UK.

Deakin, M (ed.) 2013, *SMART Cities: Governing, Modelling and Analysing the Transition*, Routledge, Oxon, UK.

Deakin, M 2014a, 'From the city of bits to e-topia: Space, citizenship and community as global strategy', *International Journal of E-Adoption*, vol. 6, no. 1, pp. 16–33.

Deakin, M 2014b, 'Smart cities: The state-of-the-art and governance challenge', *Triple Helix*, vol. 1, no. 1, pp. 1–16.

Deakin, M 2015, 'Smart cities and the internet: From mode 2 to triple helix accounts of their evolution', in Vesco, A (ed.) *Smart Cities Research Handbook: Social, Environmental and Economic Sustainability*, IGI Global, Hershey, PA.

Deakin, M, Al Waer, H 2011, 'The transition from intelligent to smart cities', *International Journal of Intelligent Buildings*, vol. 3, no. 2, pp. 140–152.

Deakin, M, Cruickshank, P 2013, 'SCRAN: The network', in Deakin, M (ed.) *Smart Cities: Governing, Modelling and Analysing the Transition*, Routledge, Oxon, UK.

Deakin, M, Leydesdorff, L 2013, 'The triple helix of smart cities: A neo-evolutionist perspective', in Deakin, M (ed.) *Smart Cities: Governing, Modelling and Analysing the Transition*, Routledge, Oxon, UK.

Deakin, M, Lombardi, P, Cooper, I 2011, 'The IntelCities CoP for the capacity-building, co-design, monitoring and evaluation of eGov services', *Journal of Urban Technology*, vol. 18, no. 2, pp. 17–38.

Deakin, M, Campbell, F, Reid, A 2014, 'Manchester as a digital powerhouse: Governing the ICT-related developments, measuring e-government efficiency', *Public Administration and Information Technology*, vol. 5, no. 1, pp. 91–212.

Etzkowitz, H 2002, *The Triple Helix of University-Industry-Government: Implications For Policy and Evaluation*, Science Policy Institute, Stockholm, Sweden.

Etzkowitz, H 2008, *The Triple Helix: University-Industry-Government Innovation in Action*, Routledge, Oxon, UK.

Giffinger, R, Kramar, H, Haindl, G 2008, 'The role of rankings in growing city competition', in *Proceedings of the XI. EURA*, Conference, 9–11 October 2008, Milan, Italy.

Komninos, N, Pallot, M, Schaffers, H 2013, 'Special issue on smart cities and the future internet in Europe', *Journal of the Knowledge Economy*, vol. 13, no. 2, pp. 119–134.

Kourtit, K, Deakin, M, Caragliu, A, Del Bo, C, Nijkamp, P, Lombardi, P, Giordano, S 2014, 'An advanced triple helix network framework for smart city performance', in Deakin, M (ed.) *Smart Cities: Governing, Modelling and Analysing the Transition*, Routledge, Oxon, UK, pp. 196–215.

Leydesdorff, L, Deakin, M 2011, 'The triple helix of smart cities: A neo-evolutionist perspective', *Journal of Urban Technology*, vol. 18, no. 2, pp. 53–63.

Lombardi, P, Giordano, S 2012, 'Evaluating the European smart cities visions of the future', *International Journal of the Analytic Hierarchy Process*, vol. 4, no. 1, pp. 27–40.

Lombardi, P, Giordano, S, Farouh, H, Yousef, W 2012, 'Modelling the smart city performance', *Innovation: the European Journal of Social Science Research*, vol. 25, no. 2, pp. 137–150.

Lombardi, P, Del Bo, C, Caragliu, A, Deakin, M, Nijkamp, P 2011, 'An advanced triple helix network model for smart cities performance', in Ercoskun, O (ed.) *Green and Ecological Technologies for Urban Planning*, IGI Global, Hershey, PA.

Nijkamp, P, Kourtit, K 2011, *Urban Europe Joint Programme Initiatives*, Free University, Amsterdam, the Netherlands.

Schaffers, H, Komninos, N, Pallot, M, Trousse, B, Nilsson, M, Oliveira, A 2011, 'Smart cities and the future internet: Towards cooperation frameworks for open innovation', in Domingue, J *et al.* (eds) *Future Internet Assembly*, Lecture Notes in Computer Science 6656, pp. 431–446.

Acknowledgements

This book is, to a degree, the result of the knowledge generated from a number of international research projects that I have been leading or been involved with in the course of the last 25 years on the topics and domains of urban and environmental planning, development, management and technologies. As an urbanist, I have tremendously enjoyed the time spent on putting this book together. This has involved meticulous and intense desktop research, field surveys at the investigated cases, conferring with a number of experts from the relevant fields and case study smart cities, and writing up the findings over a two-and-half-year period.

I am hopeful that the book will contribute to a better perception of the symbiosis between technology and city development by generating new insights. I believe, as much as solutions and suggestions, the issues and questions raised in this book will trigger many scholars and practitioners to investigate these issues further and address the questions. I also trust that it will create an awareness, particularly among urban administrators and policymakers of our cities, of the need to carefully support the development and investment in appropriate technologies, through appropriate processes, in order to achieve a truly smart and sustainable urban development. This will eventually help to make the world a better place for all.

I would like to thank a number of individuals and organisations that have been as passionate as I have been about writing and publishing this book, and who supported the research, policy development, advocacy and project work on the areas related to technology and city development topic.

First, I wish to thank two organisations that I am affiliated to: Queensland University of Technology and World Capital Institute, for making financial and in-kind resources available for the preparation of this book.

Second, my thanks go to the publishing team at Routledge, who had the foresight to recognise the value and relevance of this monograph, and who have been extremely supportive during the evolution of the book.

Third, I would like to sincerely thank Mark Deakin and Nicos Komninos who have contributed to this project with a Foreword and an Afterword. They have generously shared their knowledge and have given freely and willingly of their extremely invaluable and scarce time.

Last, I am extremely grateful to my wife, Susan, and daughter, Ela, the most loving people I have ever known, for their understanding and support, particularly during the many times I spent working on the book after office hours.

Part I

Background

Part I of the book provides an overview of and background on the role of knowledge, innovation and technology in the development process of human civilisation and urbanisation. It also provides an in-depth and comprehensive understanding of both theoretical and practical aspects of technology adoption, and their implications on our cities in the course of history. Chapter 1 focuses on the theoretical and practical underpinnings that underline the interplay between technological progress and evolution of cities. The Chapter specifies the rationale, scope, aim, objectives and key research questions of the book, and offers an overview information on the rest of the Chapters and the author of the book. Chapter 2 elaborates the historical significance of knowledge, innovation and technology in economic growth, social progress and urban development, and provides evidence by focusing particularly on the following periods: (i) the pre-industrial era including Stone Age, Bronze Age, Iron Age, the Middle Ages, and the Renaissance and the Age of Enlightenment; (ii) the industrial era; and (iii) the post-industrial era.

1   Introduction

Science is the most reliable guide in life.
(Mustafa Kemal Atatürk, the founding father of Turkey)

Theoretical and practical underpinnings

The twenty-first century is recognised as the 'century of cities', as more than half of the world's population now lives in cities, and the importance of urban environments has become even greater in recent decades (Didsbury 2004). The beginning of the twenty-first century also marked the expansion of the knowledge economy that is becoming a global phenomenon. As Gabe *et al.* (2012: 1179) put it, 'it would be an understatement to suggest that knowledge plays a key role in today's economy; for much of the developed world, it might be more accurate to assert that knowledge is today's economy'. In the global knowledge economy, cities are viewed as the centres of knowledge, as loci of cultures that produce and valorise knowledge, or as playing a major role in the governance of knowledge, in particular, humanising knowledge by integrating different types of knowledge and protecting values of a local and regional nature (Yigitcanlar *et al.* 2015). However, cities since ancient times have always been the cradle of civilisation and knowledge generation in various forms, such as analytical (science-based), synthetic (engineering-based) and symbolic (arts-based) knowledge (Carrillo *et al.* 2014). Marketable knowledge and its associated products and processes are generated, mostly in urban agglomerations, through the complex activities involving science, technology, arts, innovation and creativity. The intensity of these activities has increased exponentially, particularly since the invention of computers. The Electronic Numerical Integrator and Computer (ENIAC), completed by Presper Eckert and John Mauchly in 1945, is considered to be the first machine to incorporate the full set of traits of a modern computer (see Isaacson 2014).

The combination of the computer and distributed networks since the 1960s has led to a 'digital revolution' that today allows anyone to create, disseminate and access any information anywhere, anytime and from any smart device. According to Isaacson (2014), the birth of the 'digital age' is a result of a research ecosystem that was nurtured by government spending and military-industry-academia collaboration, along with an alliance of community organisers, communal-minded hippies, do-it-yourself hobbyists and homebrew hackers. Strictly speaking, 'the collaborative creativity has marked the digital age by establishing collaboration between humans and machines' (Isaacson 2014: 5). This interaction has changed the way some services are delivered. For instance, today the world's largest taxi company, Uber, owns no vehicles; the world's most popular media owner, Facebook, creates no content; the world's most valuable retailer, Alibaba, has no inventory; and the world's largest accommodation provider, Airbnb, owns no real estate. Besides, owing to rapid developments in the digital age, technology is widely seen as an effective apparatus to help us solve some of the most challenging problems the world is facing today, particularly, when the human element is strongly considered along with the technological capabilities (Stimmel 2016).

Today, without exception, all parts of the world are confronted by various environmental, social and economic crises, e.g. life threatening natural disasters, loss of biodiversity, destruction of natural ecosystems, regional disparities, socio-economic inequity, and digital and knowledge divides that are mainly caused by rapid population increase and expansion of resource consumption, combined with industrialisation, urbanisation, mobilisation, agricultural intensification and excessive consumption-driven lifestyles (see Epstein and Buhovac 2014; Yigitcanlar and Dizdaroglu 2015; Yigitcanlar and Teriman 2015). Rapid advancement in digital technologies has given us the hope that the impacts of global scale environmental, social and economic crises can be eased with the help of appropriate technology (Yigitcanlar and Lee 2014). In particular, the application of smart urban technologies in cities can potentially produce a number of benefits. The following are among some of the prospects (Harrison and Donnelly 2011):

- reducing resource consumption, notably energy and water, hence contributing to reductions in carbon dioxide emissions;
- improving the usage of existing infrastructure capacity, hence improving quality of life and reducing the need for traditional construction projects;
- making new services available to citizens and commuters, such as real-time guidance on how best to exploit multiple transportation modalities;
- improving commercial enterprises through the publication of real-time data on the operation of city services;
- revealing how demands for energy, water and transportation peak on a city scale so that city administrators can collaborate to smooth these peaks and improve resilience.

Hollands (2008) is among the many scholars advocating that cities should reap these benefits of smart urban technologies through the application of a wide range of electronic and digital technologies to communities and cities; the use of information technologies to transform life and work within a region; and the embedding of such ICTs in the city and territorialisation of such practices in a way that brings ICTs and people together so as to enhance the innovation, learning, knowledge and problem solving that the technologies offer. Moreover, Hollands

(2008) puts networked infrastructures at the core of smart urban technologies as a means to enable social, environmental, economic and cultural development, such infrastructures including mobile and landline phones, satellite TVs, computer networks, electronic commerce, and wired and wireless internet services. Currently, smart urban technologies are becoming more and more feasible for cities as a result of the rapid progress in the technology innovation domain in the twenty-first century. These innovative technology developments include (Harrison and Donnelly 2011):

- the widespread use of digital sensors and digital control systems for monitoring and management/operation of urban infrastructure. These comprise traffic sensors, building management systems, digital utility meters and so forth;
- the growing penetration of fixed and wireless networks that allow such sensors and systems to be connected to distributed processing centres, and for these centres in turn to exchange information among themselves;
- the development of information management techniques, specifically standardised semantic models, that allow the low-level information to be interpreted by the processing centres and for these processing centres to interpret each other's information;
- the development of both computing power and new algorithms that allow these flows of information to be analysed in near real-time in order to provide operational performance improvement and other insights.

One of the world's largest smart city technology solution companies, IBM (2010), promotes the 'smart cities movement' and utilisation of smart urban technologies to transform our cities' systems to optimise the use of finite resources. Additionally, today other technology giants are also in the smart city business, such as Cisco and Samsung, along with a number of national telecommunications companies. These companies lead the promotion of smart cities by collaborating with local governments in smart city application delivery, e.g. Incheon, Tianjin, Amsterdam, Barcelona, Abu Dhabi, Istanbul, Rio de Janeiro, San Francisco, Auckland, Brisbane and many others. These efforts have resulted in smart cities being claimed to provide an effective model for the cities of the twenty-first century, especially with their innovative technology applications and management capabilities, accompanied by the stimulus and location for the world's creativity and innovation. Furthermore, they provide a high quality of life and a low impact on the environment (see Angelidou 2014; Heo *et al.* 2014). According to Caragliu *et al.* (2011), these cities are 'smart' when it comes to investments in human and social capital, and traditional (e.g. transport) and modern (e.g. ICT) communication infrastructure that fuel sustainable economic development and a high quality of life, because of their wise management of natural resources through participatory action and engagement.

As for Kourtit and Nijkamp (2012), smart cities encompass modern urban production factors in a common framework by utilising advanced ICTs and social and environmental capitals to form competitive cities in the information and knowledge age. In other words, they are based on a promising mix of human capital (e.g. skilled labour force), infrastructural capital (e.g. high-tech telecommunication facilities), social capital (e.g. intense and open network linkages) and entrepreneurial capital (e.g. creative and risk-taking business activities) (Yigitcanlar and Lee 2014), which make them, in theory, an ideal city model. Manville *et al*. (2014) define smart cities as being based on the six dimensions of smart, 'economy, mobility, environment, people, living, and governance'. Similarly, Lombardi *et al*. (2012) employ smart, 'governance, economy, human capital, living, and environment' as the key indicators in assessing the performance of smart cities. The smart city concept is distinguished from other similar ideas, i.e. a digital or intelligent city, where it focuses on factors of human capital and education as drivers of urban growth, rather than singling out the role of ICT infrastructure (Lee *et al*. 2013).

Even the movement of smart cities is not that new. At present, there is not a single fully-fledged smart city erected on the surface of the planet. While the smart city concept is well and good in theory, in practice there are numerous challenges in building truly smart cities. These challenges can be grouped under the following categories: technological and technical issues (e.g. technical barriers due to the size of the city and users), economic issues (e.g. requiring massive financial investments), societal issues (e.g. smart cities becoming enclaves for urban elites), natural and built environmental issues (e.g. producing insignificant environmental sustainability outcomes), governance or management issues (e.g. limited public participation and bottom-up approach), and wider application of the smart city model (e.g. problematic nature of wide-scale retrofitting) (see Yigitcanlar 2015). While our cities and societies are being wired with technology to become smarter and more sustainable, we need to find ways to effectively address all of the abovementioned challenges. Until then, smart cities will not provide an opportunity to reshape our cities and societies to make them more sustainable and thus smart. As stated by Townsend (2013):

> we don't yet know how to build a smart city the way we built the internet. But it's clear from what we now know about the best ways to build cities and create new technologies that we need to start the search for ways to do it.
>
> (Townsend 2013: 111)

Underlined by Stimmel (2016), while searching ways to build truly smart cities, which is somehow the happy marriage of 'technology and the city', we need to adopt an approach that not only incorporates the issues of building technologically advanced and ecologically sustainable cites but also comprehends the shifts in human living within these environments.

Rationale and scope

The scope of this book focuses on investigating and revealing the interplay between smart urban technologies and city development. This is still relatively uncharted territory and thus has the potential to generate new insights and knowledge, which forms the *raison d'être* of this book. There are a number of authoritative works that have influenced this book. In other words, *Technology and the City* is to a degree a healthy combination of Mumford's (1961), Deakin and Al Waer's (2012), Kaku's (2012), Townsend's (2013), Isaacson's (2014), Komninos's (2014) and Stimmel's (2016) ideas discussed in their seminal books. The author, being an urbanist and also working in the technology space for quite some time, instinctively channelled himself to build on the pivotal works in the spheres of urban history, urban technology, urban planning and development, and sustainable urban futures. The overall aim of *Technology and the City* is to:

- underline the growing importance of smart technologies and systems in building cities in the twenty-first century, which is a largely uncharted territory of research;
- provide an in-depth and comprehensive understanding of both theoretical and practical aspects on smart urban technology adoption, and its implications and prospects for our cities.

The book addresses the following questions with the abovementioned aims in mind:

- What is the role of smart urban technologies and systems in the development of the twenty-first century cities?
- How can smart urban technologies and systems be adopted in the planning, development and management processes of cities to provide desired urban futures?

In line with the aims and research questions listed above, the objectives of this book are explicitly to:

- discuss the role of technology and its economic, sociocultural, spatial and institutional impacts on cities in a historical perspective;
- define the key conceptual and practical issues of smart urban technology and system adoption in cities;
- determine and share smart urban technology and system experiences of the successful cities across the globe;
- pinpoint new technology directions for cities to further benefit in providing desired smart urban futures.

In order to deliver aforementioned aims and objectives and address the research questions, the main themes of the book include the followings:

- theoretical and practical underpinnings of urban technologies;
- history of technology and development;
- smart urban information technologies;
- smart urban infrastructures and systems;

- smart city practices;
- magnitudes of smart urban technologies and systems for cities;
- prospects of smart urban technologies and systems for cities;
- smart urban futures.

Organisation of the book

This book is organised in four Parts and seven Chapters. The book is also rein-forced with a Foreword (by Mark Deakin) and an Afterword (by Nicos Komninos) written by the eminent experts of the field, with these additional Chapters located at the very beginning and very end of the book. Each Part, i.e. background, sys-tems, applications and implications, is structured so as to build on the previous one, presenting an inductive approach, from technology to urban infrastructure or system, and from there to the city as a whole in a chronological manner.

Following the Foreword, which focuses on 'capturing the state-of-the-art on smart cities', and this introductory Chapter, the book focuses on elaborating the historical significance of technology for economic growth, social progress and urban development. In Chapter 2, the book introduces the role of technology played in our civilisation from the Ice Age up to the end of the twentieth century. This Chapter raises a number of critical issues and insights, including technolo-gies mostly being a product of survival, competition, greed and wars, rather than a tool specifically designed to improve the quality of life and place. The Chapter focuses on the following periods: (i) the pre-industrial era, including the Stone Age, Bronze Age, Iron Age, the Middle Ages, and the Renaissance and the Age of Enlightenment; (ii) the industrial era; and (iii) the post-industrial era.

Afterwards, the book introduces and assesses the role and importance of the most prominent smart urban information technologies. In Chapter 3, the book looks at the most prominent technologies of the new millennium that provide a foundation for new urban infrastructure and services development as well as new urban space formation. These include: (i) infrastructural information technologies, such as the World Wide Web, broadband and mobile broadband; (ii) locational and sensing technologies, such as geographic information sci-ence technologies, radio frequency identification, ubiquitous sensor network and context-aware computing; (iii) ubiquitous computing and augmented reality technologies, such as mobile and built ubiquitous computing environment, and mobile augmented reality technologies; and (iv) convergence technologies, such as internet and media convergence, marketing convergence and telecommunications convergence.

Next, the book demonstrates how these technologies are used in various smart urban systems. In Chapter 4, the book focuses on the key urban systems and gives an example from each of them to provide a clearer understanding of the utilisa-tion, benefits and also challenges of the relevant technology system applications. Prospects and constraints analyses are also included to provide useful insights, particularly highlighting critical issues on technology acceptance, adoption and risks. The smart urban systems explored in the Chapter include: (i) smart urban transport systems; (ii) smart urban grid systems; (iii) smart urban water and waste systems; (iv) smart urban emergency and safety systems; and (v) smart urban participatory decision systems.

Thereafter, the book showcases the most significant smart city best practices from across the globe that make effective use of these technologies and systems. In Chapter 5, it includes a case study section with ten best practices from around the world. The explored so-called best practices are introduced with skepticism, and their achievements and promises are critically evaluated. The smart city initiatives selected for the exploration in the Chapter include: (i) Incheon and Tianjin from the South East Asian context; (ii) Amsterdam and Barcelona from the European context; (iii) Abu Dhabi and Istanbul from the Middle Eastern context; (iv) Rio de Janeiro and San Francisco from the North and South American context; and (v) Auckland and Brisbane from the Oceanian context.

Finally, the book discusses the magnitudes and prospects of smart technologies and systems for our cities and societies. In Chapter 6, it deals with the magnitudes of smart technology applications for cities from four different perspectives, namely: (i) economic development; (ii) sociocultural development; (iii) spatial development; and (iv) institutional development. The Chapter has a critical take on the technology revolution, for instance for those who see technology solutions as a single panacea to the climate change issue. Chapter 7 then focuses on the potential development patterns of life, technology and cities until the beginning of twenty-second century. The Chapter particularly speculates on the: (i) future of life on the planet Earth; (ii) future of smart technologies; and (iii) future of smart cities. Finally, the book concludes with the Afterword, which focuses on 'smart urban futures'.

References

Angelidou, M 2014, 'Smart city policies: A spatial approach', *Cities*, vol. 41, no. 1, pp. 3–11.

Caragliu, A, Del Bo, C, Nijkamp, P 2011, 'Smart cities in Europe', *Journal of Urban Technology*, vol. 18, no. 2, pp. 65–82.

Carrillo, J, Yigitcanlar, T, Garcia, B, Lonnqvist, A 2014, *Knowledge and the City: Concepts, Applications and Trends of Knowledge-Based Urban Development*, New York: Routledge.

Deakin, M, Al Waer, H 2012, *From Intelligent to Smart Cities*, New York: Routledge.

Didsbury, HF 2004, *Thinking Creatively in Turbulent Times*, Bethesda, MD: World Future Society.

Epstein, MJ, Buhovac, AR 2014, *Making Sustainability Work: Best Practices in Managing and Measuring Corporate Social, Environmental, and Economic Impacts*, San Francisco, CA: Berrett-Koehler Publishers.

Gabe, T, Abel, J, Ross, A, Stolarick, K 2012, 'Knowledge in cities', *Urban Studies*, vol. 49, no. 6, pp. 1179–1200.

Harrison, C, Donnelly, IA 2011, 'A theory of smart cities', in *Proceedings of the 55th Annual Meeting of the International Society for the Systems Sciences*, 17–22 July 2011, Hull, UK.

Heo, T, Kim, K, Kim, H, Lee, C, Ryu, J, Leem, Y, Ko, J 2014, 'Escaping from ancient Rome: Applications and challenges for designing smart cities', *Transactions on Emerging Telecommunications Technologies*, vol. 25, no. 1, pp. 109–119.

Hollands, R 2008, 'Will the real smart city stand up: Creative, progressive, or just entrepreneurial?' *City*, vol. 12, no. 1, pp. 302–320.

IBM 2010, *Smarter Cities For Smarter Growth: How Cities Can Optimize Their Systems For the Talent-Based Economy*, New York: IBM Global Business Services.

Isaacson, W 2014, *The Innovators*, New York, Simon and Schuster.

Kaku, M 2012, *Physics of the Future: How Science Will Shape Human Destiny and Our Daily Lives by the Year 2100*, London: Pelican Books.

Komninos, N 2014, *The Age of Intelligent Cities: Smart Environments and Innovation-For-All Strategies*, New York: Routledge.

Kourtit, K, Nijkamp, P 2012, 'Smart cities in the innovation age', *Innovation: The European Journal of Social Science Research*, vol. 25, no. 2, pp. 93–95.

Lee, J, Phaal, R, Lee, S 2013, 'An integrated service device-technology roadmap for smart city development', *Technological Forecasting and Social Change*, vol. 80, no. 1, pp. 286–306.

Lombardi, P, Giordano, S, Farouh, H, Yousef, W 2012. 'Modelling the smart city performance', *Innovation: The European Journal of Social Science Research*, vol. 25, no. 2, pp. 137–149.

Manville, C, Cochrane, G, Cave, J, Millard, J, Pederson, JK, Thaarup, RK, Kotterink, B 2014, *Mapping Smart Cities in the EU*, European Union, Brussels, Belgium.

Mumford, L 1961, *The City in History: Its Origins, Its Transformations, and Its Prospects*, New York: Harcourt, Brace and World.

Stimmel, C 2016, *Building Smart Cities: Analytics, ICT, and Design Thinking*, New York: CRC Press.

Townsend, AM 2013, *Smart Cities: Big Data, Civic Hackers, and the Quest For a New Utopia*, New York: WW Norton and Company.

Yigitcanlar, T 2015, 'Smart cities: An effective urban development and management model?' *Australian Planner*, vol. 52, no. 1, pp. 27–34.

Yigitcanlar, T, Lee, S 2014, 'Korean ubiquitous-eco-city: A smart-sustainable urban form or a branding hoax?', *Technological Forecasting and Social Change*, vol. 89, no. 1, pp. 100–114.

Yigitcanlar, T, Dizdaroglu, D 2015, 'Ecological approaches in planning for sustainable cities: A review of the literature', *Global Journal of Environmental Science and Management*, vol. 1, no. 2, pp. 71–94.

Yigitcanlar, T, Teriman, S 2015, 'Rethinking sustainable urban development: Towards an integrated planning and development process', *International Journal of Environmental Science and Technology*, vol. 12, no. 1, pp. 341–352.

Yigitcanlar, T, Inkinen, T, Makkonen, T 2015, 'Does size matter? Knowledge-based development of second-order city-regions in Finland', *disP-The Planning Review*, vol. 51, no. 3, pp. 62–77.

2   A historical perspective on technology and urbanisation

*We've arranged a civilisation in which most crucial elements profoundly depend
on science and technology.*

(Carl Sagan, author of *Mars and the Mind of Man*)

Introduction

Throughout the civilised history of humankind, urban and socioeconomic developments, along with the climatic conditions, have gone hand in hand with and
been intensely supported by new knowledge creation and technological innovation. In other words, society shapes and is shaped by economic factors, generating new knowledge, advancing technology and the environment we live in.
Technology is concerned with knowledge and collection of techniques, methods and processes that are used in manufacturing goods, providing services and
accomplishing scientific investigations. However, in the earlier periods of our
civilisation it was basically the knowledge and techniques required for survival.
This Chapter provides a historical perspective on and evidence of knowledge
generation and technological innovation and their impacts on and relations with
economic growth, societal progress and urban development. The investigation
starts with the appearance of *homo sapiens* about 200,000 years ago and continues
until the present time, the early years of the new millennium, and presents and
discusses the findings by focusing in particular on the following periods: (i) the
pre-industrial era, including the Stone Age, Bronze Age, Iron Age, the Middle
Ages, and the Renaissance and the Age of Enlightenment; (ii) the industrial era;
and (iii) the post-industrial era.

The pre-industrial era

Our species, *homo sapiens* or modern humans, are contemporaries of *neander-
thals* and *denisovans*, descended from *homo heidelbergensis*, and have a blood-
line connected to that of ancient humans *homo erectus* that dates back over two
million years. Homo sapiens first began to evolve nearly 200,000 years ago in

Africa during the Ice Age as a result of a dramatic climatic change. Even though we evolved only relatively recently, we have been able to spread throughout the world with complex culture and technology and occupy a range of different environments. Perhaps the greatest inventors of all time were the prehistoric people of the pre-industrial era. During the Ice Age, they came up with the most basic, but at the same time the most crucial inventions to survive. For instance, they discovered that the great enemy, which is fire, could be forced to obey and make their lives better. Fire kept them warm and helped them to easily chew the tough meat of wild animals. Animal hide clothing was worn in cooler areas and body adornments sewn onto clothing included ivory, shell, amber, bone and tooth beads, and pendants. They invented many different tools and weapons, such as the spinning wheel, bone hammer, flint knife and axe, stone adze, arrowhead, flakes, scrapers and points, in order to hunt or defend themselves, move heavy objects and build shelters. They developed the ability to communicate through talking and have real conversations with each other by using words. This advanced ability to communicate significantly contributed not only to their survival, by developing tactics in hunting against much stronger animals or enemies, but also to the passing on of learnt knowledge to others. They created pictures to make magic, as they believed painting pictures of animals would make them appear and so they could hunt them (Gombrich 2008). Musical instruments used for entertainment included Palaeolithic bone flutes and whistles. Bigger populations often accumulated more cultural attributes than isolated groups. Burials were practised with the inclusion of valued objects such as tools and body adornments. During the last period of the Ice Age, the Earth gradually grew warmer and became more habitable for our prehistoric ancestors (Bahn 1997) and marked the beginning of the Stone Age.

The Stone Age

Early *homo sapiens* originated in the first part of the Stone Age, which is the Palaeolithic or Old Stone Age (White *et al.* 2003). Anatomical changes indicating modern language capacity, the systematic burial of the dead, the music, early art and the first use of increasingly sophisticated multipart stone tools, arose during this period (Wolpoff 1997). Throughout this era, which lasted until approximately about 12000 BC, Palaeolithic people formed nomadic hunter-gatherer societies, which tended to be very small and egalitarian. Some of these societies that were fortunate to have abundant resources or advanced food-storage techniques, also developed sedentary lifestyles with complex social structures such as chiefdoms and social stratification (Hill *et al.* 2011). The second part of the Stone Age, which is called Mesolithic or the Middle Stone Age, took place between about 20000 and 9500 BC, which is an indicative timespan (like most of the later presented eras) as different communities in parts of the world experienced different rates of progression in their development. Interestingly, similar inventions sometimes took place in different parts of the world simultaneously, e.g. the spinning wheel, or sometimes at different dates but with no obvious connection, e.g. printing appeared first in China, but not until six centuries later in Europe. Quite often, inventions that appeared in one place stimulated the others to make different, but interrelated inventions (Pacey 1990). The era of the Stone Age is characterised in most areas of the world by composite tools such as micro-liths and micro-burins, fishing tackles, stone adzes, canoes and bows (Clark 2014). This era was a transitional period between hunter-gatherer and agricultural practices, with some Mesolithic people continuing with intensive hunting and others starting to practise the initial stages of farming and domestication (Zvelebil 2009). The last part of the Stone Age is the Neolithic or the New Stone Age that began about 10200 BC and ended between 4500 and 2000 BC. This was a significant period in the development of human technology and it commenced with the beginning of first farming practices, which produced the 'Neolithic Revolution' (Mulligan 2012). This era is a progression of behavioural and cultural characteristics and changes, including the use of wild and domestic crops and domesticated animals. Some scholars refer to this period as the era of 'Early Agricultural Village Communities' (Kuijt 2000).

In neglecting small tribal and nomadic shelters and settlements built by primitive hunter-gatherer societies, it would not be wrong to refer to the Neolithic period as the peak of the agricultural society that gave birth to civilisation and led to the formation of the first cities' urbanisation processes (Yigitcanlar 2011). Around this period, in a number of fertile parts of the world, cities or more correctly city-states were established (Creekmore and Fisher 2014). The well-known ones include, but are not limited to, Eridu, Uruk, Ur, Agade, Hattusa, Troy, Babylon, Nineveh, Persepolis, Pergamum, Jerusalem, Petra, Ephesus and Palmyra (from the Near East); Memphis, Thebes, Amarna, Carthage, Alexandria, Meroe, Leptis Magna and Aksum (from Africa); Knossos, Mycenae, Athens, Akragas, Paestum, Rome, Pompeii, Nimes, Pont Du Gard and Trier (from Europe); Mohenjo-Daro, Linzi, Xianyang, Pataliputra and Anuradhapura (from Asia); and Caral, La Venta, Momte Alban, Teotihuacan, Tikal and Palenque (from the Americas). Even though the building technologies of the time were quite primitive, fascinatingly, they managed to build colossal structures. For instance, during the building of the Great Pyramids during the 400-year span from about 2700 to 2300 BC, Egyptians did not even have metal tools with which to work the stone. Their only tools for cutting, whittling and chipping were their knives and chisels that were made of obsidian, a black volcanic glass (Van Doren 1992).

The Bronze Age

The Bronze Age refers to a period between approximately 3300 and 700 BC, when the most advanced metalworking, at least in systematic and widespread use, included techniques for smelting copper and tin from naturally occurring outcroppings of ores, and then combining them to cast bronze (Coles and Harding 2014). During this era, Bronze Age people used metals to make themselves weapons, jewellery and cauldrons. The extensive use of metals correspondingly led to the development of extensive trade networks. Furthermore, the invention of viable writing systems coincided with this era (Symington 1991). The process of building up a body of knowledge available essentially to all human beings accelerated with the invention of writing (Van Doren 1992). From this era, the Phoenician alphabet, used by the civilisation of Phoenicia (located in Tyre and Sidon cities in modern-day Lebanon), was one of the first consonantal alphabets with a strict and consistent form, from which almost all modern phonetic alphabets are derived (Gombrich 2008). Following on from the Neolithic agricultural revolution, the urban revolution took place during the Bronze Age and southern Mesopotamia in particular grew and flourished. According to Smith (2012), in this region:

> several harvests a year become possible, generating an abundance of food. There was also a constant flow of traders moving between the Fertile Crescent in the north and the Persian Gulf, bringing goods made of obsidian, metal and pottery. By 3200 BC, this region became the most densely populated farming area in the world.
>
> (Smith 2012: 31)

These were the important conditions that brought about the rise of cities in the region. During the Bronze Age, Judaism was founded by Abraham around 2000–1800 BC in Mesopotamia. Judaism is a monotheistic religion in which Jews believe in one God, Yahweh or Jehovah, which was an innovation, in a sense, for the belief system of the time. The religion has a strong sense of morality, which is reflected in the Ten Commandments and the Torah (or holy books) that were received by Moses.

The Iron Age

The Bronze Age was followed by an era that saw the prevalent use of iron. The Iron Age stretched from approximately 1200 BC to AD 800 (Gombrich 2008). This era refers to the advent of ferrous metallurgy that involves processes and alloys based on iron. The adoption of iron coincided with other changes in the cultures of the time, often including more sophisticated agricultural practices, religious beliefs and artistic styles. The majority of people at that time lived on farms or in small villages. Occasionally, Iron Age people lived in larger settlements, such as hill-forts, a type of fortification used as a barricaded refuge that defended the human settlement and took advantage of a rise in elevation for defensive purposes; and oppida, a fortified settlement usually built on an elevated position like a hill (Hawkes 1931). Even though these cities shaped the ancient world, they bear little resemblance to cities as we understand them today. Nonetheless, they laid the foundations for life as we know it, e.g. the birth of literature, drama, painting, sculpture, architecture, legislation and so on (Norwich 2014). For instance, the Sumerians gave us the first cities (i.e. Eridu and Uruk), the first irrigated agriculture, the first written language, our measurement of time (i.e. 60 seconds to a minute) and the first standing armies with professional soldiers (Smith 2012). These cities not only built urban settlements but also erected the greatest monuments of the ancient world, showcasing their technology, power and authority, e.g. the Seven Wonders of the Ancient World: the Great Pyramid of Giza, the Hanging Gardens of Babylon, the Statue of Zeus at Olympia, the Temple of Artemis at Ephesus, the Mausoleum at Halicarnassus, the Colossus of Rhodes and the Lighthouse of Alexandria. Besides the colossal public buildings of the early cities, generally, their architecture was modest, and natural and built environments were integrated and cities housed only a few tens of thousands of people (Van Doren 1992). However, as stated by Mumford (1961: 74), 'most of the major physical organs of the city had been created by 2000 BC'.

During the Iron Age, ancient Greece was at its peak around the fifth and fourth centuries BC. The conquests of Alexander the Great of Macedonia made Hellenistic civilisation flourish from Central Asia to the western end of the Mediterranean Sea. Political reforms in Athens in the sixth and fifth centuries BC, founded as they were on the philosophical bedrock of justice and wisdom, paved the way for Athens to become a unique city (Hughes 2014). Situated at the heart of the Hellenistic civilisation in Athens, the solidarity and self-determination of the world's first true democracy was brought to life, although only for free adult males. Geographic features of the land separated ancient Greece into small regions, so-called *poli* meaning city (more correctly city-state) or citizen, which also was the form of government in Greece, including its colonies. Most of the city-states were small in size accommodating fewer than 20,000 people due to geographical restrictions. Athens and Sparta were the largest city-states. At its peak in around the fifth century BC, the population of Athens was about 300,000 people and the city was fully integrated with the surrounding natural environment (Gomme 1933). Small city-state size also made people form close communities. The typical layout of the city-states was as follows: Centre of life was the 'Agora' and open space for business, gatherings, hosting political discussions, festivals, athletic contests, statues, temples and public buildings. Many city-states had a fortified hilltop, 'Acropolis' or highest city, used for military purposes at first, but later had temples and palaces, such as the Parthenon in Athens. For ancient Greece, there was no one king or administration in common; each city-state governed themselves. Religion and sports were the glue that kept them together. Every four years Olympic Games were organised in honour of Zeus in his sanctuary in Olympia (the first one was in 776 BC) with the participation of Dorians, Ionians, Spartans and Athenians. Greek city-states advanced urban development not only with their famous urban planning principles, i.e. settlements were laid out on orthogonal principles, with streets forming a checkerboard pattern of identical units, but they also contributed significantly to the knowledge pool of humankind by forming the nucleus of many sciences, which triggered the appearance of a new social class, the *bourgeoisie* (Yigitcanlar 2011).

This era laid the foundations for modern maths, astronomy and philosophy. For instance, Greek mathematician, Pythagoras of Samos, developed his Pythagorean Theorem. Greek mathematician, Thales, predicted a solar eclipse. Eudoxus of Cnidus made the first to attempt to provide a mathematical explanation for the planets. Socrates (credited as one of the founders of Western philosophy), Zeno of Elea (known for his/Zeno's paradoxes), Democritus (known for his formulation of an atomic theory of the universe), Anaxagoras (determined the Milky Way as a concentration of distant stars), Gorgias (introduced the idea of paradoxical thought and expression), Empedocles (originator of the cosmogenic theory that all matter is made up of four elements: water, earth, air and fire), Anaximander (developer of evolutionary ideas such as that the Earth floats unsupported and rain results from the humidity generated by the sun's heat), Anaximenes of Miletus (practised material monism to identify one specific underlying reality made up of a material thing), Heraclitus of Ephesus (advocated ever-present change in the universe), Hippocrates of Kos (the father of Western medicine), Solon of Athens (creator of the Solonian Constitution of Athens, which incorporated the first elements of formalised civil democracy in world history), Aeschylus (author of Greek tragedies), Pindar (the most famous one of the canonical nine lyric poets of ancient Greece), Herodotus of Halicarnassus (the father of history), Thucydides (one of the first historians and the father of the school of political realism), Thespis (founder of Greek theatre) were only a few among the many Greek philosophers, poets, writers, statesmen and law-givers who were renowned in the following centuries for their wisdom. Under Aristotle's extraordinary pupil, Alexander the Great, the Greeks conquered Egypt and the East, and marked the apex of Greek power, an empire stretching from the Balkans to modern-day Pakistan. However, after the death of Alexander the Great there began a period of slow decline. The success of Alexander the Great is seen as a result of being influenced by Aristotle's teachings, taking scientists with him on his military campaigns, perfecting Macedonian military style, the Phalanx, using innovative and daring battle tactics, and forming an army that was professional and strongly equipped with light auxiliaries, archers, a siege train and a cavalry (Fox 2006).

The Romans replaced the Greek power in the region by adopting many aspects of their civilisation. For instance, the Romans adopted Greek gods by renaming them. They also used the Greek alphabet, copied the Macedonian order of battle and Spartan steel weapons and armour, learnt poetry and drama from Greek authors, studied Greek philosophy and imitated Greek art (Van Doren 1992). In other words, they turned Greek theory into Roman practice. The Roman Empire at its peak at around AD 100 covered the whole of the Mediterranean Sea and most of the Black Sea reaching as far as Scotland, the Caspian Sea, the Atlantic, the Sahara and the Persian Gulf. One of the major contributions of Romans was introducing a common law to the entire Empire. In about 450 BC, Roman law was codified and used. The law was the legal system of ancient Rome, including Roman military jurisdiction and the legal developments spanning over a thousand years of jurisprudence from the 12 Tables. Today, Roman law continues to be an influence upon almost all legal systems in the Western world (Riggsby 2010). Along with this law, the concept of citizenship, borrowed from the Greeks, was perfected and applied across the Empire. A Roman citizen living abroad always retained his privileged status. The second major contribution was the Roman roads. Romans used concrete widely, which made possible the paved and durable Roman roads (Lechtman and Hobbs 1986). They excelled in where and how to build roads and how to make them last. The Roman Empire had about 164,000 kms of paved roads across their 5.2 million km^2 territory (Tellier 2009). Some of these roads still exist today. According to Gombrich (2008):

> [t]he Romans did not build these roads out of consideration for the people living there. On the contrary, their aim was to send new troops to all parts of the empire in the shortest possible time. The Romans were superb engineers.
>
> (Gombrich 2008: 84)

Additionally, the Romans made major advancements in sanitation; public baths were used for both hygienic and social purposes. Many Roman houses came to have flush toilets and indoor plumbing and a complex sewer system (Nielsen 1993). The imperial capital Rome's power and wealth drew people from all over the Empire, creating a population at about one million, making it the first city to reach a million of population (Tellier 2009). Many aqueducts were built using the 'Arch' technology to bring water into the city from faraway water sources. Some of the aqueducts built in different parts of the Empire still survive to this day (Hodge 2002). With rapid urbanisation, Rome became an urban sprawl that grew without central or long-term planning, the product of a republican political system in which individuals held power for a year at a time. The Theatre of Pompey, the Colosseum and the Roman Forum were among the largest buildings in the ancient world at the time (Pollard 2014). These buildings were the result of genius designs and building technologies and remain as testaments to Roman engineering and culture. Urban planning and design of Roman cities followed clear regulations for the development of public and military services, and cities were basically composed of a number of identical components, laid out in a particular way, i.e. parallel and equidistant and separated by streets (Yigitcanlar 2011).

Romans further built on the foundations that were laid during the Greek era of maths, astronomy and philosophy. For instance, Gaius Julius Caesar reformed the calendar, the Julian calendar, with 12 months and leap years. Titus Lucretius Carus, a Roman poet and philosopher, was known for his epic philosophical poem *On the Nature of Things*, which is about the tenets and philosophy of Epicureanism. It played an important role both in the development of atomism and in the efforts of various figures during the Age of Enlightenment to construct a new Christian humanism. Marcus Tullius Cicero, a Roman philosopher, politician, lawyer, orator, political theorist, consul and constitutionalist, believed in a government of laws not of men, and articulated an early, abstract conceptualisation of rights, based on ancient law and custom. Lucius Annaeus Seneca, a Roman Stoic philosopher, statesman and dramatist, was a tutor and later advisor to Emperor Nero. His plays became influential during the Renaissance. According to Van Doren (1992):

> [a]udiences remained fascinated by the kind of cruel, violent, and dramatically crude plays that Seneca had written, supposing he was imitating the great Greeks. Audiences are fascinated today. It is Senecan rather than Sophoclean or Shakespearian drama that we watch, with avid interest, on television.
>
> (Van Doren 1992: 80)

Publius Cornelius Tacitus was a senator, consul and governor and considered to be one of the greatest Roman historians. He authored the Annals and the Histories that examine the reigns of the Roman Emperors Tiberius, Claudius, Nero and those who reigned in the Year of the Four Emperors. As said by Van Doren (1992: 81), 'he is the ancestor of such cultural institutions as *People* magazine, although he never falls to the depths reached by the *National Enquirer*'. Additionally, during the early Roman period, Christianity, an Abrahamic, monotheistic religion based on the life and oral teachings of Jesus Christ, was born (in present-time Israel). Jesus added a kind of supernumerary law based on love to the Jewish law. The refusal of the Jews to accept Christ as not merely one of the prophets but as the son of God and one of the three persons of God, the Father, Son and Holy Ghost, created a deep and unbridgeable gulf between the two religions (Van Doren 1992). Christianity began to transition to the dominant religion of the Roman Empire (from paganism) during the reign of the Emperor Constantine the Great (337–306 BC).

During the Iron Age at the opposite end of the world, in the east, India was a prominent centre of learning since ancient times. The ancient cultures of India were among the first to discover the powerful means of maintaining social order through the use of the caste system. This was used especially to control a large population in which there were severe differences in wealth, power and privileges (Van Doren 1992). The Indian subcontinent has been a major contributor to the world and has excelled in fields of astronomy, numerology, arithmetic, mineralogy, metallurgy, logic, information and technology. Some of these inventions include: zero (which was invented independently by the Babylonians, Mayans and Indians), Fibonacci numbers, binary code, the decimal system, the quadratic formula, the value of 'pi' (discovered by Baudhayana), the time taken by the Earth to orbit the sun (Bhaskaracharya calculated this in the fifth century), yoga, ink, crucible steel, dock, diamonds, numerous medical treatments including surgery (such as cataract, artificial limbs, caesareans, fractures, urinary stones, brain and plastic surgery conducted by Sushruta), natural fibres, chess, buttons, the ruler (made of ivory), shampoo, prefabricated home and movable structures, and cotton gin (McNeil 2002). Furthermore, India at the time (or more precisely, modern-day Nepal) was the home of Siddhartha Gautama, known as the 'Enlightened one' or 'Buddha', on whose teachings Buddhism was founded in the late sixth century BC. For many, Buddhism, in its origins at least, is an offshoot of Hinduism, the oldest religion in the world dating back to 2300–1500 BC. Hinduism is about understanding Brahma, existence, from within the 'self' or 'soul', whereas Buddhism is about finding the 'not soul' or 'not self'. In Hinduism, attaining the highest life is a process of removing the bodily distractions from life, allowing one to eventually understand the 'self' or 'soul' nature within. In Buddhism, one follows a disciplined life to move through and understand that nothing in oneself is 'me', such that one dispels the very illusion of existence (Diffen 2015). Buddha is undoubtedly one of the most influential figures in world history and his teachings have affected everything from a variety of other faiths to literature to philosophy in India and the Western world (Kornfield 2004). Buddhism continues to play a vital role in the politics of many Asian countries as its emphasis on social equity and its doctrine that many human ills are caused by poverty, have inspired liberal reform movements (Van Doren 1992). Furthermore, Buddhism all around the world is practised by many today beyond a religion as a way or philosophy of living, leading a moral life that is mindful and aware of thoughts and actions.

Much like India, China has also been the source of a long list of significant contributions to humanity through innovations, scientific discoveries and inventions. This includes the four great inventions, namely papermaking, the compass, gunpowder and printing containing both woodblock and movable types (Needham *et al*. 1963). Other notable inventions include, but are not limited to: iron and steel smelting, the discovery and mining of coal, alcoholic beverages and the process of fermentation, the bell, coffin, dagger axe, potter vessel, lacquer, millet cultivation, noddle, rowing oar, plastromancy, triangular ploughshare, rammed earth, pottery steamer, pottery urn, rice cultivation, sericulture, soybean cultivation, wet field cultivation, acupuncture, banknote, hydraulic-powered armillary sphere, belt drive, belt hook, cast iron bomb, borehole drilling, bristle toothbrush, chemical warfare, chopsticks, civil service examinations, coke as fuel, crank handle, dental amalgam, dominoes, fireworks, gas cylinder, football, hand grenade, horse collar and harness, kite, matches, oil well, playing cards, porcelain, restaurant menu, seismometer, tea, tofu, toilet paper and unmanned hot air balloons (Deng 2011). The invention of the compass helped Chinese envoys to sail into the Indian Ocean from late second century BC. The principal vessels carrying goods to and from China were called Chinese 'kun-lun bo' or 'kunlun ships'. With these boats, which had woven sails averaging 50 m in length and were capable of transporting between 500 and 1,000 people and a cargo of between 250 and 1,000 tons, the Chinese explored the Indian Ocean and the continent of Africa including Madagascar and Egypt (Elfasi and Hrbek 1988). Qin Shi Huang, the King of the state of Qin, conquered all other States and united China in 221 BC and became the first emperor of united China. After the unification, Emperor Qin (or Ch'in where the name China comes from) ordered the building of a network of roads to connect the existing walls, which were built to stop nomadic tribes attacking from the north and northwest, and to extend them further as a front line defence against possible invasion. The Great Wall of China (which with all of its branches measures some 21,196 km) connected numerous state walls, built during the previous four centuries, which were a network of small walls linking river defences to impassable cliffs (Kafka 2007). In the minds of the Chinese, this was a barrier to protect civilisation from barbarism. This great monument still stands today. What is more, Emperor Qin organised a complex state bureaucracy based on Confucian principles. Confucius, who lived during the sixth and fifth centuries BC, was an influential Chinese philosopher, teacher and political figure known for his popular aphorisms and his models of social interaction. The philosophy of Confucius emphasised personal and governmental morality, correctness of social relationships, justice and sincerity. Although the Chinese often follow Confucianism in a religious manner, arguments continue over whether it is a religion (Kaizuka 2002). Around the same time as Confucius, Lao-Tzu (or Laozi), who was a philosopher and poet of ancient China, founded the philosophical Taoism. Taoism emphasises living in harmony with the Tao, meaning way, path or the ordering principle that makes cosmic harmony possible. Philosophical Taoism is rational, contemplative and non-sectarian, and it accepts death as a natural returning to the Tao. Religious Taoism is magical, cultic, esoteric and sectarian, and it emphasises health and healing as ways to gain long life or even immortality. Tai chi and the medical practice of Qigong are modern manifestations of Taoism (Wong 2011).

The Middle Ages

In European history, the Middle Ages, also called as the Medieval period, lasted from the fifth to the fifteenth century. It began with the end of rule across Europe by the Roman Empire as a result of the collapse of the Western Roman Empire in AD 476. By AD 285, the Roman Empire had grown so vast that it was no longer feasible to govern all the provinces from the central seat of Rome. The Emperor, Diocletian, divided management of the Empire into halves with the Eastern Empire governed out of Byzantium (later on called Constantinople) and the Western Empire governed from Rome, but with both parts under his emperorship. In AD 395, on his deathbed, Theodosius I, the last emperor of the united Roman Empire, gave the sovereignty of each part of the Empire to his sons, Arcadius and Honorius, and officially formed two new empires. In the late fourth century, the Western Roman Empire crumbled after a nearly 500-year run as the world's greatest superpower. Invasions by Barbarian tribes, economic troubles and overreliance on slave labour, the rise of the Eastern Roman Empire (Byzantine), overexpansion and military overspending, government corruption and political instability, the arrival of the Huns and the migration of the Barbarian tribes, Christianity and the loss of traditional values, and the weakening of the Roman legions were among the main reasons for the collapse of the Western Roman Empire (Veyne 1997).

The catastrophic climate change event in 536, a series of severe volcanic eruptions in Central and South America, put so much dust into the atmosphere that it depressed the temperature of the Earth for years. This can also be regarded as the trigger that ended the classical world and marked the beginning of the Middle Ages. This climate event blotted the sun out and resulted directly and indirectly, in climate chaos, famine, migration, war and massive political change on all continents (Gräslund and Price 2012). The climatic event worked as a funnel and reinforced an already existing downturn in Europe (Larsen *et al.* 2008). During the Early Middle Ages (from the fifth to tenth century) Europeans suffered from poverty and many died of starvation. During the High Middle Ages (around the eleventh, twelfth and thirteenth centuries), the world experienced a climate slightly warmer than in the preceding period, the so-called 'Medieval Warm Period' or 'Medieval Climate Optimum' (Hughes and Diaz 1994). In Europe, this warmer climate had positive effects. The harvests were great and the population increased rapidly. Under these conditions, art, literature and even science were developing apace. The most visible achievements of this period are undoubtedly the construction of the many cathedrals all over Europe. This was a golden period for European architecture and art. For instance, the establishment of churches and monasteries led to the development of stone architecture that elaborated vernacular Roman forms, from which the term 'Romanesque' is derived. In 1215, King John of England signed a great Charter of Liberties (the Magna Carta) in which he assured the protection of church rights, protection for the barons from illegal imprisonment, access to swift justice and limitations on feudal payments to the Crown. This was to be implemented through a council of 25 barons. This charter, which protected the freedom of the individual, became part of English political life and was typically renewed by each monarch in turn (Gombrich 2008). The Late Middle Ages (the fourteenth and fifteenth centuries) began with the 'Little Ice Age', a period between about 1300 and 1870, which caused cold winters, failed harvests and resulted in 'the Great Famine' (Mann 2002). Furthermore, the arrival of the Black Death in Europe in 1347 pushed the European population into a century-long demographic decline and caused long-term changes in the economy and society. As a result of the epidemic, 30–40 per cent of the European population perished (Pamuk 2007). Gunpowder, the printing press and the compass, adopted from the East, helped Europe to find a way forward. The use of gunpowder in battles affected military organisation. Gutenberg's movable type printing press made possible not only the Reformation but also a dissemination of knowledge that would lead to a gradually more egalitarian society. The compass, along with other innovations such as the cross-staff and the mariner's astrolabe, and advances in shipbuilding enabled the navigation of the world's oceans and the early phases of colonialism (Koenigsberger 2014). Other notable inventions were eyeglasses and the weight-driven clock. In terms of architecture, Gothic architecture remained the norm, particularly in northern Europe, and the gothic cathedral was further elaborated. The end of the Middle Ages coincided with the capture of Constantinople (Istanbul) by the Turks in 1453, the end of the Hundred Years' War between the English and the French in 1453, the Muslims' being ejected from Spain in 1492, the discovery of America by Columbus in 1492 and the beginning of Protestant Reformation in 1517.

Although this period was a 'Dark Age' for Europeans, it was the beginning of the rise of Islam and the rebirth of the Middle Eastern (or Mesopotamian) civilisation. During the so-called 'Islamic Golden Age', much of the Muslim world was ruled by various caliphates, experiencing a scientific, economic and cultural flourishing. Around 610, Muhammad received his first direct message from God (Allah) in Mecca (in present Saudi Arabia) saying he is the messenger or prophet of God. Later on all of the messages he received were collected and written down and became the holy book Qur'an (or Koran), the sacred scriptures of the new religion Islam (a monotheistic and Abrahamic religion). His emigration from Mecca to Medina in 622 marked the start of the Muslim era and saw the beginning of the Islamic calendar. He managed to unite all of the Arabs of the Middle East and North Africa into one nation. During the Umayyad Caliphate, most of the Byzantine and Persian empires, North Africa and Spain were conquered (661–750). In 732, the Arab raiding party was defeated near Tours in southern France effectively ending Muslim penetration of Western Europe from Spain.

The reign of Caliph al-Mamun (813–833) saw the enthusiastic promotion of science and philosophy. In 825, Muhammad ibn Musa al-Khwarizmi produced his famous star tables. In 848, Albumazar or Aby Mashar completed his masterpiece *The Introduction to Astrology* in Baghdad. Averroes or Ibn Rushd, a Muslim philosopher, exerted enormous influence over Western thought with his commentaries of Aristotle's works, which had been mostly forgotten in the West. His main achievement was the reconciliation of Aristotelianism with Islam and Latin translations of Averroes's work, which, beginning in the thirteenth century, led to the legacy of Aristotle being recovered in the Latin West. Avicenna or Ibn Sina, a Muslim philosopher and physician, is regarded as one of the most significant thinkers, writers and authorities on medicine of the 'Islamic Golden Age'. His most famous works are *The Book of Healing*, a philosophical and scientific encyclopaedia, and *The Canon of Medicine*, a medical encyclopaedia that became a standard medical text at many medieval universities and remained in use as late as 1650 (Lyons 2010). Mawlānā Jalāl ad-Dīn Muhammad Rūmī was a thirteenth century Persian poet, jurist, Islamic scholar, theologian and Sufi mystic. He was also an evolutionary thinker in the sense that he believed the spirit after devolution from the divine Ego undergoes an evolutionary process by which it comes nearer and nearer to the same divine Ego, in a modern sense idea of life being creative and evolutionary being similar (Sharif 1966). Rumi believed passionately in the use of music, poetry and dance as a path for reaching God, and he is the founder of Sufi whirling that is performed by dervishes, and Sufi meditation called Muraqaba (Lewis 2000). Rumi's poems are still highly popular and read widely across the world.

After the defeat of the Great Seljuk Empire by Mongols in Anatolia (Asia Minor) in 1256, Seljuk Turks founded the Ottoman Empire (or Turkish Empire) in 1299. With conquests in the Balkans between 1362 and 1389, the Ottoman sultanate was transformed into a transcontinental empire and claimant to caliphate (the last one). The Ottoman Turks overthrew the Byzantine Empire with the 1453 conquest of Constantinople (present-day Istanbul) under the command of the Emperor Sultan Mehmed the Conqueror (or Mehmed II). During the sixteenth and seventeenth centuries, in particular at the height of its power under the reign of Suleiman the Magnificent, the Ottoman Empire was a powerful multinational, multilingual empire controlling much of Southeast Europe, Western Asia, the Caucasus, North Africa, the Horn of Africa and the Silk Road and spice trade routes. The economically important trade routes blocked by the Turks spurred Europe's exploration, which was motivated initially by searching for a sea route around Africa to India and triggered the Age of Discovery. With Istanbul as its capital and control of lands around the Mediterranean basin, the Ottoman Empire was at the centre of interactions between the Eastern and Western worlds for over six centuries. The famous Islamic educational institutions, the madrasa (college) were widespread in the Empire. Hezarfen Ahmed Çelebi, a Turkish polymath, was the first aviator to have made a successful flight with artificial wings in 1630. Lagari Hasan Çelebi launched himself in the air in a seven-winged rocket, which was composed of a large cage with a conical top filled with gunpowder in 1633.

The flight was estimated to have lasted about 20 seconds and the maximum height reached was around 300 m. This was the first known example of a manned rocket and an artificially powered aircraft. Taqi al-Din Muhammad ibn Ma'ruf al-Shami al-Asadi (1526–1585) was a renowned Turkish scientist, astronomer, engineer and inventor. One of his books, *The Sublime Methods of Spiritual Machines* (1551), described the workings of a rudimentary steam engine and steam turbine, predating the more famous discovery of steam power by Giovanni Branca in 1629. The Istanbul Observatory was built during the reign of Sultan Murad III (1574–1595), which was comparable to Tycho Brahe's (1546–1601) Uranienborg Observatory built in 1576. Piri Reis, a famous admiral of the Turkish fleet, drew one of the earliest world maps in 1513 on gazelle skin, primarily detailing the western coast of Africa, the eastern coast of South America and the northern coast of Antarctica. The map was considered the most accurate in the sixteenth century (Ihsanoglu 2004). Other significant philosophers, poets, Sufi mystics and thinkers of this Turk era include Mawlānā Jalāl ad-Dīn Muhammad Rūmī (1207–1273), Haji Bektash Veli (1209–1271), Yunus Emre (1238–1320), and Pir Sultan Abdal (1480–1550).

The Renaissance and the Age of Enlightenment

The Renaissance, a cultural movement started in Italy (more precisely in Florence) in the fourteenth century and lasting until the seventeenth century, is considered as the bridge between the Middle Ages and modern history. The literal meaning of Renaissance being 'rebirth', this period in European civilisation was characterised by a surge of interest in and rediscovery of classical Greek and Roman scholarship and values after a long period of cultural decline and stagnation. This movement had a great influence on and shaped European literature, philosophy, art, music, politics, science, religion and other aspects of intellectual inquiry (Gombrich 2008). Dante Alighieri's great poem the *Divine Comedy* in 1300 marks the end of the Middle Ages and the beginning of the Renaissance, as Dante was the culmination of everything that a thousand years of obsession with God could produce (Van Doren 1992).

The Renaissance was a period in which multitalented 'universal men' or 'Renaissance men' consciously sought to use the classical past as an inspirational model for creating a new age of enlightenment in fields as diverse as science, art and politics (Johnson 2005). In particular, the Renaissance humanism, which was not only a philosophy but also a way or method of learning, brought the combination of reasoning and empirical evidence to education. Humanist scholars, including Niccolò Machiavelli, Thomas More, Pico della Mirandola, Cicero, Quintilian and Desiderius Erasmus, shaped the intellectual landscape of the era (Nauert 2006). Art was the spirit of the Renaissance and in the hands of artists (painters, sculptors and architects, some polymath), such as Leonardo da Vinci, Masaccio, the brothers Pietro and Ambrogio Lorenzetti, Fra Angelico, Sandro Botticelli, Perugino, Piero della Francesca, Raphael, Titian, Giovanni Pisano, Donatello, Andrea del Verrocchio, Lorenzo Ghiberti, Michelangelo, Leon

Battista Alberti, Filippo Brunelleschi, Andrea Palladio, Michelozzo and Filarete, the dignity of humanity found expression in the arts. In this period, art was based on observation of the visible world and practised according to mathematical principles of balance, harmony and perspective (Johnson 2005). Dante Alighieri (the first author who wrote in his native language, Italian, instead of Latin or Greek), Francesco Petrarca, Giovanni Boccaccio, Niccolò Machiavelli, Ludovico Ariosto, Michel de Montaigne, William Shakespeare, Miguel de Cervantes, Baldassare Castiglione, Benvenuto Cellini, Geoffrey Chaucer, John Donne, Ben Jonson, Christopher Marlowe, Thomas More, François Rabelais, Pierre de Ronsard, Jacopo Sannazzaro, Philip Sidney, Edmund Spenser and Lope de Vega are notable examples of remarkable Renaissance writers and thinkers.

In this era, attempts to bypass the Turk controlled Silk Road and spice trade routes resulted in the discovery and exploration of the new continent, America, by Christopher Columbus. Leonardo da Vinci made substantial discoveries in anatomy, civil engineering, optics and hydrodynamics. Rene Descartes is considered the father of modern philosophy. Nicolaus Copernicus is acknowledged as the founder of modern astronomy. Galileo was one of the chief founders of modern science with his greatest impact being the telescope and the laws of motion that changed the way people viewed the universe. Gerhard Kremer or Gerardus Mercator's maps and globes increased trade, exploration and people's knowledge of the world. Johannes Kepler attained fame in astronomy, because of his three planetary laws, and made fundamental contributions in the fields of optics and mathematics. Architect Filippo Brunelleschi made advances in mathematics in order to design buildings. Francis Bacon is called the father of empiricism as his works established and popularised inductive methodologies for scientific inquiry, often called the Baconian method, or simply the scientific method. Johannes Gutenberg's movable type metal printing press democratised learning and allowed a faster propagation of ideas. The particular innovation in Gutenberg's press was that he mechanised the transfer of ink from movable type to paper, which set his printing press apart from his predecessors in China (Hall 2013). The Renaissance had a profound effect on contemporary theology as the foremost theologians of the time were followers of the humanist method, i.e. Erasmus, Zwingli, Thomas More, Martin Luther and John Calvin. The Protestant Reformation began in 1517 with Martin Luther's *The 25 Theses* criticising many of the doctrines and devotional catholic practices. This new movement influenced the Church of England decisively and the national church was made independent under Henry VIII in the early 1530s for political rather than religious reasons. The Protestant Reformation, with its emphasis on the individual need for grace, provided an opportunity for everyone to be able to read the Bible and determine its meanings (Cameron 2012). This new self-centredness also had other effects, such as the rise of capitalism (Van Doren 1992). As stressed by Van Doren (1992), the Greek idea of the city-state came to life in Italian communes in Milan, Pisa, Venice and Florence, and was then adopted by other European city-states, such as Bruges. They overthrew their feudal lords and grasped the power themselves. Freedom was enjoyed by the formation of a new class of urban merchants and traders to produce wealth. Florence became the banker of Europe, and its citizens achieved a glory and splendour of art and architecture belonging to all its people. The revitalised idea of a city-state ruled by its people, the model Renaissance city, spread all across Europe (Martines 1988). Rulers of Renaissance cities aimed to achieve grand effects through architecture. During this era, architects began to systematically study the shaping of urban space, as though the city itself were a piece of architecture that could be given an aesthetically pleasing and functional order. Bold geometry was used, large public areas were built and parts of old cities were rebuilt to create elegant squares, long street vistas and symmetrical building arrangements. Venice is a good example of Renaissance architecture, the vast wealth generated through trade used to build magnificent Renaissance palaces, churches, piazzas and picturesque canals (Argan 1969).

The Age of Enlightenment or Age of Reason is an era from about the 1650s to the 1780s in which cultural and intellectual forces in Western Europe emphasised reason, analysis and individualism rather than traditional lines of authority. European politics, philosophy, science and communications were radically reoriented during the course of this era. Many relatively small advances during the Renaissance triggered larger ones and, through a snowball effect, the Age of Enlightenment came to life. Seventeenth-century precursors, such as Francis Bacon, Thomas Hobbes, Renee Descartes, Galileo Galilei, Johannes Kepler and Gottfried Wilhelm Leibniz borrowed ideas from their predecessors and built on them to come up with groundbreaking findings. For instance, the revision of the scientific method during this period set the stage for others' landmark discoveries – such as Isaac Newton in physics. This approach also ensured centuries of philosophising and innovation (Durant and Durant 1961). The biggest inventions of this time were the invention of the meaning of science and scientific method. In his essay *What is Enlightenment?*, written in 1784, the German philosopher Immanuel Kant summed up the era's motto as 'Dare to know and have courage to use your own reason (understanding)'. Sir Isaac Newton is considered one of the most important scientists in history that lived in the Age of Enlightenment. He defined the three laws of motion and universal gravitation, and his conception of the universe based upon natural and rationally understandable laws became one of the seeds for Enlightenment ideology. Philosopher Jean-Jacques Rousseau wrote his masterpiece *The Social Contract* in 1762 – later on called Social Contract Theory. In this work, he proposed a form of governance system based on a small-scale and straightforward democracy principle that directly reflects the will of the citizens. Closer to the end of his career, he prepared a writing on deeply personal reflection on his life – *Confessions*. His opposition to the empirical philosophers, such as Voltaire, along with his unprecedented intimate perspective contributed to the burgeoning of the 'Romantic era'. This era or in other words 'romanticism' is characterised by an emphasis on emotion, individualism, glorification of the past and nature, and instinct instead of reason (Delon 2013). This movement was also a reaction to the Industrial Revolution. The prevailing principles of the Age of Enlightenment also gave birth to another undercurrent – 'skepticism'. Philosophical skepticism revolved around the idea that the perceived world is relative to the beholder and, as such, no one can be sure whether any truths actually exist. In other words, skeptics questioned the notion that absolutely certain knowledge is possible as knowledge requires justification, and it is not possible to have an adequate justification. For example, David Hume questioned whether human society could really be perfected through the use of reason and denied the ability of rational thought to reveal universal truths (Sparknotes 2015). Furthermore, a number of novel religious ideas developed with the Enlightened faith, including 'Deism (knowledge of God based on the application of our reason on the designs/laws found throughout nature)' and 'Atheism (the rejection of belief in the existence of deities)'. The era promoted the concept of strictly separating the state from religious institutions, and people of different religions and beliefs being equal before the law (Secularism), a concept that is often credited to the writings of English philosopher, John Locke (Israel 2001).

During the Age of Enlightenment many European cities, such as Padua, Bologna, Naples, Rome, Paris, London and Glasgow, had created an intellectual infrastructure of supporting institutions such as universities, reading societies, libraries, periodicals, museums and masonic lodges. The intellects, forming an early information society, spent a great deal of energy disseminating their ideas in cosmopolitan cities in many venues, some of them quite new, such as private salons and coffeehouses in Paris, Milan, Turin and Venice. The Café Procope in Paris was a centre of Enlightenment as it hosted celebrities of the time, such as Voltaire and Rousseau (Darnton 2000). In the Baroque era, the tendency to make a statement through architecture grew and monumental architectural and landscape ensembles were designed and built. Ambitious monarchs constructed new palaces, courts and bureaucratic offices. In Baroque cities, the grand scale was sought in urban public spaces such as long avenues, radial street networks, monumental squares, geometric parks and gardens (Zucker 1955). Examples of this city-building model include Louis XIV's Palace of Versailles and Pierre L'Enfant's plan for Washington DC.

The American and French Revolutions were directly inspired by the Enlightenment ideals. However, what suddenly and ultimately ended the Age of Enlightenment was the French Revolution that took place in 1789. Although the French Revolution attempted to implement orderly representative assemblies in accordance with Enlightenment thought, regrettably it quickly turned into chaos and violence. According to many scholars of the time, Enlightenment-induced breakdown of norms was the root cause of the instability, and the violence was proof that the masses could not be trusted to govern themselves (Chartier 2004). Nonetheless, the discoveries and theories of the intellects from this era still continued to influence Western societies for centuries to come (Zafirovski 2010). Notable intellects of this era include: Francis Bacon, Thomas Hobbes, Baruch Spinoza, John Locke, Balthasar Bekker, Robert Hooke, Isaac Newton, Gottfried Leibniz, Pierre Bayle, Bernard le Bovier de Fontenelle, Jean Meslier, Giambattista Vico, Dimitrie Cantemir, Justus Henning Boehmer, Benito Jerónimo Feijóo y Montenegro, Christian Wolff, Ludvig Holberg, George Berkeley, Emanuel Swedenborg,

Montesquieu, François Quesnay, Voltaire François-Marie Arouet, Henry Home, Lord Kames, Marquis of Pombal, Émilie du Châtelet, Benjamin Franklin, Carl von Linné Carl Linnaeus, GL Buffon, La Mettrie, Thomas Reid, Mikhail Lomonosov, David Hume, Ruđer Bošković, Antonio Genovesi, Jean-Jacques Rousseau, Denis Diderot, James Burnett, Lord Monboddo, Claude Adrien Helvétius, Alexander Sumarokov, Jean le Rond d'Alembert, Baron d'Holbach, Adam Smith, Immanuel Kant, George Mason, Zaharije Orfelin, Jovan Rajić, Gotthold Ephraim Lessing, Moses Mendelssohn, Edmund Burke, Anders Chydenius, Francisco Javier Clavijero, Stanisław August Poniatowski, Joseph Haydn, Josef Vratislav Monse, Christlieb Feldstrauch, Ignacy Krasicki, Joseph-Louis Lagrange, Edward Gibbon, Luigi Galvani, Thomas Paine, Thomas Abbt, Cesare Beccaria, Dositej Obradović, James Boswell, Antoine Lavoisier, Marquis de Condorcet, Ekaterina Dashkova, Thomas Jefferson, Denis Fonvizin, Johann Gottfried von Herder, Gaspar Melchor de Jovellanos, Nikolay Novikov, Olympe de Gouges, Francesco Mario Pagano, Adam Weishaupt, Alexander Radishchev, Johann Wolfgang von Goethe, Hugo Kołłątaj, James Madison, Alexander Hamilton, José Celestino Mutis, Wolfgang Amadeus Mozart, Jan Śniadecki, Mary Wollstonecraft, Leandro Fernández de Moratín, José Gaspar Rodríguez de Francia, Wilhelm von Humboldt, Jędrzej Śniadecki, Vasyl Karazin and Giacomo Leopardi.

The industrial era

The 'scientific revolution' of the sixteenth and seventeenth centuries, and the ideas generated by Galileo, Descartes and Newton, together with a host of scientific contemporaries changed the way of thinking and production methods. The most important invention of the era was the 'factory', a great machine that combined human and mechanical elements to mass-produce goods. Factories applied Descartes' 'geometrical method' of breaking down any situation or operation into the smallest constituent parts and then attempting to deal with each of them mathematically. Adam Smith's famous pin factory is a good example of very large numbers of very small steps adding to the steady progress towards a goal (Van Doren 1992). The concept of the factory gave birth to the Industrial era, and industrialisation marked a shift to power, special-purpose machinery, factories and mass production. The era was also referred to as the Fordist era, named after Henry Ford, which was a notion of a modern economic and social system based on an industrialised and standardised form of mass production (Batchelor 1994). This new system of mass production brought a great change in the organisation of work and production, and the change was revolutionary. The 'Industrial Revolution', which took place during the eighteenth and nineteenth centuries, was a period during which predominantly agrarian, rural societies in England first and then major European countries and America became industrial and urban. During this time and following the Civil War, the 13th Amendment to the United States Constitution abolished slavery in 1865.

The Industrial Revolution is by far the most important milestone in economic history (De Vries 1994). The iron and textile industries, along with the development of the steam engine, played central roles in the Industrial Revolution, which also saw improved systems of transportation, communication and banking (More 2002). This era provided enormous social progress, great gains in health, literacy, social gains and mobility. Developments in the textile and iron industries played central roles in the Industrial Revolution. James Hargreaves invented the spinning jenny (engine), a machine that enabled an individual to produce multiple spools of threads simultaneously. Samuel Compton significantly improved the spinning mule. Edmund Cartwright's power loom mechanised the process of weaving cloth. Abraham Darby discovered a cheaper, easier method to produce cast iron, using a coke-fuelled as opposed to charcoal-fired furnace.

In the 1850s, Henry Bessemer developed the first inexpensive process for mass-producing steel. Thomas Newcomen developed the first practical steam engine, which was used to pump water out of the mines. James Watt improved on Newcomen's steam engine to power machinery, locomotives and ships. Innovation in the transportation industry helped the boom in the Industrial Revolution. In the early 1800s, Richard Trevithick constructed the first railway steam locomotive. In 1830, England's Liverpool and Manchester Railway became the first to offer regular, timetabled passenger services. In 1820, John McAdam developed a new process for road construction, 'macadam', making roads smoother, more durable and less muddy. Robert Fulton built the first commercially successful steamboat, and by the mid-nineteenth century, steamships were carrying freight across the Atlantic. In 1837, William Cooke and Charles Wheatstone patented the first commercial electrical telegraph, which made communication easier. In 1866, a telegraph cable was successfully laid across the Atlantic. A stock exchange was established in London in the 1770s, and the New York Stock Exchange was founded in the early 1790s. Adam Smith, regarded as the founder of modern economics, promoted an economic system based on free enterprise, the private ownership of means of production and a lack of government interference. Perhaps one of the most significant inventions of this era was electricity. The Greeks knew about electricity, but it was not even remotely understood until Benjamin Franklin's investigation of the phenomenon in the 1750s. Later on, Alessandro Volta demonstrated the battery, Sir Humphrey Davy showed how electricity produced heat, Hans Christian Ørsted discovered that electric currents create magnetic fields, Michael Faraday demonstrated the inverse action and James Clerck Maxwell demonstrated electromagnetism. Nikola Tesla designed the modern alternating-current electricity supply system. In 1879, Thomas Alva Edison invented the long-lasting practical electric light bulb (he also invented phonograph and the motion picture camera). Edison's rival direct-current (DC) electric power was chosen over Tesla's alternating-current (AC) system and, by the end of the 1880s, small electrical stations based on Edison's designs were in a number of cities in the United States, but each station was able to power only a few city blocks. However, it did not take long for electricity to become widespread in all cities. In 1888, George Eastman introduced the famous box camera, with its handy roll of negative film and with the promise of cheap and widely available film processing.

The introduction of photography revolutionised the arts of drawing, painting, engineering and architecture (Van Doren 1992).

Millions of people migrated during the Industrial Revolution. Most travelled to find work, but some were transported for their crimes or migrated to escape Britain's poor living conditions. During the Industrial Revolution in Britain, there was high unemployment, up to 75 per cent in some trades (Ashton 1970). For many of those that did work, life was extremely arduous. There are countless examples available of harsh working conditions, particularly in coalmines. Every amenity of urban life was sacrificed to the requirements of industrial production. As the new towns and cities rapidly developed during the Industrial Revolution, the need for cheap housing, near the factories, increased. Most employers ruthlessly exploited their workers by erecting poor, and often unsanitary, shoddily built houses. In the early years of the industrial era, sewerage infrastructure was largely non-existent. Many dwellings had water closets, which emptied into cesspools under dwellings or in backyards, while some had bucket privies collected by dung carts or disposed of in the street (Morgan 2004). Pollution was a part of daily life. Following cholera, tuberculosis and typhoid epidemics, measures for public health and safety were extended. The Public Health Act in 1847 established the General Board of Health in England, and in New York State, the Tenement House Act of 1879 served the same purpose. The first system of water supply by gravity flow was installed, pumping systems were in general use, and methods for the disposal and treatment of sewage improved (Lines 1990).

Industrialisation also had a profound impact on the natural world. While humans had always exploited natural resources, it was in the eighteenth century that this came to be done on a massive and organised scale. Huge areas of land were cleared to make way for factories and large-scale farms. Timber was devoured for housing and construction, and coal became the dominant source of fuel (Allen 2006). The Industrial Revolution caused the birth of a new discipline to find a panacea to the ills of the industrial development-related activities. The year 1909 was a milestone in the establishment of 'urban planning discipline and practice' as a modern governmental function; it saw the passage of Britain's first Town Planning Act (Benevolo 1967).

In 1898, Ebenezer Howard prepared plans for a 'garden city' (or in its modern meaning a new town) as an ideal of a planned residential community. This small and planned garden city, girdled by greenbelts, was to serve as the master key to a higher and more cooperative stage of civilisation based on ecologically balanced communities. This was a response to the need for improvement in the quality of urban life, which had become marred by overcrowding and congestion due to uncontrolled growth since the beginning of the Industrial Revolution (Hall and Tewdwr-Jones 2010). The main elements of a garden city were the: purchase of a large area of agricultural land within a ring fence; planning of a compact town surrounded by a wide rural belt; accommodation of residents, industry, and agriculture within the town; limitation of the extent of the town and prevention of encroachment upon the rural belt; and a natural rise in land values to be used for the town's own general welfare. The garden city movement was very influential in British urban planning theory and practice and internationally, since when it has represented a remarkable blend of acceptance of and protest against urban changes and the rise of the suburbs (Buder 1990). Efforts to improve the urban environment included recognition of the need for recreation areas, such as parks, to provide visual relief and places for healthful play or relaxation. New York's Central Park, envisioned in the 1850s and designed by architects, Calvert Vaux and Frederick Law Olmsted, became a widely imitated model (Rosenzweig and Blackmar 1992). In Paris in the 1850s, Georges-Eugène Haussmann became the greatest of the planners on a grand scale, using Baroque principles of urban design, advocating straight arterial boulevards, advantageous vistas and a symmetry of squares and radiating roads. He built new parks and gardens for the recreation and relaxation of the Parisians, particularly those in the new neighbourhoods of the expanding city, and new train stations to connect the city to the rest of the country (Jordan 1995). Although most of the ideas for the changes in Paris came from Napoleon III, Haussmann had an exceptional capacity for work ensuring that the plans were carried out expeditiously. The resulting urban form was widely emulated throughout the rest of continental Europe. Urban planning scholars, such as Lewis Mumford, argued that the real purpose of Haussmann's boulevards was to make it easier for the military to crush popular uprisings of the time (Mumford 1961). The 'city beautiful' movement was coined in the US principles set out by Daniel Burnham. The movement was first showcased in Chicago during the World's Columbian Exposition in 1893. The archetype of the city beautiful, characterised by grand malls and majestically sited civic buildings in Greco-Roman architecture, was replicated in civic centres and boulevards throughout the country, contrasting with and in protest against the surrounding disorder and ugliness (Wilson 1994). In this era, the most influential factor in shaping the physical form of the contemporary city was transportation technology, e.g. trains and automobiles. In 1768, Nicolas-Joseph Cugnot built the first steam-powered automobile capable of human transportation. In 1807, François Isaac de Rivaz designed the first car powered by an internal combustion engine fuelled by hydrogen. In 1886, the first petrol or gasoline powered automobile, the Benz Patent-Motorwagen, was invented by Karl Benz (Eckermann 2001). Transportation networks became the focus of planning activities, especially as subway systems were constructed in London (in 1890), Glasgow (in 1896), Budapest (in 1896), Chicago (in 1897), Paris (in 1900), Boston (in 1901), Berlin (in 1902) and New York (in 1904). Local governments started to invest in road infrastructure and widening and extending roads. In 1903, the Wright brothers invented the first successful aeroplane in the United States. Many western cities formed planning departments. The colonial powers transported European concepts of city planning to the cities of the developing world.

Karl Max, Walt Whitman, Herman Melville, Charles Baudelaire, Gustave Flaubert, Emile Zola, Friedrich Nietzsche, George Eliot, Thomas Hardy, Oscar Wilde, Charles Darwin and Sigmund Freud were among the major intellects of the industrial era that made significant contributions to political thinking, literature, arts and science. According to Van Doren (1992), the world in 1914 can be divided into four economic zones. The first one constitutes the highly industrialised countries, such as Britain, Germany, the United States, Japan and Belgium. Mostly industrialised countries, such as Sweden, Italy and Austria, form the second group. The third zone includes countries that had begun to industrialise, such as Russia. The last group was the developing world countries, such as the Balkan Nations, the Ottoman Empire, Latin America and colonial territories in Asia and Africa. For the first time in history, a small proportion of the population of the globe (industrialised countries) had the power to control the rest of the world; and the competition and conflict between these countries to expand their domination eventually caused WWI. The total number of military and civilian deaths during this war amounted to over 16 million, ranking it among the deadliest conflicts in human history. However, the influenza pandemic of 1918–1919, known as 'Spanish Flu' or 'La Grippe', killed more people than the war, somewhere between 20 and 40 million people. The war led to technological advancements and innovations including tanks, machineguns, barbwire, flamethrowers, poisoned gas, tracer bullets, interrupter gear, air traffic control, depth chargers, hydrophones, aircraft carriers, pilotless drones, mobile x-ray machines and sanitary napkins (Ross 2003).

After WWII, governments in European countries launched large-scale housing and redevelopment programs within their war devastated cities. The principles of the modernist planning movement were adopted in these programs. The movement based its philosophy on the ideas of Siegfried Giedion, Le Corbusier and the Bauhaus international art school. The signature design principles of these projects included high-rise buildings to be separated by green spaces, which became a norm for contemporary urban development. The form of the buildings in these programs reflected both the need to produce large-scale, relatively inexpensive projects, and the architects' preference for models that exploited new materials and technologies that also could be replicated elsewhere in the world (Encyclopaedia Britannica 2015). Traditionally, up until then, governments relied on regulatory devices as a means of restricting private developers. However, these programs, for the first time, involved government bodies directly in housing development, which gave the public sector a more effective means of controlling the pattern of urban growth through its investments (Freestone 2000). In contrast to Europe, in the United States housing construction continued to be privately planned and financed. Nevertheless, the federal government encouraged the development through tax subsidies and government-guaranteed mortgage loans for homeowners. Planning of the suburban development took place at the municipal level in the form of zoning and subdivision approvals. The public sector also took care of the planning and financing of the major infrastructure development in cities (Hall 2014). WWII started as the cumulative effect of a number of factors, including the conditions created by the peace agreements of WWI, the rise of totalitarian and militaristic regimes of Germany, Italy and Japan, and the Great Depression in the USA.

It was the deadliest war in history with over 60 million people killed, which was over 3 per cent of the world's population. Technology played a crucial role in determining the outcome of the war. Electronics rose to prominence quickly during the war as equipment designed for communications and the interception of those communications was becoming critical. For instance, the German 'Enigma' encryption machine was an electro-mechanical rotor cypher machine, invented by Arthur Scherbius, which was used for enciphering and deciphering secret messages. 'Colossus', designed by Tommy Flowers, was the first electronic computer to solve a problem posed by mathematician, Max Newman, at the Government Code and Cypher School at Bletchley Park in the UK. Alan Turing's use of probability in cryptanalysis contributed to its design. Turing, British pioneering computer scientist, mathematician, logician, cryptanalyst, philosopher and mathematical biologist, devised a number of techniques for breaking the German Enigma machine (Hodges 2012). He was highly influential in the development of computer science, providing a formalisation of the concepts of algorithm and computation with the Turing machine, which can be considered a model of a general-purpose computer. He is widely considered as the father of theoretical computer science and artificial intelligence (Downey *et al.* 2014). Albert Einstein won the Nobel Prize for physics in 1921 for his famous 'General Theory of Relativity' that hypothesised gravitation not as a force as suggested by Newton but as a curved field in a space-time continuum that is created by the presence of mass, $E = mc^2$ (Isaacson 2007). The great triumph of Einstein's work also springs from his understanding of Maxwell's description of electrodynamics. This discovery then led to the development of nuclear power, and then the atomic bomb, whose use over Japan marked the end of WWII in 1945. Penicillin, jerry cans, the pressurised cabin, radio navigation, radar, synthetic rubber and synthetic oil, the V-2 rocket, jet engine, ballpoint pen, nylon, Teflon, jeep, colour television, aerosol spray, helicopters, microwave oven and the kidney dialyses machine, are among the other inventions of the time.

The post-WWII economic policies, so-called Keynesian economics, in the capitalist Western nations were successful in generating rapid growth with high employment. Keynesian economics theory, developed by British economist, John Maynard Keynes, was an attempt to understand the Great Depression. It advocates a mixed economy, predominantly private sector-driven, but with a role for government intervention during recessions. The 'Golden Age of Capitalism' ended with the collapse of the Bretton Woods system in 1971, the 1973 oil crisis and the 1973–1974 stock market crash (Marglin and Schor 1992). By the second half of the twentieth century, technology, science and inventions had progressed at an accelerated rate. In the 1950s, one of the remarkable discoveries of the time was DNA (Deoxyribonucleic acid). In 1953, James Watson and Francis Crick suggested the first correct double-helix model of DNA structure and jointly (with Maurice Wilkins) received the Nobel Prize in Physiology or Medicine in 1962. Philo Taylor Farnsworth invented electronic television in 1927 in San Francisco, and it became the dominant media in the 1950s. Also during this decade the first credit card, Diners, was invented by Ralph Schneider, Edward Teller built the hydrogen bomb, the first patent for the barcode was issued to Joseph Woodland and Bernard Silver, the transistor radio was invented by Texas Instruments, the solar cell was invented by Chaplin, Fuller and Pearson, Optic fibre was invented, computer hard disk, modem and language Fortran were invented, Gordon Gould invented the laser, and Jack Kilby and Robert Noyce invented the microchip. In the 1960s, humanity had entered the space age when, in 1961, Russian cosmonaut, Yuri Gagarin, became the first human in space, and in 1969, American astronauts, Neil Armstrong and Edwin Aldrin, walked on the moon. During this decade the halogen lamp, audio cassette, fibre-tip pen, video disk, the first computer game (Spacewar), computer language BASIC, compact disc, soft contact lenses, electric fuel injection cars, handheld calculators, computer mouse, the first computer with integrated circuits, computer RAM (random access memory), the first internet (ARPANET) for military use only, ATM machines and barcode scanner were among the leading inventions. This decade witnessed a battle between private sector and academia in designing what we call today 'internet'; telecommunications companies backed the 'X.25', and academic computer scientists the 'internet'. Due to a simpler, collaborative and ad hoc approach, the internet has become the norm, which was the triumph of distributed innovation over a centralised one (Townsend 2013).

The 1970s started the age of the practical computer, made possible by the invention of the floppy disk (by Alan Shugart) and the microprocessor (by Faggin, Hoff and Mazor). In the 1970s, printers (daisy-wheel, dot-matrix, ink-jet and laser), liquid-crystal display (LCD), videocassette and recorder, magnetic resonance imaging (MRI), artificial heart, word processor, spread sheet, the first video game (pong), gene splicing, ethernet (local computer network), mobile phones, Walkman and Cray super computer were invented. The 1980s saw the rise of the multinational corporation and scientific developments, particularly in the worlds of computers (e.g. Apple and Microsoft) and health sciences (e.g. human growth hormone was genetically engineered and the first patent for a genetically engineered animal was granted). During this decade, hepatitis-B vaccine, soft bifocal contact lens, synthetic skin, scanning tunnelling microscope, the computer operating system MS-DOS, the first personal computer (IBM-PC), CD-ROM, the term 'virtual reality', Apple Lisa, Apple Macintosh, MS Windows, high-temperature super-conductor, the first 3D video game, digital cellular phones, Doppler radar, Indiglo nightlight and high-definition television were invented. The 1990s witnessed remarkable developments in the various areas of science and technology, the introduction of the internet for public use, the rise of Microsoft, invention of genetic engineering, and cloning and stem cell research. During the last decade of the twentieth century, the World Wide Web (WWW), internet protocol (HTTP), WWW language (HTML), digital answering machine, Pentium processors, Java computer language, DVD, web TV, gas-powered fuel cell, the smart pill and HIV protease inhibitor were invented.

The classical urban models, developed in the late 1950s and 1960s on the basis of 'urban and central place theories', faithfully reflected the world of that time. On a broader inter-urban or regional scale, in a world of relatively self-contained agrarian regions, central urban places exchanged goods and services with their rural hinterlands. On a narrower intra-urban scale, was a world of centralised cities in which central business districts acted as dominant nodes, connected by traditional radial public transport lines to the suburbs that depended on them for services and that supplied their labour forces (Hall 1997). The primary goal of city planning in the mid-twentieth century emphasised that land use, transport and housing should be designed in relation to each other. In the United States, the 'rational model' that experts would evaluate alternatives in relation to a specified set of goals and then choose the optimum solution, was seen as a promising approach. However, it was soon criticised on the grounds that the human consequences of planning decisions could not be neatly quantified and added up and decisions made isolated from public opinion (Benevolo 1980). In the latter half of the twentieth century, rapid population growth and increased industrial activities started to create serious environmental challenges. Modernist planning fell into decline in the 1970s when the construction of cheap, uniform tower blocks ended in most countries, such as Britain and France. Similarly, sprawling suburban development became problematic in the provision of infrastructure in many countries, such as Australia, Canada, New Zealand and the United States. The concept of 'sustainability' emerged in the early 1970s in response to growing concerns about the impact of development practices on the state of the environment (Yigitcanlar *et al.* 2015). The debate on sustainability started with the United Nations (UN) Stockholm Conference on the Human Environment in 1972. In this conference, a declaration was produced emphasising the international concern for environmental protection. The declaration proclaimed that environmental problems had become a growing global concern, and thus international cooperation among nations, governments and nongovernmental organisations is required to deal with this matter. In 1980, the International Union for the Conservation of Nature and Natural Resources prepared the World Conservation Strategy, which was the first attempt to promote the principles of the sustainable use of natural resources. In 1983, the UN established the World Commission on Environment and Development, which was charged with developing a global agenda for the conservation of natural resources. The commission published a report known as the Brundtland Report in 1987, and the term 'sustainable development' was first introduced in this report. The report proposed sustainable development as a global goal to achieve a harmonious balance of the three components of urban development: social welfare, economic development and environmental protection. In 1992, the UN Conference on Environment and Development was organised. The Conference produced Agenda 21, which provides a comprehensive plan of action for sustainable development. In 1996, the UN HABITAT II Conference was held in Istanbul. This conference produced a Habitat Agenda, which was signed by 171 countries to show their commitment towards ensuring a better living environment for their citizens. In 1997, the Kyoto Protocol was signed in the UN Framework Convention on Climate Change, which was a legally binding emission target for industrialised countries to achieve (Yigitcanlar and Dizdaroglu 2015). Along with the sustainable urban development agenda in the 1980s, the New Urbanism movement, also referred to as smart growth or neo-traditionalism, an urban design movement that promotes walkable neighbourhoods containing a range of housing and job types, influenced many aspects of real estate development, urban planning and municipal land-use strategies that has attracted popular attention through its alternative views of suburban development (Katz *et al.* 1994). Furthermore, in the late 1990s, the concept of participatory planning, which involves residents and stakeholders in the decision-making process for their locales, is included in the planning agendas of some cities, particularly in the Anglophone countries.

The post-industrial era

The dramatic consequences of human activities, which have been happening since the beginning of the Industrial era through population increase, sprawling urbanisation and polluting industrialisation, transportation and food production activities, started to take their toll on the planet during the post-industrial era. Large-scale extinction events, desertification, deforestation, loss of biodiversity, climatic changes, topsoil loss, flooding, famine, disease outbreaks and insect plagues (e.g. bees) are among the significant changes and challenges that we have been facing throughout many parts of the world. Moreover, in recent years, their impacts have been increasing at an accelerating rate (Kalnay and Cai 2003). In this new era, the number of megacities, a metropolitan area with a total population in excess of 10 million people, has reached 36. Tokyo, hosting almost 38 million people and being the largest, is followed by Delhi, Seoul, Shanghai and Mumbai. In the list there are 22 entries from Asia, 5 from Europe, 3 from North America, 3 from South America and 3 from Africa, indicating the urbanisation quantum (and also externalities) of the continent of Asia.

Besides these issues, the post-industrial period is characterised as an era in the development of an economy or nation in which the relative importance of manufacturing lessens and that of services, information and research grows. The era is also referred as the post-Fordist era that is characterised by small-batch production; economies of scope; specialised products and jobs; new information technologies; emphasis on types of consumers in contrast to previous emphasis on social class; the rise of the service and the white-collar worker; and the feminisation of the work force (Amin 2011). This period, already upon us, commenced during the 1990s. The late twentieth-century society of technically advanced nations was based largely on the production and consumption of services and information instead of goods. In other words, cities of this era were characterised by a growing proportion of talented workers and the service orientation of activities, while the role of agriculture and industrial manufacturing has been diminishing in these post-industrial Western nations. In the twenty-first century, dynamic processes of economic and spatial restructuring are radically altering urban economies, and knowledge has become a precious local and regional resource for post-industrial territories, which were severely affected by the economic and social implications of structural change. To compensate for the loss of industrial monopolistic power, and to remain competitive in a world economy, the new global division of labour forces cities to concentrate on developing knowledge as a critical local and regional resource. Subsequently, preparing for a 'knowledge economy and society' has become a new political challenge (Cooke and Leydesdorff 2006). Naturally, the development paths of cities differ significantly, but the transition from a natural and physical resource-based manufacturing orientation to a knowledge-based service orientation has been a trend in many cities worldwide (Yigitcanlar and Lonnqvist 2013). The concept of knowledge economy, which is grounded in the 'endogenous growth theory', emerged from an increasing recognition of the requirement for the generation, circulation and use of knowledge within national and urban economies for increased competitiveness (Yigitcanlar 2014a). In the era of the global knowledge economy, the world is becoming increasingly integrated, and knowledge is becoming the driving force for economic growth, societal development and improvement in the competitiveness of not only the industrial system and firms (Konstadakopulos 2003) but also the urban regions (May and Perry 2011).

With the advent of the twenty-first century, most of the world's population have become urban residents. The UN (UN 2013) has estimated that, by 2050, about 70 per cent of the world's population will be living in cities, which makes the twenty-first century the 'century of cities'. In this new era, cities compete in a global knowledge economy, seeking constantly to redefine their economic roles as old functions are lost and new functions are sought to take their place. According to Hall (1997), since the 1990s the post-industrial nature of the economy and society influenced the emergence of a new kind of city: globalised (connected to other cities in global networks); tertiarised and even quaternarised (a process that is distinctly characterised by the substantial effect of technological and organisational change on economic development); informationalised (using information as a raw material); and polycentric (dispersing residences and decentralising employment into multiple centres or edge cities). Consequently, so-called 'global cities' have started to play a dominant role in controlling the world economy, through banking and related financial institutions, or through the headquarters of major multinational corporations, or through ownership of the media, e.g. London, New York, Tokyo. Contemporary cities that seek to achieve a similar performance to these global cities focused increasingly on innovation as the key driver to sustainable growth and competitiveness (Pancholi *et al*. 2014). The expansion of the knowledge economy, globalisation and the growing global competitiveness has imparted the importance of creativity and innovation in local economies (Carrillo *et al*. 2014). In other words, technological innovation and knowledge generation have become critical elements, more than ever, in the contemporary urban and economic development as the economic future of cities increasingly depends on the capacity to attract, generate, retain and foster creativity, knowledge and innovation. Accordingly, 'knowledge-based development' has become a new urban policy approach to boost the innovation and knowledge creation basis of our cities (Yigitcanlar 2014b). However, augmenting the innovation and knowledge creation basis of cities requires more than focusing on economic measures. The knowledge economy excellence of cities is also a result of effective investment in people and ideas that create a vibrant and liveable environment, where knowledge is produced, exchanged and marketed (Lonnqvist *et al*. 2014).

Today, cities are undoubtedly the engines of economic growth, as the lion's share of the innovations and entrepreneurship take place in cities that foster economic growth (Pancholi *et al*. 2014). Rapid urbanisation, along with globalisation and knowledge economy in the twenty-first century, has led to the new century being referred to as the century of cities. This new era has marked the beginning of the novel advancements in the field of ICT. The rapid development of ICTs has made a significant impact on the overall socioeconomic fabric of our cities and has created an urgent need for urban planners and administrators to explore new ways of strategising planning and development that encompass the needs and requirements of the knowledge economy and society (Yigitcanlar and Sarimin 2015). Furthermore, global environmental and climatic issues, global financial crises, terrorism, peak oil, increasing number of megacities, Middle Eastern social unrest and many other global and regional crises have marked the early twenty-first century as a difficult period. These problems have also given us a wakeup call for us to rethink where society is heading and how we need to plan and manage our cities to avoid or minimise their impacts. Due to tough competition in the era of knowledge economy, cities are now required to become entrepreneurial, work in partnership with the private sector and find ways to deal with the new responsibilities given to them. As a result of environmental matters, cities are now required to become eco-cities or eco-friendly cities, produce as few carbon emissions as possible, adopt sustainable transport, infrastructure and urban development approaches, find ways to mitigate climate change and deal with the increasing public health investment needs and aging population issues. In terms of social and governance issues, cities are required to become more transparent and inclusive in decision making, support social equity, work together with the communities towards a common future and manage institutions to work better with each other, prepare their vision and objectives, and become more strategic and dynamic in nature (Yigitcanlar 2011).

In the mid-1990s, as a response to the aforementioned changes and challenges, Knight (1995: 225–226) coined the term, 'knowledge-based development of cities' that refers to, 'the transformation of knowledge resources into local development, which could provide a basis for sustainable development'. Yigitcanlar (2011: 354) demarcated its more popular synonymous 'knowledge-based urban development' (KBUD) as potentially, 'the new development paradigm of the knowledge era that aims to bring economic prosperity, environmental sustainability, a just sociospatial order and good governance to cities'. According to many KBUD scholars (e.g. Carrillo *et al*. 2014), when applied appropriately, KBUD could produce a balanced and sustainable approach that is sought for the development of post-industrial cities, e.g. Melbourne (see Yigitcanlar *et al*. 2008), in order to deal with the contemporary problems of our time, such as global climate change and global financial crises. Today, popularisation of the KBUD has fuelled localised urban development strategies and actions within numerous developed and emerging economies across the world (Yigitcanlar and Bulu 2015). These established and emerging primate and second-tier 'knowledge cities' include, but are not limited to: Austin, Bangalore, Barcelona, Boston, Bilbao, Birmingham, Brisbane,

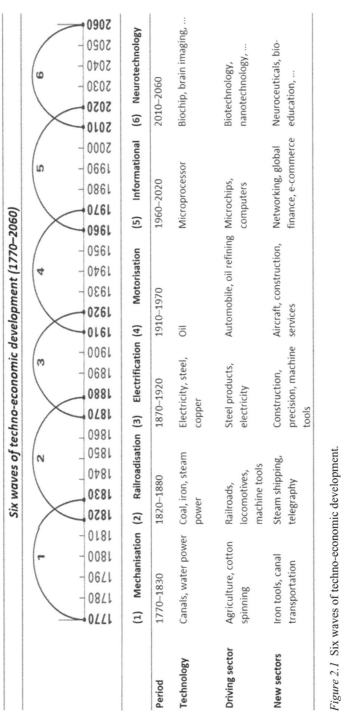

Six waves of techno-economic development (1770–2060)

	(1) Mechanisation	(2) Railroadisation	(3) Electrification	(4) Motorisation	(5) Informational	(6) Neurotechnology
Period	1770–1830	1820–1880	1870–1920	1910–1970	1960–2020	2010–2060
Technology	Canals, water power	Coal, iron, steam power	Electricity, steel, copper	Oil	Microprocessor	Biochip, brain imaging, ...
Driving sector	Agriculture, cotton spinning	Railroads, locomotives, machine tools	Steel products, electricity	Automobile, oil refining	Microchips, computers	Biotechnology, nanotechnology, ...
New sectors	Iron tools, canal transportation	Steam shipping, telegraphy	Construction, precision, machine tools	Aircraft, construction, services	Networking, global finance, e-commerce	Neuroceuticals, bio-education, ...

Figure 2.1 Six waves of techno-economic development.

Source: Lynch 2009.

Copenhagen, Curitiba, Dubai, Espoo, Helsinki, Hong Kong, Istanbul, Kuala Lumpur, Manchester, Manizales, Melbourne, Mondragon, Monterrey, Montreal, Munich, San Francisco, Stockholm, Ottawa, Oulu, Seattle, Seoul, Sheffield, Shenzhen, Singapore, Sydney, Tallinn, Tampere, Toronto, Turku, Valencia, Vancouver, Vienna and Zurich (for more information, see Carrillo *et al.* 2014).

Since the Industrial Revolution, there has been a relatively consistent pattern of 50-year waves of techno-economic change, which impacted both societal and urban development. The fifth wave of information technology diffusion is nearing an end (see Figure 2.1), while a sixth wave is emerging with converging advancements across the nano-bio-info-cogno (NBIC) space (Yigitcanlar 2011). According to Lynch (2009), the sixth wave is neurotechnology, which revolves around enhancing human performance and will help in widening the global knowledge society and hopefully, producing the panacea to global problems and financial, social and climatic crises. The era of knowledge economy encouraged research, development, innovation and investment in the areas and industries of, in particular, ICT and media, pharmaceutical and biosciences, entertainment and art, eco-sciences and green technologies and so on. Subsequently, some of the most significant inventions of the twenty-first century include: Apple iPod, iPad, iPhone, iTunes, Skype, Facebook, Twitter, YouTube, Nintendo Wii, Wi-Fi, Amazon Kindle, Google Android, Spotify, 4G phone service, 3D printing, cell transplantation, driverless car, Mars' Opportunity and Curiosity rovers, Exacto self-guided bullets, Abiocor system (a fully functional artificial heart that mimics the function of the native heart), Braingate to enable tetraplegic people to control a robotic arm through the mere power of thought, Nissan Leaf electric car, advancements in genetic engineering, advancements in nanotechnology, hypersonic transportation and a spray-on skin gun that uses a person's own stem cells for regenerating skin tissue.

Summary

The short history of mankind is the history of the progress and development of human knowledge, creativity and technology (Van Doren 1992). When we consider the urbanisation and civilisation progress achieved through human intelligence and creativity with development and utilisation of technology during predominantly the last five millennia, it is not hard to agree with Smith (2012), who refers to humankind as *homo urbanus*, the city builder ape that shapes our environment. By creating, using and transferring accumulated knowledge and technology, humankind managed to increase their population during the Ice Age from only about a few hundred thousand (facing the risk of extinction) to a few million during the Stone Age, to about 300 million during the Iron Age up to the end of the pre-industrial era, to a billion in 1830 and two billion in 1930. From there, the world's population grew to four billion by 1975 during the industrial era, and from there to seven billion in 2013 during the post-industrial era. Population projections from the UN (UN 2013) suggest the world's population might reach nine billion before the end of the first half of the century, in 2048.

However, this rapid population increase, coupled with unsustainable human activities, is resulting in the scarcity and inequitable share of the limited natural and financial resources. Adding to this global climate change, which refers to the significant and lasting changes in the statistical distribution of weather patterns, such as increased Earth surface temperature or the increasing number and frequency of extreme rainfall events or extreme droughts (Goonetilleke *et al.* 2014), and global financial crises, human civilisation may yet have a few more major obstacles to tackle for survival. While according to some scholars more radical changes are needed, such as adopting fully sustainable living by all (Turner 2008), for others, human intelligence, knowledge and technology are essential means to finding a viable solution to the ever-growing catastrophic problems (Grubb 2004).

References

Allen, RC 2006, *The British Industrial Revolution in Global Perspective: How Commerce Created the Industrial Revolution and Modern Economic Growth*, Nuffield College, Oxford, UK.

Amin, A (ed.) 2011, *Post-Fordism: A Reader*, John Wiley & Sons, London.

Argan, GC 1969, *The Renaissance City*, George Braziller, New York.

Ashton, TS 1970, *The Industrial Revolution 1760–1830*, Oxford University Press, London.

Bahn, PG 1997, *Journey through the Ice Age*, University of California Press, Los Angeles, CA.

Batchelor, R 1994, *Henry Ford, Mass Production, Modernism, and Design*, Manchester University Press, Manchester, UK.

Benevolo, L 1967, *The Origins of Modern Town Planning, Great Britain*, Routledge, New York.

Benevolo, L 1980, *The History of the City*, MIT Press, Cambridge, MA.

Brundtland, G, Khalid, M, Agnelli, S, Al-Athel, S, Chidzero, B, Fadika, L, Hauff, V, Lang, I, Shijun, M, de Botero, MM, Singh, M 1987, *Report of the World Commission on Environment and Development: Our Common Future*, UN, New York.

Buder, S 1990, *Visionaries and Planners: The Garden City Movement and the Modern Community*, Oxford University Press, Oxford, UK.

Cameron, E 2012, *The European Reformation*, Oxford University Press, Oxford, UK.

Carrillo, J, Yigitcanlar, T, Garcia, B, Lonnqvist, A 2014, *Knowledge and the City: Concepts, Applications and Trends of Knowledge-Based Urban Development*, Routledge, New York.

Chartier, R 2004, *The Cultural Origins of the French Revolution*, Duke University Press, Durham, NC.

Clark, JGD 2014, *The Mesolithic Settlement of Northern Europe*, Cambridge University Press, London.

Coles, JM, Harding, AF (eds) 2014, *The Bronze Age in Europe: An Introduction to the Prehistory of Europe c. 2000–700 BC*, Routledge, New York.

Cooke, P, Leydesdorff, L 2006, 'Regional development in the knowledge-based economy', *Journal of Technology Transfer*, vol. 31, no. 1, pp. 5–15.

Creekmore, A, Fisher, KD (eds) 2014, *Making Ancient Cities: Space and Place in Early Urban Societies*, Cambridge University Press, London.

Darnton, R 2000, 'An early information society: News and the media in eighteenth-century Paris', *American Historical Review*, vol. 105, no. 1, pp. 1–35.

De Vries, J 1994, 'The industrial revolution and the industrious revolution', *The Journal of Economic History*, vol. 54, no. 2, pp. 249–270.

Delon, M (ed.) 2013, *Encyclopedia of the Enlightenment*, Routledge, New York.

Deng, Y 2011, *Ancient Chinese Inventions*, Cambridge University Press, Cambridge, MA.

Diffen 2015, *Buddhism vs. Hinduism*, accessed on 30 July 2015 from http://www.diffen.com/difference/Buddhism_vs_Hinduism

Downey, R, Avigad, J, Brattka, V, Blum, L, Buhrman, H, Fokina, EB, Welch, PD 2014, *Turing's Legacy*, Cambridge University Press, Cambridge, MA.

Durant, W, Durant, A 1961, *The Age of Reason Begins: The Story of Civilization: Part VII: A History Of European Civilization (1558–1648)*, Simon and Schuster, New York.

Eckermann, E 2001, *World History of the Automobile*, Society of Automotive Engineers, Warrendale, PA.

Elfasi, M., Hrbek, I (eds) 1988, *General History of Africa: Africa from the Seventh to the Eleventh Century*, UNESCO, Heinemann, CA.

Encyclopaedia Britannica 2015, *Urban Planning*, accessed on 14 August 2015 from http://www.britannica.com/topic/urban-planning/Postwar-approaches

Fox, RL 2006, *Alexander the Great*, Penguin, London.

Freestone, R (ed.) 2000, *Urban Planning in a Changing World: The Twentieth Century Experience*, Taylor and Francis, New York.

Gombrich, EH 2008, *A Little History of the World*, Yale University Press, New Haven, CT.

Gomme, A 1933, *The Population of Athens in the Fifth and Fourth Centuries B.C.*, Blackwell, Oxford, UK.

Goonetilleke, A, Yigitcanlar, T, Ayoko, G, Egodawatta, P 2014, *Sustainable Urban Water Environment: Climate, Pollution and Adaptation*, Edward Elgar, Cheltenham, UK.

Gräslund, B, Price, N 2012, 'Twilight of the gods? The "dust veil event" of AD 536 in critical perspective', *Antiquity*, vol. 86, no. 332, pp. 428–443.

Grubb, M, 2004, 'Technology innovation and climate change policy: An overview of issues and options', *Keio Economic Studies*, vol. 41, no. 2, pp. 103–132.

Hall, MB 2013, *The Scientific Renaissance 1450–1630*, Courier Corporation, Toronto, ON.

Hall, P 1997, 'Modelling the post-industrial city', *Futures*, vol. 29, no. 4, pp. 311–322.

Hall, P 2014, *Cities of Tomorrow: An Intellectual History of Urban Planning and Design since 1880*, John Wiley & Sons, London.

Hall, P, Tewdwr-Jones, M 2010, *Urban and Regional Planning*, Routledge, New York.

Hawkes C 1931, 'Hill-forts', *Antiquity*, vol. 5, no. 17, pp. 60–97.

Hill, KR, Walker, RS, Božičević, M, Eder, J, Headland, T, Hewlett, B, Wood, B 2011, 'Co-residence patterns in hunter-gatherer societies show unique human social structure', *Science*, vol. 331, no. 6022, pp. 1286–1289.

Hodge, AT 2002, *Roman Aqueducts and Water Supply*, Bristol Classical Press, Bristol, UK.

Hodges, A 2012, *Alan Turing: The Enigma*, Random House, New York.

Hughes, B 2014, 'Athens: Birthplace of democracy', in Norwich, JJ (ed.) *Cities That Shaped the Ancient World*, Thames and Hudson, London, pp. 126–131.

Hughes, MK, Diaz, HF 1994, 'Was there a "Medieval Warm Period", and if so, where and when?', *Climatic Change*, vol. 26, no. 2–3, pp. 109–142.

Ihsanoglu, E 2004, *Science, Technology and Learning in the Ottoman Empire*, Ashgate, Burlington, VT.

Isaacson, W, 2007, *Einstein: His Life and Universe*, Simon and Schuster, New York.

Israel, JI 2001, *Radical Enlightenment: Philosophy and the Making of Modernity 1650–1750*, Oxford University Press, Oxford, UK.

Johnson, GA 2005, *Renaissance Art: A Very Short Introduction*, Oxford University Press, Oxford, UK.

Jordan, DP 1995, *Transforming Paris: The Life and Labors of Baron Haussman*, Free Press, New York.

Kafka, F 2007, *The Great Wall of China*, Penguin, London.

Kaizuka, S 2002, *Confucius: His Life and Thought*, Courier Corporation, New York.

Kalnay, E, Cai, M 2003, 'Impact of urbanization and land-use change on climate', *Nature*, vol. 423, no. 6939, pp. 528–531.

Katz, P, Scully, VJ, Bressi, TW 1994, *The New Urbanism: Toward an Architecture of Community*, McGraw-Hill, New York.

Knight, R 1995, 'Knowledge-based development: policy and planning implications for cities', *Urban Studies*, vol. 32, no. 2, pp. 225–260.

Koenigsberger, HG 2014, *Medieval Europe 400–1500*, Routledge, New York.

Konstadakopulos, D 2003, 'The emerging knowledge-based economies of the Atlantic regions', *Journal of Transatlantic Studies*, vol. 1, no. 1, pp. 59–86.

Kornfield, J 2004, *Teachings of the Buddha*, Shambhala Publications, Boston, MA.

Kuijt, I 2000, 'People and space in early agricultural villages: Exploring daily lives, community size, and architecture in the late pre-pottery Neolithic', *Journal of Anthropological Archaeology*, vol. 19, no. 1, pp. 75–102.

Larsen, LB, Vinther, BM, Briffa, KR, Melvin, TM, Clausen, HB, Jones, PD, Nicolussi, K 2008 'New ice core evidence for a volcanic cause of the AD 536 dust veil', *Geophysical Research Letters*, vol. 35, no. 4, pp. 1–19.

Lechtman, HN, Hobbs, LW 1986, 'Roman concrete and the Roman architectural revolution', in Kingery, WD (ed.) *High-Technology Ceramics: Past, Present, and Future – The Nature of Innovation and Change in Ceramic Technology*, The American Ceramic Society, Westerville, OH, vol. 3, pp. 81–128.

Lewis, F 2000, *Rumi Past and Present, East and West: The Life, Teachings and Poetry of Jala al-Din Rumi*, Oneworld Publications, London.

Lines, C 1990, *Companion to the Industrial Revolution*, Facts on File Ltd, Oxford, UK.

Lonnqvist, A, Kapyla, J, Salonius, H, Yigitcanlar, T 2014, 'Knowledge that matters: Identifying regional knowledge assets of Tampere Region', *European Planning Studies*, vol. 22, no. 10, pp. 2011–2029.

Lynch, Z 2009, *The Neuro Revolution: How Brain Science Is Changing Our World*, St. Martin's Press, New York.

Lyons J 2010, *The House of Wisdom: How Arabs Transformed Western Civilization*, Bloomsbury, London.

Mann ME 2002, 'Little Ice Age', in MacCracken, M and Perry, JS (eds) *Encyclopaedia of Global Environmental Change*, John Wiley & Sons, Ltd, Chichester, UK, vol. 1, pp. 504–509.

Marglin, SA, Schor, JB (eds) 1992, *The Golden Age of Capitalism: Reinterpreting the Postwar Experience*, Oxford University Press, Oxford, UK.

Martines, L 1988, *Power and Imagination: City-States in Renaissance Italy*, Taylor and Francis, New York.

May, T, Perry, B 2011, 'Contours and conflicts in scale', *Local Economy*, vol. 26, no. 8, pp. 715–720.

McNeil, I (ed.) 2002, *Encyclopedia of the History of Technology*, Routledge, New York.

More, C 2002, *Understanding the Industrial Revolution*, Routledge, New York.

Morgan, K 2004, *The Birth of the Industrial Britain: Social Change, 1750–1850*, Pearson Education Ltd, Harlow, UK.

Mulligan, G 2012, 'Settling down or moving on? The settlement of the Irish Neolithic landscape', *New Hibernia Review*, vol. 16, no. 1, pp. 94–112.

Mumford, L 1961, *The City in History: Its Origins, Its Transformations, and Its Prospects*, Harcourt, Brace and World, New York.

Nauert, CG 2006, *Humanism and the Culture of Renaissance Europe*, Cambridge University Press, Cambridge, MA.

Needham, J, Wang, L, Lu, GD 1963, *Science and Civilisation in China*, Cambridge University Press, Cambridge, MA.

Nielsen, I 1993, *Thermae et Balnea: The Architecture and Cultural History of Roman Public Baths*, Aarhus University Press, Aarhus, Denmark.

Norwich, JJ 2014, 'Introduction: The birth of urban life', in Norwich, JJ (ed.) *Cities That Shaped the Ancient World*, Thames and Hudson, London, pp. 6–13.

Pacey, A 1990, *Technology in World Civilization: A Thousand-Year History*, MIT Press, Boston, MA.

Pamuk, Ş 2007, 'The black death and the origins of the "Great Divergence" across Europe, 1300–1600', *European Review of Economic History*, vol. 11, no. 3, pp. 289–317.

Pancholi, S, Yigitcanlar, T, Guaralda, M 2014, 'Urban knowledge and innovation spaces: Concepts, conditions and contexts', *Asia Pacific Journal of Innovation and Entrepreneurship*, vol. 8, no. 1, pp. 15–38.

Pollard, N 2014, 'Rome: Augustus' city of stone', in Norwich, JJ (ed.) *Cities That Shaped the Ancient World*, Thames and Hudson, London, pp. 144–151.

Riggsby, AM 2010, *Roman Law and the Legal World of the Romans*, Cambridge University Press, London.

Rosenzweig, R, Blackmar, E 1992, *The Park and the People: A History of Central Park*, Cornell University Press, New York.

Ross, S 2003, *The Technology of World War I*, Raintree Steck-Vaughn, New York.

Sharif, MM (ed.) 1966, *A History of Muslim Philosophy*, Royal Book Company, Karachi, Pakistan.

Smith, PD 2012, *City: A Guidebook for the Urban Age*, Bloomsbury, London.

Sparknotes 2015, *The Enlightenment (1650–1800)*, accessed on 14 August 2015 from http://www.sparknotes.com/history/european/enlightenment/summary.html

Symington, D 1991, 'Late Bronze Age writing-boards and their uses: Textual evidence from Anatolia and Syria', *Anatolian Studies*, vol. 41, no. 1, pp. 111–123.

Tellier, LN 2009, *Urban World History: An Economic and Geographical Perspective*, University of Québec Press, Montreal, QC.

Townsend, AM 2013, *Smart Cities: Big Data, Civic Hackers, and the Quest for a New Utopia*, WW Norton and Company, New York.

Turner, N 2008, *The Earth's Blanket: Traditional Teachings for Sustainable Living*, DandM Publishers, Vancouver, BC.

UN 2013, *World Population Prospects: The 2012 Revision*, Population Division of the Department of Economic and Social Affairs of the United Nations Secretariat, New York.

Van Doren, C 1992, *A History of Knowledge: Past, Present and Future*, Random House Publishing, Toronto, ON.

Veyne, P 1997, *The Roman Empire*, Harvard University Press, Boston, MA.

White, TD, Asfaw, B, DeGusta, D, Gilbert, H, Richards, GD, Suwa, G, Howell, FC 2003, 'Pleistocene homo sapiens from middle awash, Ethiopia', *Nature*, vol. 423 no. 6941, pp. 742–747.

Wilson, WH 1994, *The City Beautiful Movement*, Johns Hopkins University Press, Baltimore, MD.

Wolpoff, MH 1997, *Race and Human Evolution*, Simon and Schuster, New York.

Wong, E 2011, *Taoism*, Shambhala Publications, Boston, MA.

Yigitcanlar, T 2011, 'Position paper: Redefining knowledge-based urban development', *International Journal of Knowledge Based Development*, vol. 2, no. 4, pp. 340–356.

Yigitcanlar, T 2014a, 'Position paper: Benchmarking the performance of global and emerging knowledge cities', *Expert Systems with Applications*, vol. 41, no. 12, pp. 5549–5559.

Yigitcanlar, T 2014b, 'Innovating urban policymaking and planning mechanisms to deliver knowledge-based agendas: A methodological approach', *International Journal of Knowledge-Based Development*, vol. 5, no. 3, pp. 253–270.

Yigitcanlar, T, Lonnqvist, A 2013, 'Benchmarking knowledge-based urban development performance: Results from the international comparison of Helsinki', *Cities*, vol. 31, no. 1, 357–369.

Yigitcanlar, T, Bulu, M 2015, 'Dubaization of Istanbul: Insights from the knowledge-based urban development journey of an emerging local economy', *Environment and Planning A*, vol. 47, no. 1, pp. 89–107.

Yigitcanlar, T, Dizdaroglu, D 2015, 'Ecological approaches in planning for sustainable cities: A review of the literature', *Global Journal of Environmental Science and Management*, vol. 1, no. 2, pp. 159–188.

Yigitcanlar, T, Sarimin, M 2015, 'Multimedia super corridor, Malaysia: Knowledge-based urban development lessons from an emerging economy', *VINE: The Journal of Information and Knowledge Management*, vol. 45, no. 1, pp. 126–147.

Yigitcanlar, T, O'Connor, K, Westerman, C 2008, 'The making of knowledge cities: Melbourne's knowledge-based urban development experience', *Cities*, vol. 25, no. 2, pp. 63–72.

Yigitcanlar, T, Dur, F, Dizdaroglu, D 2015, 'Towards prosperous sustainable cities: A multiscalar urban sustainability assessment approach', *Habitat International*, vol. 45, no. 1, pp. 36–46.

Zafirovski, M 2010, *The Enlightenment and Its Effects on Modern Society*, Springer Science and Business Media, London.

Zucker, P 1955, 'Space and movement in High Baroque city planning', *Journal of the Society of Architectural Historians*, vol. 14, no. 1, pp. 8–13.

Zvelebil, M (ed.) 2009, *Hunters in Transition: Mesolithic Societies of Temperate Eurasia and Their Transition to Farming*, Cambridge University Press, London.

Part II
Systems

Part II of the book provides a comprehensive review and demonstration of smart urban information technologies and smart urban systems. Chapter 3 presents the most prominent smart urban information technologies and recent technological innovations: (i) infrastructural information technologies, such as the World Wide Web, broadband and mobile broadband; (ii) locational and sensing technologies, such as geographic information science technologies, radio frequency identification, ubiquitous sensor network and context-aware computing; (iii) ubiquitous computing and augmented reality technologies, such as mobile and built ubiquitous computing environments, and mobile augmented reality technologies; and (iv) convergence technologies, such as internet and media convergence, marketing convergence and telecommunications convergence. Chapter 4 introduces and elaborates the most common smart urban systems and gives examples from their successful adoption in contemporary urban contexts: (i) smart urban transport systems; (ii) smart urban grid systems; (iii) smart urban water and waste systems; (iv) smart urban emergency and safety systems; and (v) smart urban participatory decision systems. This part aims to define the key conceptual and practical issues of smart urban technology and system adoption in smart cities. By doing so, it addresses the first research question of the book, i.e. What is the role of smart urban technologies and systems in the development of twenty-first-century cities?

3 Smart urban information technologies

Any sufficiently advanced technology is indistinguishable from magic.
(Sir Arthur C Clarke, author of *2001: A Space Odyssey*)

Introduction

Cities are human-made systems of systems. They are highly complex urban systems that are composed of many subsystems that are also complex in nature, such as economy, society, built environment, natural environment and governance. Each of these subsystems has their own subsystems as well. For example, built environment consists of subsystems like buildings, infrastructures, amenities and so on. Furthermore, each of these subsystems also has their own subsystems and are interconnected with other systems, e.g. an infrastructure subsystem consists of many subsystems, including the transportation infrastructure where it is also linked to the energy provision system. Moreover, each subsystem impacts and is impacted by the other, thus increasing the complexity level even further. Such intertwined structures of systems in cities make them greatly complex environments in terms of social, natural and artificial aspects (Portugali 2011). Today, the adoption of technology is a global phenomenon, and the intensity of its usage is impressive all across the world. In particular, smart urban information technologies play a critical role in supporting the decision-making, design, planning, development and management operations of these complex urban environments (Yigitcanlar and Lee 2014; Yigitcanlar 2015). This Chapter introduces the state-of-the-art smart urban information technologies, and their use and contributions in dealing with complexity and uncertainty and in generating sustainable and liveable urban environments. These technologies are presented and discussed under the main categories of: (i) infrastructural information technologies, such as the World Wide Web, broadband and mobile broadband; (ii) locational and sensing technologies, such as geographic information science technologies, radio frequency identification, ubiquitous sensor network and context-aware computing; (iii) ubiquitous computing and augmented reality technologies, such as mobile and built ubiquitous computing environments, and mobile augmented reality technologies; and (iv) convergence technologies, such as internet and media convergence, marketing convergence and telecommunications convergence.

Infrastructural information technologies

ICTs play an increasingly important role in the decision-making, design, planning, development and management operations of complex systems in our cities. In particular, the advent of internet and multimedia applications with high bandwidth and quality of service requirements has initiated a new era in ICT. In this new era infrastructural information technologies, in other words technologies supporting the World Wide Web (in short, web) and broadband internet delivery, form a backbone platform for all urban, business, education, health and social services to run efficiently and effectively, such as e-business, social media, e-governance, e-learning, e-health, municipal and environmental services. Without exception, the development and/or adoption of such mainstay technologies have become high priorities for governments all around the world (Papacharissi and Zaks 2006). Web 1.0, web 2.0, web 3.0, ultra-broadband convergence networks and fourth and fifth generation mobile network (4G/5G network) wireless broadband applications are introduced below as exemplary innovative infrastructural information technologies within the context of web, broadband and mobile broadband.

World Wide Web

Internet was the result of some visionary thinking by people, such as JCR Licklider of MIT (see Licklider and Clark 1962), in the early 1960s, who realised the potential in allowing computers to share information on research and development in scientific and military fields. In 1969, the very first message was sent from University of California Los Angeles (UCLA) to the second network node at Stanford Research Institute (SRI) over the Advanced Research Projects Agency Network (ARPANET), a US Department of Defense project. In 1984, the ARPANET project was completed by forming the US Military Network (MILNET) for unclassified Defense Department communications. In 1989, the internet's first node was installed in UCLA, a year later ARPANET was decommissioned and private connections to the internet by commercial entities became possible (Isaacson 2014). Since then, much progress has been made in the technology space with the popularising of the internet and the advent of the web for over the past 25 years. In 2015, over 3.15 billion people had access to the internet, making more than 43 per cent of the world's population an internet user (Internet Live Stats 2015). Originally, web 1.0 started in 1989 as a broadcast medium for graphical academic documents, and it quickly diverged from there. It continued its outrageous growth pattern until 2001's 'Dot Com bubble burst'. In 2004, the economic hangover ended and gave birth to web 2.0. This is essentially a variety of websites and applications that allow people to create and share online information or material they have, and to collaborate and communicate with other people. According to Goodchild (2007b):

> [t]he early web was primarily one-directional, allowing a large number of users to view the contents of a comparatively small number of sites, the new

web 2.0 is a bi-directional collaboration in which users are able to interact with and provide information to central sites, and to see that information collated and made available to others.

(Goodchild 2007b: 27)

According to Berthon *et al.* (2012), web 2.0:

[t]echnologies have caused three effects: (i) A shift in locus of activity from the desktop to the web; (ii) A shift in locus of value production from the firm to the consumer; and (iii) A shift in the locus of power away from the firm to the consumer.

(Berthon *et al.* 2012: 262)

Common application areas of web 2.0 are wikis, blogs, tagging and social bookmarking, social networking, audio blogging and podcasting, education, gaming, RSS and syndication, and content hosting and multimedia sharing services.

Some of the leading examples of web 2.0 include: Wikipedia, Google Maps, Google Docs, Webblogs, My Yahoo!, MSN Web Messenger, Delicious, Flickr, MySpace, Facebook, Linkedin, Instagram, Twitter, Plaxo, Buble.us, Snipshot, OpenStreetMap, Second Life and YouTube. In order to remove the frustration in the time spent waiting for pages to reload and refresh web 1.0's HTML-based websites, the delivery of web 2.0 applications and services are driven by the widespread adoption of technologies including Ajax and JavaScript frameworks, such as YUI Library, Dojo Toolkit, MooTools, jQuery, Ext JS and Prototype JavaScript Framework (Anderson 2007). Web 2.0 has proven its strength in many ways, especially in community empowerment and resistance building. For instance, many social resistance movements are planned and organised across the world by using web 2.0 applications such as Twitter and Facebook, e.g. Occupy Wall Street (DeLuca *et al.* 2012), Arab Spring (Wolfsfeld *et al.* 2013) and Gezi Park Resistance (Gökçe *et al.* 2014). At present, the web is entering a new phase of evolution. The third generation of the web, or web 3.0, is the evolution of the web as an extension of web 2.0 that has a connective intelligence, connecting data, concepts, applications and ultimately people, and hence embeds intelligence in anything that exists online. While some call it a 'semantic web', according to Spivack (2007) the semantic web is just one of several converging technologies and trends web 3.0 will have. It is enabled by the convergence of several key emerging technology trends, ubiquitous connectivity, network computing, open technologies, open identity and the intelligent web (Spivack 2015).

Broadband

Broadband technology has emerged as the natural next step in internet evolution and diffusion (see Papacharissi and Zaks 2006). Broadband is a wide bandwidth data transmission with an ability to simultaneously transport multiple signals and traffic types. Data transmission happens through various mediums: (i) cable modem is a type of network bridge and modem that provides bi-directional data communication via radio frequency channels on a hybrid fibre-coaxial (HFC) and radio frequency over glass (RFoG) infrastructure, and is primarily used to deliver broadband internet access; (ii) asymmetric digital subscriber line (ADSL) is a data communications technology that enables faster data transmission over twisted-pair copper telephone lines than a conventional voice band modem can provide; (iii) optical fibre is a flexible, transparent fibre made by drawing glass to a diameter slightly thicker than that of a human hair and is used as a means to transmit light between the two ends of the fibre and finds wide usage in fibre-optic communications, where they permit transmission over longer distances and at higher bandwidths than wire cables, also referred as fibre-to-home-network (FTHN); and (iv) wireless broadband is delivered through fixed wireless that is also referred as Local Multipoint Distribution Service (LMDS), high-speed satellite and 3G/4G networks. Beyond web surfing, multimedia applications and data download, broadband also enables telephony services using voice-over-internet protocol (VoIP), high-definition TV (HDTV), Smart TV and video on demand (VoD) (Andrews *et al.* 2007). The benefits and problems of broadband are widely discussed in the literature (see Firth and Mellor 2005).

On the one hand, in the global knowledge economy, broadband holds a critical position in the progress of economic and social indicators by connecting consumers, businesses and governments and by facilitating social interaction (OECD 2001; Xavier 2003). On the other hand, the take up rate of the technology in less developed countries and in some populations of the developed nations have left some people disadvantaged due to being unable to access broadband for several reasons, such as availability, affordability and awareness, which is widening the ever-growing digital/knowledge divide (Katz and Rice 2002). Frieden (2005) provides invaluable lessons on the role of governments and the private sector in broadband development from Canada, Japan, Korea and the United States. The most advanced broadband technology is the Ultra-Broadband convergence Network (UBcN). It is a conduit through which broadband services, applications and content flow to reflect a robust high-speed internet infrastructure actualised through an internet protocol (IP) packet-based integrated network for high quality convergence services through dynamic accesses with three key objectives: media convergence, widespread connectivity or access, and coordination among the network stakeholders (Menon 2011). UBcN is the most notable attempt by any government to create an enhanced digital environment to keep apace of new ICT convergence trends. The project was started in 2004, initially as BcN, and developed in Korea through the full support of the government due to the magnitude and scope of its potential impact. UBcN aims for the convergence of television, telecom and internet networks into a single network with transmission speeds of 50–100Mb/s. Furthermore, through UBcN, a ubiquitous networking is envisaged that any electronic devices, such as fridges and digital TVs, could be used as network consoles to enable internet access (Shin and Kweon 2011), and moving one step closer to achieving the 'internet-of-things'. The current stage of the project is targeting a further increase in broadband subscribers having access to speeds of over 1Gb/s, along with upgrades to the backbone network, which was a plan that was established to link the public sector to a sensor network (Shin and Jung 2012). Nevertheless, it is argued that, in general, the primary driving force for developing the broadband was the arrangement, or outlay, of technological equipment to improve technical capabilities in the country, in particular, UBcN is designed primarily to serve the demands of the major corporate suppliers and industries at the expense of the public interest and funding (Shin 2007). Moreover, 'the [U]BcN has been criticized as an insufficient telecom infrastructure in terms of its ontologically bounded accountability . . . [as] ontologically bounded accountability characterizes the [U]BcN as a public good, or public utility, such as public health, education and public safety' (Shin and Jung 2012: 579).

Mobile broadband

Much like wired broadband, wireless broadband has also enjoyed rapid mass-market adoption (Andrews *et al.* 2007). The demand for faster mobile broadband is an outcome of the widening of mobile networks. The first generation mobile network (1G) was the analogue mobile phone that worked like the traditional telephone system. The second generation one (2G) was rolled out in the early 1990s. It was using digital signalling that occupied a channel when being used. In 2001, the third generation (3G) brought more frequencies and also a more advanced compression to provide a larger bandwidth (Townsend 2013). In 2007, the fourth generation mobile networks (4G) were launched in Korea, providing better use of mobile web access, IP telephony, gaming services, high-definition mobile TV, video conferencing, 3D television and cloud computing. The forthcoming fifth generation (5G) mobile network, planned to be launched in Korea in 2017, and most of the developed countries by 2020, will provide better speeds and coverage than the current 4G.

Wireless mobile phone services grew from 11 million subscribers in 1990 to more than 4.5 billion in 2014, with about 1.75 billion of them being smartphone users (Statista 2015). Major reasons for smartphones becoming so widespread include increasing functionality, decreasing prices and advancing mobile and wireless broadband technology, networks and coverage. Mobile broadband is a technology that provides high-speed wireless internet or computer networking access over a wide area. As stated by Andrews *et al.* (2007: 19–20), '[m]obile broadband offers the additional functionality of portability, nomadicity, and mobility . . . [and] attempts to bring broadband applications to new user experience scenarios and hence offer the end user a very different value proposition'. Today, the mobile broadband market is evolving rapidly, with the 4G network and wireless system currently in use following the introduction of smart mobile phones, with operators introducing a number of new standards and technologies for users, e.g. Wideband Code Division Multiple Access (W-CDMA), High-Speed Downlink Packet Access (HSDPA), Wireless Broadband (WiBro), Worldwide Interoperability for Microwave Access (WiMAX) and Long-Term Evolution (LTE or 4G LTE). Among these technologies, 4G LTE has become a standard for wireless communication of high-speed data for mobile phones and data terminals in the 2010s. It is based on the GSM/EDGE (Global System for Mobile Communications/Enhanced Data rates for GSM Evolution) and UMTS/ HSPA (Universal Mobile Telecommunications System/High-Speed Packet Access) network technologies, increasing the capacity and speed using a different radio interface, together with core network improvements.

Korea with 62 per cent 4G LTE penetration was the leading country with Japan, Australia and the United States around a 20 per cent penetration rate in 2013 (Robertson 2013). In terms of 4G LTE speed, Spain with 18.24 mbps had the top download speed, followed by Finland, Denmark and Korea above 16 mbps in 2015 (Murphy 2015). Furthermore, the developments for 5G wireless are underway. The European Commission's Horizon 2020 plan includes investment for 5G research and development, and the Korean government is funding the development of a national 5G network to be completed by 2020. Both proposals indicate the transformative effects and massive economic benefits of 5G technology (Gold 2015). 5G technology is to offer: (i) significantly faster data speeds, e.g. 4G networks are capable of achieving peak download speeds of one gigabit per second – with 5G this would increase to 10Gbps; (ii) ultra-low latency, which is the time it takes one device to send a packet of data to another device, e.g. with 4G the latency rate is around 50 milliseconds – 5G will reduce that to about one millisecond, which is particularly important for industrial applications and driverless cars; and (iii) a more connected world, e.g. beyond smartphones, the internet-of-things, such as wearables, smart home appliances, connected cars, is expected to grow exponentially by 2025, and 5G is to provide that capacity to a network that can accommodate billions of connected devices (Cha 2015).

Locational and sensing technologies

Location plays a key role in determining the type and nature of human activities or natural phenomena. It can also determine consumers' information needs and their product, amenity and service choices (Rao and Minakakis 2003). Fortunately, the proliferation of ICTs, mobile computing devices and the internet has fostered the widespread use of locational technologies, where systems based on these technologies track and use the physical location of the investigated objects or phenomena. Locational technologies, such as technologies of geographic information sciences and global positioning systems, are among the critical smart urban information technologies that provide foundations for the development and delivery of location-based services, which are a general class of computer program-level services that use location data to control features such as online social networking applications, parcel and vehicle tracking services, environmental monitoring services and so on. Furthermore, as part of the locational technologies, advancements in the sensing technology field along with the convergence among mobile computing and communication devices and embedded technology have sparked the development of 'context-aware' applications, with location being the most essential context (Ni *et al.* 2004). Particularly since the mid-1990s, there has been an unprecedented growth in the number of products and services using sensors, a device that responds to an input quantity by generating a functionally related output usually in the form of electrical or optical signals (Cherifi *et al.* 2011). The developments in the sensing technology not only result in new technological products and trends, such as context-aware sensors and networks, but also support a smart environment that delivers the safest and most convenient conditions to users, such as self-sensing places and smart homes (Ding *et al.* 2011). Sensing technologies, such as radio frequency identification, ubiquitous sensor network and context-aware computing are integral smart urban information technologies.

Geographic information science technologies

Geographic information sciences are among the disciplines that directly contribute to increasing the intelligence of cities and support the development of smart cities, by using digital applications for the dematerialisation of information and knowledge for the communities and territories to undergo digital transformation and become smart (Komninos 2002). Volunteered geographic information (VGI), crowdsourcing, spatial data infrastructures (SDI), open data, Big Data, digital urban models, geographic information system (GIS) and geodesign offer a wide range of concepts, methods and technologies providing effective support for the implementation of smart urban technologies and the development of smart cities (Roche 2014). GIS, a domain within the academic discipline of geographic information sciences, is a system designed to capture, store, manipulate, analyse, manage and visualise all types of spatial or geographical data and is a widely used technology for scientific investigations, resource management, asset management, environmental impact assessment, urban planning, community health monitoring, cartography, criminology, marketing, traffic planning and so on (Lee *et al.* 2008a). Web-based or mobile public participatory and collaborative GIS applications provide a user-friendly interface and platform for citizen involvement in decision-making processes (Baum *et al.* 2010; Batty *et al.* 2012). Similarly, VGI technology helps in the collection of user/volunteer collected vital information and after validating and qualifying the information, ensures its coherence and smooth integration within municipal SDI (Goodchild 2007a; Goodchild and Li 2012). By using VGI technology, individuals can create their own personal maps of a community or specific place, by using WikiMapia, OpenStreetMap, Google Map Maker, Google Maps, Google Earth or other web 2.0 applications capable of geotagging information, for authorities to take action (see Chapter 4 for more info on VGI). These participatory models lead to the formation of open data applications and new technology development for warehousing, handling and analysing such Big Data (Zikopoulos and Eaton 2011). Big Data is information assets mainly characterised by a high volume, variety, velocity, variability, veracity and complexity that require specific technology and analytical methods for its transformation into value (Gordon 2013). Currently, available technologies for Big Data include A/B testing, crowdsourcing, data fusion and integration, genetic algorithms, machine learning, natural language processing, signal processing, simulation, time series analysis and visualisation (Chen and Zhang 2014).

Another important geographical information science technology is global positioning systems (GPS), initiated by the US Department of Defense in 1978 and offered free of charge and accessible worldwide. It is a widely used system for navigation worldwide and a useful tool for map making, land surveying, commerce and scientific uses. As stated by Goodchild (2007b: 24–25), GPS 'has revolutionized the processes of surveying, allowing the rapid and accurate determination of absolute position on the Earth's surface, and remote sensing provides a massive and constant flow of Earth imagery'. Thus, it has become a universal utility as the cost of integrating the technology into vehicles, machinery, computers and mobile phones has decreased, and it will revolutionise location-tracking technology as commercial usage increases (Bajaj *et al.* 2002). GPS provides a precise time reference used in many applications, including the scientific study of earthquakes and the synchronisation of telecommunications networks (Lee *et al.* 2008b). It is an excellent lateration framework for determining geographic positions, and today it is used for a variety of applications including but not limited to tracking package delivery, mobile commerce, emergency response, exploration, surveying, law enforcement, recreation, wildlife tracking, search and rescue, roadside assistance, stolen vehicle recovery, satellite data processing and environmental and resource management. GPS technology can determine the position of an object or user by triangulation/trilateration via at least three satellites, and with four or more satellites in view, it can determine the object/user's latitude, longitude and altitude as well as speed, bearing track, trip distance, distance to destination, and sunrise and sunset time (Bajaj *et al.* 2002). The worldwide satellite constellation has reliable and widespread coverage and, assuming a differential reference or use of the wide area augmentation system, allows receivers to compute the location with marginal errors (Hightower and Borriello 2001). However, GPS, being a satellite dependent system, suffers from an inherent problem of accurately determining the location of objects, particularly ones located inside buildings (Ni *et al.* 2004).

Radio frequency identification

Even though radio frequency identification (RFID) has only become widespread since the mid-2000s due to cost-related issues, the utilisation of this technology dates back to the 1940s when the British employed RFID principles in WWII to identify their aircraft using the identification friend or foe system. Today, RFID is an integral part of our lives and increases productivity and convenience, mainly as a result of GPS technology being unavailable in indoor locations. We have seen the large-scale adoption of the technology by major organisations, such as Walmart, Tesco and the US Department of Defense (Want 2006). Furthermore, in many countries, worldwide RFID technology is commonly used for instance for electronic toll collection, and with some integration of sensors with tags, is used to report on a wide range of environmental conditions (De Donno *et al.* 2014). In simple terms, RFID is a short-range radio technology used to communicate mainly digital information between a stationary location and a movable object, or between movable objects (Landt 2005). In other words, RFID is a means of transmitting, storing and retrieving data through electromagnetic transmission to a radio frequency compatible integrated circuit from a distance. An RFID system has several basic components including a number of readers, active or passive tags or transponders, and communication between them (Ni *et al.* 2004). Active RFID tags contain a battery and provide a greater range. They could be carried by a person for personal identification; passive RFID tags have no power source and are often attached to an object to detect user-object interaction (Ding *et al.* 2011). All RFID tags contain an integrated circuit for storing and processing information, modulating and demodulating a radio frequency signal and other specialised functions, and an antenna for receiving and transmitting the signals (Lee *et al.* 2008a). As a sensing technology, RFID automatically identifies people, animals or objects using radio waves from small sensor devices and are used in various applications such as to identify animals, label airline luggage, time marathon runners, make toys interactive, prevent theft, locate lost items and so on. There are two types of RFID, near-field and far-field. As stated by Shrestha *et al.* (2011):

> [b]ased on types of objects and applications, inductively coupled near-field operation or electromagnetically coupled far-field operation are used to transfer information between reader and tag. Far-field communication is widely used due to its long read range. Near-field reading can be useful for objects having metals and liquids in their vicinity because normal far-field tags' performance is affected by the presence of these objects.
>
> (Shrestha *et al.* 2011: 1274)

One of the most intriguing aspects of RFID technology is that it can convey information that extends beyond data stored in an internal memory and include data that on-board sensors create dynamically. For example, a passive force sensor supplies information and alerts the system when a package is dropped, or a sensor alerts when temperature changes beyond the safe range (Want 2006). RFID that has access to wireless networks and is connected to the internet enables ubiquitous sensing (Lee *et al.* 2008a). The privacy issue is raised as a major concern to be dealt with immediately (Want 2004; Garfinkel *et al.* 2005). For instance, today technology is being used extensively, including in common products incorporating smart tags, where they can be tracked beyond the intended use of manufacturers and retail stores.

Ubiquitous sensor networks

A ubiquitous sensor network (USN) is an omnipresent environment providing communication opportunities among small embedded devices with sensing capabilities; basically a network of intelligent sensors (El Zabadani 2006). Sensor network is a key technology for building a ubiquitous system. Small enough to guarantee the pervasiveness needed for smart infrastructure, sensor devices are associated with the development of networks that provide valuable information to be used in a great variety of sensor applications. USNs are numerous, easily accessible, often invisible computing devices, frequently mobile or embedded in the environment, connected to an increasingly ubiquitous network infrastructure and composed of a wired core and wireless edges to obtain information through any devices anytime and anywhere (Lee *et al.* 2008a). A USN consists of: (i) a sensor network that comprises sensors, independently energy supplied, used for collecting and transmitting information about their surrounding environment; (ii) an access network that has intermediary or sink nodes collecting information from groups of sensors and facilitating communication with a control centre or with external entities; (iii) a network infrastructure that is based on future next generation networks; (iv) a USN middleware that is software for the collection and processing of large volumes of data; and (v) a USN applications platform that is a technology platform to enable the effective use of a USN in a particular application (Tafa 2011).

Today, USNs and their applications are emerging rapidly as an exciting new paradigm to provide an intelligent and ubiquitous communication and network technology and reliable and comfortable life services (Kim *et al.* 2012). There are a number of application areas of USN that are currently in use including: (i) facility status monitoring solutions for monitoring facilities and equipment; (ii) quality control and instrumentation solutions for taking measurements during production to monitor the manufacturing process and conduct quality control; (iii) temperature and humidity monitoring solutions for warehouses to monitor the storage conditions of warehouses for food and pharmaceutical products; (iv) building management solutions that offer detailed temperature and humidity controls, while making it easy to add or remove sensors; (v) positioning management solutions for management positioning and asset management, involving vehicles and construction materials; (vi) disaster prevention solutions for tracking the status of disasters and to secure escape routes, as well as crime prevention solutions for preventing crime in the home and at various facilities, including the implementation of counter-terrorism strategies; and (vii) distribution solutions for monitoring the status of temperatures, humidity and vibrations during the transportation of food products and precision instruments (Tomioka and Kondo 2006). As stated by Perera *et al.* (2014: 447), 'with the advances in sensor hardware technology and cheap materials, sensors are expected to be attached to all the objects around us, so these can communicate with each other with minimum human intervention'. This brings us to the importance of context-aware computing to interpret sensor data after which we suggest appropriate actions.

Context-aware computing

In ubiquitous environments, one of the important factors is context awareness. Context is used or having influence when interacting between entities. Context-aware computing is a technology solution that is used for acquiring and utilising information about the context of a device to provide services that are appropriate to the particular users, places, events and times. In other words, it is a system that extracts, interprets and uses context information and adapts its functionality to the current context of use (Byun and Cheverst 2004). For example, through context-aware computing, a system can be aware of the location of a mobile phone and a concert schedule and the phone can be conditioned to always vibrate when in a concert hall (Lee *et al.* 2008a). Another example is that in a hospital the bed 'knows' the nurse, the patient and the medicine tray and displays relevant information according to this context, such as a medicine schema or patient record (Bricon-Souf and Newman 2007). Moreover, as Cheskin Research's (2002: 8) report underlines, 'your email needs and expectations are different whether you are at home, work, school, commuting, the airport, etc. and different devices are [available] to suit your needs for accessing content depending on where you are, your situated context'. As in these examples, the context basically refers to the physical and social situation in which computational devices are embedded (Schilit and Theimer 1994; Svanaes 2001).

Context-aware computing consists of four main contextual elements. The first one is the 'computing context', which comprises network connections, communication costs, nearby computing resources such as displays, printers, and so on. The second one is the 'user context', which comprises users' profiles, their locations, orientations, movements, other nearby people or objects, current and time-tabled activities and so on. The third is the 'physical context', which comprises place, temperature, lighting, noise levels, weather and traffic conditions and so on. The last element is the 'time context', which includes the context history (Dey *et al.* 2001). There are two types of context-aware models that exist. The first one is the 'active context awareness', which is an application that automatically adapts to discovered context by changing the application's behaviour. The second one is the 'passive context awareness', which presents the new or updated context to an interested user or makes the context persistent for the user (Chen and Kotz 2000). Context-aware computing is essential for making use of collected sensor data. Understanding and interpreting sensor data through context-aware computing is critical as, today, the number of sensors deployed around the world is growing at a rapid pace. Moreover, these sensors continuously generate enormous amounts of data, and the collection, modelling, reasoning and distribution of context in relation to sensor data play a critical role in forming a smart environment (Perera *et al.* 2014), especially in the age of the 'internet-of-things' where everyday objects have network connectivity, which allows them to send and receive data. Supervised and unsupervised learning, rules, fuzzy logic, ontological reasoning and probabilistic reasoning are among the major context reasoning or decision models, which provide a method of deducing new knowledge and understanding, based on the available context, and which are used to make sense of the sensor data. Perera *et al.* (2014) provide an extensive comparison of these techniques in terms of their prospects, constraints and applicability for context-aware computing.

Ubiquitous computing and augmented reality technologies

Intelligent environments, also known as ambient intelligence, have become increasingly important since the start of the twenty-first century, where these environments are characterised by certain capacities such as omnipresence, transparency and intelligence (Molina *et al.* 2008). Emerging ubiquitous or pervasive computing technologies offer 'anytime, anywhere, anyone' computing by decoupling users from devices (Billsus *et al.* 2002; Hong *et al.* 2009). The term 'ubiquitous computing' or 'ubiquitous technology', coined by Xerox PARC Chief Scientist, Weiser (1991), refers to the ubiquity of information technology and computer power, which in principle pervade all everyday objects. It suggests countless very small, wirelessly intercommunicating microprocessors, which can be more or less invisibly embedded into objects (Friedewald and Raabe 2011). Equipped with sensors, these computers can record the environment of the object in which they are embedded and provide that object with information processing and communication capabilities. Such objects have a new, additional quality. They know, for example, where they are, which other things are in the vicinity and what happened to them in the past (Yigitcanlar and Lee 2014). Ubiquitous technology is often wireless, mobile and networked, making its users more connected to the world around them and the people in it. Typical ubiquitous technology devices include small mobile computers, further developments of today's mobile telephones, so-called wearables such as intelligent textiles or accessories, as well as computerised implants. The following features characterise ubiquitous technologies: decentralisation or modularity of the systems and their comprehensive networking; embedding of the computer hardware and software in other equipment and objects of daily use; mobile support for the user through information services anywhere and anytime; context awareness and adaptation of the system to current information requirements; and automatic recognition and autonomous processing of repetitive tasks without user intervention (Gabriel *et al.* 2006).

Ubiquitous technologies can pervade all spheres of life and are vital for the development of a widespread infrastructure system that provides a range of services to the public in a smart city. These technologies, for instance, increase comfort in the private home area; improve energy efficiency; make roads safer with intelligent vehicles; raise work productivity in the office with adaptive personal assistance systems; and in the medical field, monitor the health of the user with implantable sensors and micro-computers (Aarts and Encarnaçao 2005). More specifically, for example, the technology of telematics, i.e. any integrated use of ICT, allows us to send, receive and store traffic information via telecommunication devices. More commonly, telematics has been applied specifically to the use of global positioning system technology integrated with computers and mobile communications technology. Transport telematics applications are contributing to safer, cleaner and more efficient transport by helping travellers, freight distributors and transport operators avoid delays, congestion and unnecessary trips by diverting traffic from overcrowded roads to alternative modes. These functions help in controlling rail, sea and inland waterways; reducing accidents; increasing productivity; gaining extra capacity from existing infrastructure; encouraging integrated transport, thus reducing energy use; and reducing environmental pollution (Lee 1999). They could provide potential savings of time and energy for individual drivers, reduction of congestion for the city, and could impact on long-term land use (Yigitcanlar and Lee 2014). Ubiquitous is also referred to as pervasive; both terms are used interchangeably. Computing technologies, such as mobile and built ubiquitous computing environments and mobile augmented reality, are among the key smart urban information technologies that support the development of intelligent environments.

Mobile and built ubiquitous computing environments

Mobile ubiquitous computing environments (MUCE) consist of mobile nodes capable of roaming independently and include wearable computers, laptops, PDAs, pocket PCs, tablets, mobile phones, palmtops or any other mobile wireless devices. They are seen as major drivers in establishing communication and convergence between ICT and users to form a smart and intelligent space or environment (Lee *et al.* 2008b). For MUCE, ubiquitous computing provides an environment with 'hidden computers', where people can interact with neighbouring objects (Hsu 2010). Likewise, the rapid development of the wireless sensor networks has led to various mobile devices that can access diverse web-based applications through web 2.0 technologies, which provide a medium for the sharing and exchange of resources, such as Web feed and Web API, to support MUCE (Knights 2007). Additionally, social web 2.0 technologies enable the development of mobile ubiquitous modules that are easy to integrate into the various web standards to facilitate the sharing and exchange of widespread resources, including ubiquitous information and ubiquitous services. It facilitates substantial ubiquitous resources to store up information by using the XML-based pattern in the ubiquitous web (O'Reilly 2007). However, so far, the lack of or limited considerations of the physical space and its design have restricted MUCE's success and effectiveness, particularly in the country context of Korea, where MUCE developments are more common than in any other country (Lee *et al.* 2008b).

Ubiquitous or pervasive computing ushers in a new era of computing that integrates both cyber and physical worlds to enable people to move around and interact with computers more naturally than they currently do (Cai *et al.* 2012). Converging ICTs and physical urban environments is an important planning and design issue from the smart city perspective. The limitations of MUCE are mostly eliminated by giving emphasis to built ubiquitous computing environment (BUCE) development in order to address this issue. BUCE improved the communication between and convergence of ICTs and urban elements. Some of the exemplar BUCE developments include new urban structures and land use planning and design such as digital walls as central urban screens, ubiquitous digital streets and widespread open spaces and parks (Lee *et al.* 2008a).

Mobile augmented reality technologies

Augmented reality technologies, including mobile augmented reality, form a field of computer science that deals with the combination of real-world and computer generated data. It includes the use of motion tracking data, fiducial marker recognition using machine vision and the construction of controlled environments containing any number of sensors and actuators (Lee *et al.* 2008a). An augmented reality system basically: combines real and virtual objects in a real environment; registers and aligns real and virtual objects with each other; and runs interactively, in three dimensions, and in real time (Van Krevelen and Poelman 2010). The visualisation is achieved through three methods of augmented reality displays, based on their position between the viewer and the real environment: head-worn (e.g. special glasses), hand-held (e.g. mobile device/phone) and spatial (e.g. video projection). Mobile augmented reality systems provide an opportunity to overlay digital information onto the real world, viewed through a camera phone or glasses (such as Google Glass). Mobile augmented reality systems use digital cameras and/or other optical sensors, accelerometers, GPS, gyroscopes, solid state compasses, RFID and wireless sensors as tracking technologies. These technologies offer varying levels of accuracy and precision. As opposed to augmented reality, mobile augmented reality systems provide six degrees of freedom (6DoF), which refers to the freedom of movement of a rigid body in three-dimensional space, during movement (Olsson *et al.* 2012). At the moment, mobile augmented reality applications are mostly used in the industrial assembly, medical, tourism, education and training, sports broadcasting and defence sectors (Wu *et al.* 2013). For instance, 3D Tallinn (Estonia) helps visitors to explore the 3D medieval old town (see http://3d.tallinn.ee/home_eng.html), and there is currently a mobile phone application of the product that is at the beta testing stage. Mobile augmented reality systems are rapidly developing despite a number of limitations and challenges, such as portability and outdoor use; tracking and auto-calibration; depth perception; overload and over-reliance; and social acceptance (see Van Krevelen and Poelman 2010). However, recent technology developments, such as laser-powered displays and hand-held displays, help in efforts to overcome some of these problems. Even though augmented reality has come a long way, it still has a long way to go to become an integral part of our daily lives and the general public accepting it as a familiar user interface.

Convergence technologies

Management of ubiquitous urban infrastructure partially depends on intelligent planning support, monitoring and management systems that heavily benefit from ICT and technologies convergence. Ubiquitous infrastructure management in the areas of education, transport, power supply, sewerage and waste treatment, and water supply constantly relies on ICT convergence to enhance its quality and customer service delivery. As Brotchie *et al.* (1987: 449) point out, 'a shift, from land, material, and energy to knowledge, information, and intellect as key factors of production, increased the interdependence between manufacturing, commerce, and consumption and the new information channels [including] the traditional transport systems'. The convergence technologies used in urban infrastructure help local economic growth through e-business, improve local service delivery through e-government, advance connectivity to local and global networks through wireline and wireless devices and provide access to education through e-education. These technologies also minimise unnecessary travels and contribute to reducing greenhouse gas emissions by offsetting material and energy consumption and expediting a more efficient use of current forms of physical infrastructure. Many local governments have been investing in the latest telecommunication convergence, such as wireless internet network technologies (e.g. 4G LTE, WiMAX) in order to improve the shift from polluting manufacturing industries to clean knowledge industries. Another example is the intelligent streetlights that are being provided alongside existing streetlights that have RFID and wireline and wireless communications technologies in order to minimise energy consumption (Lee and Leem 2009). These intelligent streetlights benefit from the convergence technology of construction and information and communications, C-ICT (Yigitcanlar 2010). Technology convergence can be classified into the following fundamental groups according to their common features in implementing and processing specific information: (i) sensing, e.g. data input; (ii) network, e.g. data transfer; (iii) interface, e.g. data representation; (iv) processing, e.g. data processing; and (v) security, e.g. data safety measures (see Lee and Leem 2009).

Internet and media convergence

The internet is one of the most powerful technologies to access information in modern society. It provides a channel for users to undertake many tasks including doing business; studying online; communicating with others; entertaining, such as watching videos, TV shows, listening to music; and downloading and uploading pictures, music and videos (Cunningham and Turner 2005). For instance, people can easily access the latest audio-visual data downloaded from YouTube at anytime if they can access the internet. Technology convergence enables them to access the information regardless of time and space using a converged digital device, a so-called 'black box'. Jenkins (2006) describes technology convergence as a black box, where multiple products are integrated with one product and takes each of their technical advantages. Convergence leads to a technological shift or a new technological process, but it also integrates educational, cultural and social paradigms. Convergence also shows the way in which individuals interact with each other and use various media platforms in order to create new experiences, new forms of media and content (Cunningham and Turner 2005).

To date, technology convergence of internet media and contents significantly improves our learning activities. For example, a number of primary schools in Australia use Nintendo DS with a touch-panel interface for mathematics education. Students of these schools show higher performance levels than those who do not use such innovative education tools. Similarly, the Wii had sold over

50 million units worldwide by March 2009. In Australia, the Wii exceeded the record set by the Xbox 360 to become the fastest selling games, exercise and education console in Australian history (Moses 2006). This innovative device is based on technology convergence, which integrates a games console, moving sensor and internet browser. The integrated activities can be visible in smart cities using these converged technologies. For instance, the programmable street is provided with multiple functions, such as lighting, security monitoring, commercial advertisement, solar energy and audio-visual objects. Since the mid-2000s, convergence of ICTs has also created a new form of urban spaces. Public telephone booth and public transport ticketing offices have disappeared and been replaced by mobile phones with converged technologies. The new generation mobile phones are now equipped with more advanced features, such as touch screen, video recording, GPS navigation, internet and emailing, data storage and security mechanisms. Today, it is possible for a mobile phone to access information on urban utilities and real-time monitoring of the environment (Yigitcanlar 2009). These widespread devices can be used in real-time planning and management, and can contribute to conservation of urban natural resources (Yigitcanlar *et al.* 2008), urban growth management and sustainable urban development (Yigitcanlar 2010).

Marketing convergence

Technology convergence in the area of marketing and business is also apparent. The notion of multiplay is often used in a convergence of ICT services and products and is often adapted to smart cities planning. The multiplay is needed when an individual accesses different telecommunication services, such as broadband internet access, cable television, telephone and mobile phone services rather than traditionally only using one or two of these services (Cunningham and Turner 2005). The multiplay technology convergence consists of dual, triple or quadruple play options depending on the specific application area: a dual play service needs to provide two ICT services, such as high-speed internet (ADSL2+) and a telephone service over a single broadband connection. High-speed internet (cable modem) and TV services provided by a single broadband connection is an example for this (ANSI 1998). Convergence can be accompanied by the underlying telecommunications infrastructure. An example of this is a triple play service, where communication services are bundled, which allows consumers to access TV, internet and telephone through a single subscription (Flew 2005). A quadruple play service is similar to the triple play service of broadband internet access, television and telephone, but is based on wireless technologies. This service is sometimes referred to as the 'fantastic four' or 'grand slam' (Baumgartner 2005). The next level of service used in smart cities is the integration of RFID into the quadruple play, which adds the capability for home equipment to communicate with the outside world and schedule maintenance of its own (Fisher and Monahan 2008). RFID tags are applied to an object incorporated into a product, an animal or a person for the purpose of identifying, reading and tracking information by using radio waves. Some tags can be read from several metres away and some can be far beyond the line of sight of the reader. This technology convergence in marketing helps connect people to other consumers so that they may share their reviews and, at the same time, engage with the service providers in ways in which they have not been able to in the past (Yigitcanlar 2010).

Telecommunication convergence

Telecommunication convergence is closely related to the merging of relevant urban infrastructures, such as telecommunications infrastructure and transport systems. Convergence is a key concept in coordinating a range of urban network services, such as physical networks or components thereof that channel fluxes through conduits or media to their nodes, such as receivers (Neuman 2006). Technology convergence requires supporting super ordinate systems connected to the networks. These networks include transportation, pipes, wires and cables in the channels through which their products are sold and serviced. The highly mobile nature of portable technology provides immobile physical networks with convergence by incorporating telecommunication devices, such as portable video and media devices, GPS navigation devices, portable internet surfing and mobile telecommunications devices into a single device; this is the black box designed to remove the need to carry multiple devices while away from the office or home.

A telecommunications infrastructure network, which is interconnected by a web of sensors, actuators, wireline and wireless communications networks, and computer systems could benefit from a convergence in the form of a combination of different telecommunication media in a single operating platform (O'Brien and Soibelman 2004). Convergence in fact allows companies to no longer be confined to their own markets. Fixed, mobile and IP service providers can offer content and media services, and hardware and software providers can offer services directly to the end user (Telecom Media Convergence 2009). These days, most of the content or service providers are consistently looking for new digital infrastructure and more effective distribution channels. For instance, the 3G and 4G mobile phone technologies use technology convergence that provides the combination of telecom, data processing and imaging technologies. Previously separate technologies, such as voice including telephone features, data including productivity applications, and video including teleconferencing now share resources and interact with each other (Jenkins 2006). In a smart city environment, the present 'voiceover IP' (VoIP) and 'Bluetooth' technologies are merged into a wireless internet network, the so-called LTE/WiMAX, for seamless mobility between VoWiFi and cellular networks (Telephony Online 2009). These mobile service provisions give rise to the ability to access most of the telecommunications channels including voice, internet, video and content without requiring tethering to the network via cables (Williams 2009). Given the recent advancements in LTE/WiMAX and other leading edge technologies, it is fair to say the ability to transfer information over a wireless link at combinations of speed, distance and non-line of sight conditions is rapidly improving. Therefore, the whole range of technology conversion is becoming increasingly invisible, intangible and pervasive (Firmino *et al*. 2008) and is likely to improve the quality of the lives of its users. (Yigitcanlar 2010).

Summary

This Chapter introduced and reviewed the major smart urban information technologies that are currently in use or being developed to improve the quality of life and environment in our cities and societies. Smart urban information technologies potentially provide solutions to many of the challenges faced by our cities, societies and the environment. For instance, at present most of the developed nations are facing aging population-related problems, and smart homes help in easing some of the aged care problems. For instance, according to Ding *et al*. (2011: 135):

> [a]s the population of people with disabilities grows and the burgeoning older adult population seeks to age in place, smart home technologies can potentially provide an answer to relieve the demanding workload of care from family caregivers and healthcare providers, and support independent living. However, this review of current sensor technology for smart homes indicates most of the identified studies only demonstrate the feasibility of technological solutions in laboratory settings.

This Chapter also highlighted that technology convergence may provide new horizons for our cities and societies. So far, the implementation of convergence technologies on urban infrastructure is already clearly understood, and somehow development is underway in most parts of the developed world (Yigitcanlar 2010). Rapid new economic growth associated with new technology and new infrastructure is clearly taking its roots in the global knowledge economy (Wieman 1998; Neuman 2006). Managing and monitoring the urban infrastructure has become easier by deploying appropriate wireless infrastructures, making it accessible and inexpensive to users, and refining software, portals and so on (Aurigi 2006). Convergence technology solutions including performance monitoring, distance working and seamless production are already starting to be incorporated into broad planning initiatives, focusing on improving the efficiency of existing urban infrastructure planning, provision and management (Rheingold 2007). According to Jenkins (2006), due to the speedy progress of technology conversion, it has been long thought that, eventually, users will access all services and information from urban infrastructure networks and services through one single mobile device.

References

Aarts, E, Encarnaçao, J 2005, 'Into ambient intelligence', in Aarts, E, Encarnaçao, J (eds) *True Visions: The Emergence of Ambient Intelligence*, Springer, Berlin, Germany, pp. 1–16.
Anderson, P 2007, *What Is Web 2.0? Ideas, Technologies and Implications for Education*, JISC Technology and Standards Watch, Bristol, UK.

Andrews, JG, Ghosh, A, Muhamed, R 2007, *Fundamentals of WiMAX: Understanding Broadband Wireless Networking*, Pearson Education, New York.

ANSI 1998, *Network and Customer Installation Interfaces: Asymmetric Digital Subscriber Line (Adsl) Metallic Interface*, American National Standards Institute (ANSI), Washington, DC.

Aurigi, A 2006, 'New technologies, yet same dilemmas? Policy and design issues for the augmented city', *Journal of Urban Technology*, vol. 13, no. 3, pp. 5–28.

Bajaj, R, Ranaweera, SL, Agrawal, DP 2002, 'GPS: Location-tracking technology', *Computer*, vol. 35, no. 1, pp. 92–94.

Batty, M, Axhausen, KW, Giannotti, F 2012, 'Smart cities of the future', *The European Physical Journal Special Topics*, vol. 214, no. 1, pp. 481–518.

Baum, S, Kendall, E, Muenchberger, H, Gudes, O, Yigitcanlar, T 2010, 'Geographical information systems: An effective planning and decision-making platform for community health coalitions in Australia?', *Health Information Management Journal*, vol. 39, no. 3, pp. 28–33.

Baumgartner, J 2005, *Cable Consortium Mobilizes Quad-Play With Sprint*, accessed on 25 June 2015 from http://www.cedmagazine.com/news/2005/11/cable-consortium-mobilizes-quad-play-with-sprint

Berthon, PR, Pitt, LF, Plangger, K, Shapiro, D 2012, 'Marketing meets Web 2.0, social media, and creative consumers: Implications for international marketing strategy', *Business Horizons*, vol. 55, no. 3, pp. 261–271.

Billsus, D, Brunk, CA, Evans, C, Gladish, B, Pazzani, M 2002, 'Adaptive interfaces for ubiquitous web access', *Communications of the ACM*, vol. 45, no. 5, pp. 34–38.

Bricon-Souf, N, Newman, CR 2007, 'Context awareness in health care: A review', *International Journal of Medical Informatics*, vol. 76, no. 1, pp. 2–12.

Brotchie, J, Hall, P, Newton, J 1987, 'The transition to an information society', in Brotchie, J, Hall, P, Newton, J (eds) *The Spatial Impact of Technological Change*, Croom Helm, London, pp. 441–456.

Byun, HE, Cheverst, K 2004, 'Utilizing context history to provide dynamic adaptations', *Applied Artificial Intelligence*, vol. 18, no. 6, pp. 533–548.

Cai, H, Jiang, L, Zhang, Y 2012, 'Context and policy based fault-tolerant scheme in mobile ubiquitous computing environment', in Proceedings of the 7th IEEE Conference on Industrial Electronics and Applications, July 2012, pp. 1711–1715.

Cha, B 2015, *What Is 5g, and What Does It Mean For Consumers?*, accessed on 11 June 2015 from http://recode.net/2015/03/13/what-is-5g-and-what-does-it-mean-for-consumers

Chen, CP, Zhang, CY 2014, 'Data-intensive applications, challenges, techniques and technologies: A survey on Big Data', *Information Sciences*, vol. 275, no. 1, pp. 314–347.

Chen, GD, Kotz, A 2000, *Survey of Context-Aware Mobile Computing Research*, Dartmouth Computer Science Technical Report, TR2000–381, Hanover, Germany.

Cherifi, H, Zain, JM, El Qawasmeh, E (eds) 2011, *Digital Information and Communication Technology and Its Applications*, Springer, New York.

Cheskin Research 2002, 'Designing digital experiences for youth', *Market Insights Series*, vol. 2002, no. 4, pp. 8–9.

Cunningham, C, Turner, G 2005, 'The media and communications in Australia', in Flew, T (ed.) *New Media: An Introduction*, Allen and Unwin, Sydney, Australia, pp. 102–114.

De Donno, D, Catarinucci, L, Tarricone, L 2014, 'RAMSES: RFID augmented module for smart environmental sensing', *IEEE Transactions on Instrumentation and Measurement*, vol. 63, no. 7, pp. 1701–1708.

DeLuca, KM, Lawson, S, Sun, Y 2012, 'Occupy Wall Street on the public screens of social media: the many framings of the birth of a protest movement', *Communication, Culture and Critique*, vol. 5, no. 4, pp. 483–509.

Dey, AK, Abowd, GD, Salber, D 2001, 'A conceptual framework and a toolkit for supporting the rapid prototyping of context-aware applications', *Human–Computer Interaction*, vol. 16, no. 1, pp. 97–166.

Ding, D, Cooper, RA, Pasquina, PF, Fici-Pasquina, L 2011, 'Sensor technology for smart homes', *Maturitas*, vol. 69, no. 2, pp. 131–136.

El Zabadani, H 2006, *Self-Sensing Places*, Unpublished PhD thesis, University of Florida, Gainesville, FL.

Firmino, R, Duarte, F, Moreira, T 2008, 'Pervasive technologies and urban planning in the augmented city', *Journal of Urban Technology*, vol. 15, no. 1, pp. 77–93.

Firth, L, Mellor, D 2005, 'Broadband: Benefits and problems', *Telecommunications Policy*, vol. 29, no. 2, pp. 223–236.

Fisher, J, Monahan, T 2008, 'Tracking the social dimensions of RFID systems in hospitals', *International Journal of Medical Informatics*, vol. 77, no. 1, pp. 176–183.

Flew, T (ed.) 2005, *New Media: An Introduction*, Oxford University Press, Oxford, UK.

Frieden, R 2005, 'Lessons from broadband development in Canada, Japan, Korea and the United States', *Telecommunications Policy*, vol. 29, no. 8, pp. 595–613.

Friedewald, M, Raabe, O 2011, 'Ubiquitous computing: An overview of technology impacts', *Telematics and Informatics*, vol. 28, no. 2, pp. 55–65.

Gabriel, P, Bovenschulte, M, Hartmann, E, Gross, W, Strese, H, Bayarou, K, Haisch, M, Matthess, M, Brune, C, Strauss, H, Kelter, H, Oberweis, R 2006, *Pervasive Computing*, SecuMedia, Ingelheim, Germany.

Garfinkel, SL, Juels, A, Pappu, R 2005, 'RFID privacy: An overview of problems and proposed solutions', *IEEE Security and Privacy*, vol. 3, no. 1, pp. 34–43.

Gökçe, OZ, Hatipoğlu, E, Göktürk, G, Luetgert, B, Saygin, Y 2014, 'Twitter and politics: Identifying Turkish opinion leaders in new social media', *Turkish Studies*, vol. 15, no. 4, pp. 671–688.

Gold, J 2015, *5G Wireless: Reality Looks to Catch up With Hype*, accessed on 11 June 2015 from http://www.networkworld.com/article/2172952/wireless/5g-wireless–reality-looks-to-catch-up-with-hype.html

Goodchild, MF 2007a, 'Citizens as sensors: The world of volunteered geography', *GeoJournal*, vol. 69, no. 4, pp. 211–221.

Goodchild, MF 2007b, 'Citizens as voluntary sensors: Spatial data infrastructure in the world of web 2.0', *International Journal of Spatial Data Infrastructures Research*, vol. 2, no. 1, pp. 24–32.

Goodchild, MF, Li, L 2012, 'Assuring the quality of volunteered geographic information', *Spatial Statistics*, vol. 1, no. 1, pp. 110–120.

Gordon, K 2013, 'What is big data?', *ITNOW*, vol. 55, no. 3, pp. 12–13.

Hightower, J, Borriello, G 2001, 'Location systems for ubiquitous computing', *Computer*, vol. 8, no. 1, pp. 57–66.

Hong, JY, Suh, EH, Kim, SJ 2009, 'Context-aware systems: A literature review and classification', *Expert Systems with Applications*, vol. 36, no. 4, pp. 8509–8522.

Hsu, I 2010, 'Mobile ubiquitous attendance monitoring system using wireless sensor networks', *Education Technology and Computer IEEE*, vol. 4, no. 1, pp. 533–537.

Internet Live Stats 2015, *Internet Users in the World*, accessed on 24 June 2015 from http://www.internetlivestats.com/internet-users

Isaacson, W 2014, *The Innovators*, Simon and Schuster, New York.

Jenkins, H 2006, *Convergence Culture: Where Old and New Media Collide*, New York University Press, New York.

Katz, J, Rice, R 2002, *Social Consequences of Internet Use: Access, Involvement, and Interaction*, MIT Press, Cambridge, MA.

Kim, TH, Fang, WC, Ramos, C, Mohammed, S, Gervasi, O, Stoica, A 2012, 'Ubiquitous sensor networks and its application', *International Journal of Distributed Sensor Networks*, vol. 2012, no. 1, pp. 1–3.

Knights, MI 2007, 'Web 2.0: Web technologies', *Communications Engineer*, vol. 5, no. 1, pp. 30–35.

Komninos, N 2002, *Intelligent Cities: Innovation, Knowledge Systems and Digital Spaces*, Spon Press, London.

Landt, J 2005, 'The history of RFID', *Potentials IEEE*, vol. 24, no. 4, pp. 8–11.

Lee, S 1999, 'Internet-based planning methodology', *Journal of Korea Planning Association*, vol. 34, no. 3, pp. 49–60.

Lee, S, Leem, Y 2009, 'Philosophical and conceptual characteristics of ubiquitous city strategies and projects', in *Proceedings of the Computers in Urban Planning and Urban Management Conference*, 16–19 June 2009, Hong Kong, ROC, pp. 92–103.

Lee, S, Hoon, H, Taik, L, Yigitcanlar, T 2008b, 'Towards ubiquitous city: Concept, planning, and experiences in the Republic of Korea', in Yigitcanlar, T, Velibeyoglu, K, Baum, S (eds) *Knowledge-Based Urban Development: Planning and Application in the Information Era*, IGI Global, Hershey, PA, pp. 148–169.

Lee, S, Yigitcanlar, T, Hoon, H, Taik, L 2008a, 'Ubiquitous urban infrastructure: Infrastructure planning and development in Korea', *Innovation: Management, Policy and Practice*, vol. 10, no. 2/3, pp. 282–292.

Licklider, JCR, Clark, WE 1962, 'On-line man-computer communication', in *Proceedings of the Association for Computing Machinery (ACM) Conference*, 1–3 May 1962, New York, pp. 113–128.

Menon, S 2011, 'Policy agendas for South Korea's broadband convergence network infrastructure project', *Info*, vol. 13, no. 2, pp. 19–34.

Molina, JM, Corchado, JM, Bajo, J 2008, 'Ubiquitous computing for mobile environments', in Moreno, A, Pavon, J (eds) *Issues in Multi-Agent Systems*, Birkhäuser, Basel, Switzerland, pp. 33–57.

Moses, A 2006, *Wii Breaks Xbox 360 Sales Record*, accessed on 25 June 2015 from http://www.smh.com.au/news/games/wii-breaks-xbox-sales-record/2006/12/14/1165685799546.html

Murphy, M 2015, *These Countries Have the Fastest 4G Wireless Networks in the World*, accessed on 9 June 2015 from http://qz.com/360548/these-countries-have-the-fastest-4g-wireless-networks-in-the-world

Neuman, M 2006, 'Infiltrating infrastructures: On the nature of networked infrastructure', *Journal of Urban Technology*, vol. 13, no. 1, pp. 3–31.

Ni, LM, Liu, Y, Lau, YC, Patil, AP 2004, 'LANDMARC: Indoor location sensing using active RFID', *Wireless Networks*, vol. 10, no. 6, pp. 701–710.

O'Brien, W, Soibelman, L 2004, 'Technology and engineering dimensions: Collecting and interpreting new information for civil and environmental infrastructure management', in Zimmerman, R, Horan, T (eds) *Digital Infrastructures: Enabling Civil and Environmental Systems through Information Technology*, Routledge, London, pp. 19–36.

O'Reilly, T 2007, 'What is web 2.0: Design patterns and business models for the next generation of software', *Communications and Strategies*, vol. 1, no. 1, pp. 17–38.

OECD 2001, *The Development of Broadband Access in OECD Countries*, OECD, Paris, France.

Olsson, T, Kärkkäinen, T, Lagerstam, E, Ventä-Olkkonen, L 2012, 'User evaluation of mobile augmented reality scenarios', *Journal of Ambient Intelligence and Smart Environments*, vol. 4, no. 1, pp. 29–47.

Papacharissi, Z, Zaks, A 2006, 'Is broadband the future? An analysis of broadband technology potential and diffusion', *Telecommunications Policy*, vol. 30, no. 1, pp. 64–75.

Perera, C, Zaslavsky, A, Christen, P, Georgakopoulos, D 2014, 'Context aware computing for the internet-of-things: A survey', *IEEE Communications Surveys and Tutorials*, vol. 16, no. 1, pp. 414–454.

Portugali, J 2011, *Complexity Cognition and the City*, Springer, New York.

Rao, B, Minakakis, L 2003, 'Evolution of mobile location-based services', *Communications of the ACM*, vol. 46, no. 12, pp. 61–65.

Rheingold, H 2007, *Smart Mobs: The Next Social Revolution*, Basic Books, Cambridge, MA.

Robertson, J 2013, *Countries With the Most 4G Mobile Users*, accessed on 9 June 2015 from http://www.bloomberg.com/slideshow/2013–09–19/countries-with-the-most-4g-mobile-users.html

Roche, S 2014, 'Geographic information science I: Why does a smart city need to be spatially enabled?', *Progress in Human Geography*, vol. 38, no. 5, pp. 703–711.

Schilit, B, Theimer, M 1994, 'Disseminating active map information to mobile hosts', *Network IEEE*, vol. 8, no. 5, pp. 22–32.

Shin, D 2007, 'A critique of Korean national information strategy', *Government Information Quarterly*, vol. 24, no. 3, pp. 624–645.

Shin, D, Kweon, S 2011, 'Evaluation of Korean information infrastructure policy 2000–2010: Focusing on broadband ecosystem change', *Government Information Quarterly*, vol. 28, no. 3, pp. 374–387.

Shin, D, Jung, J 2012, 'Socio-technical analysis of Korea's broadband convergence network: Big plans, big projects, big prospects?', *Telecommunications Policy*, vol. 36, no. 7, pp. 579–593.

Shrestha, B, Elsherbeni, A, Ukkonen, L 2011, 'UHF RFID reader antenna for near-field and far-field operations', *Antennas and Wireless Propagation Letters IEEE*, vol. 10, no. 1, pp. 1274–1277.

Spivack, N 2007, *Web 3.0 Roundup: Radar Networks, Powerset, Metaweb and Others*, accessed on 25 June 2015 from http://www.novaspivack.com/technology/web-3-0-roundup-radar-networks-powerset-metaweb-and-others

Spivack, N 2015, *Web 3.0: The Third Generation Web Is Coming*, accessed on 25 June 2015 from https://lifeboat.com/ex/web.3.0

Statista 2015, *Number of Mobile Phone Users Worldwide from 2012 to 2018*, accessed on 11 June 2015 from http://www.statista.com/statistics/274774/forecast-of-mobile-phone-users-worldwide

Svanaes, D 2001, 'Context-aware technology: A phenomenological perspective', *Human–Computer Interaction*, vol. 16, no. 1, pp. 379–400.

Tafa, Z 2011, 'Ubiquitous sensor networks', in Gavrilovska, L, Krco, S, Milutinovic, V, Stojmenovic, I, Trobec, R (eds) *Application and Multidisciplinary Aspects of Wireless Sensor Networks*, Springer, London, pp. 267–268.

Telecom Media Convergence 2009, *Telecom Media Convergence*, accessed on 15 June 2009 from http://www.tmforum.org/TelecomMediaConvergence/4645/home.html

Telephony Online 2009, *Simplifying Fixed/Mobile Convergence (FMC) for Businesses*, accessed on 15 June 2009 from http://telephonyonline.com/global/commentary/simplifying-fixed-mobile-convergence-0330/?cid=hcom

Tomioka, K, Kondo, K 2006, 'Ubiquitous sensor network system', *NEC Technical Journal*, vol. 1, no. 1, pp. 78–82.

Townsend, AM 2013, *Smart Cities: Big Data, Civic Hackers, and the Quest for a New Utopia*, WW Norton and Company, New York.

Van Krevelen, DWF, Poelman, R 2010, 'A survey of augmented reality technologies, applications and limitations', *International Journal of Virtual Reality*, vol. 9, no. 2, pp. 1–20.

Want, R 2004, 'Enabling ubiquitous sensing with RFID', *Computer*, vol. 37, no. 4, pp. 84–86.

Want, R 2006, 'An introduction to RFID technology', *Pervasive Computing IEEE*, vol. 5, no. 1, pp. 25–33.

Weiser, M 1991, 'The computer for the 21st century', *Scientific American*, vol. 265, no. 3, pp. 66–75.

Wieman, C 1998, 'The high-tech transition: Technology and the prospects for improving infrastructure performance', *Journal of Urban Technology*, vol. 5, no. 2, pp. 21–46.

Williams, I 2009, *Huawei Pushes Fixed-Mobile Convergence*, accessed on 15 June 2009 from http://identitymanagement.itweek.co.uk/vnunet/news/2230131/huawei-pushes-fixed-mobile

Wolfsfeld, G, Segev, E, Sheafer, T 2013, 'Social media and the Arab spring politics come first', *The International Journal of Press/Politics*, vol. 18, no. 2, pp. 115–137.

Wu, HK, Lee, SW, Chang, HY, Liang, JC 2013, 'Current status, opportunities and challenges of augmented reality in education', *Computers and Education*, vol. 62, no. 1, pp. 41–49.

Xavier, P 2003, 'Should broadband be part of universal service obligations?', *Info*, vol. 5, no. 1, pp. 8–25.

Yigitcanlar, T. 2009, 'Planning for smart urban ecosystems: Information technology applications for capacity building in environmental decision making', *Theoretical and Empirical Researches in Urban Management*, vol. 3, no. 12, pp. 5–21.

Yigitcanlar, T 2010, 'Managing ubiquitous eco cities: Telecommunication infrastructure networks, technology convergence and intelligent urban management systems', *Ecohumanity*, vol. 2010, no. 3, pp. 25–59

Yigitcanlar, T 2015, 'Smart cities: An effective urban development and management model?', *Australian Planner*, vol. 52, no. 1, pp. 27–34.

Yigitcanlar, T, Lee, S 2014, 'Korean ubiquitous-eco-city: A smart-sustainable urban form or a branding hoax?', *Technological Forecasting and Social Change*, vol. 89, no. 1, pp. 100–114.

Yigitcanlar, T, Han, JH, Lee, SH 2008, 'Online environmental information systems', in Adam, F (ed.) *Encyclopaedia of Decision Making and Decision Support Techniques*, IGI Global, Hershey, PA, pp. 691–698.

Zikopoulos, P, Eaton, C 2011, *Understanding Big Data: Analytics for Enterprise Class Hadoop and Streaming Data*, McGraw-Hill, New York.

4 Smart urban systems

> *Some Google employees have their self-driving vehicles take them to work. These car robots don't look like something from 'The Jetsons'; the driverless features on these cars are a bunch of sensors, wires, and software. This technology 'works'.*
> (Tyler Cowen, author of *Modern Principles of Economics*)

Introduction

As stated by Goh (2015: 169), 'visions of a kind of technology-infused "smart city" are becoming reality, translated from the realm of concepts into actual urban space'. In particular, the development of smart urban systems through effective use of smart urban technologies is providing an invaluable foundation for smart cities to surface. Today, more and more governments are showing interest in smart urban system investment to make cities more efficient, sustainable and inclusive. Consequently, it is estimated that the global market for smart urban systems for transport, energy, healthcare, water and waste will be around $400 billion per annum by 2020 (BIS 2013). Building on Chapter 3, this is to say that smart urban systems will fast become an integral part of our lives. This Chapter, therefore, aims to elaborate on the key conceptual and practical issues of smart urban system adoption in cities. In order to do so, the Chapter introduces and explores the most common and advanced smart urban systems, and offers examples of their adoption in the contemporary cities of the world. The Chapter also provides a discussion on challenges and opportunities of smart urban systems. The smart urban systems presented in this Chapter include: (i) smart urban transport systems; (ii) smart urban grid systems; (iii) smart urban water and waste systems; (iv) smart urban emergency and safety systems; and (v) smart urban participatory decision systems.

Smart urban transport systems

Increasing urban populations, changing lifestyles and growing travel needs are resulting in major issues and challenges for urban administrations to deal with, e.g. congestion, accidents, comfort, productivity and pollution. A potential solution for these problems is seen as managing the traffic and transport systems intelligently (Bulu *et al.* 2014). In other words, cities can benefit from the deployment of intelligent transport systems (ITSs) for combatting transport-related problems. ITS is an advanced technology application designed to provide innovative services by transferring information between transport and infrastructure systems for an improved safety, efficiency, comfort and environmental performance. As indicated by Sussman (2008: 3), 'ITS combines high technology and improvements in information systems, communication, sensors, and advanced mathematical methods with the conventional world of surface transportation infrastructure'. It enhances road networks and transport systems through standalone applications, such as traffic management systems, information and warning systems installed in individual vehicles, and cooperative applications involving vehicle-to-infrastructure and vehicle-to-vehicle (V2V) communications, such as dedicated short range communications (DSRC), mobile networks (e.g. 4G LTE), Wi-Fi, WLAN, digital audio broadcasting (e.g. radio) and global navigation satellite system (e.g. GPS) (Hasan *et al.* 2012). ITS enables various users to be better informed and make safer, more coordinated and smarter use of transport networks by linking different modes of transport, infrastructure and traffic management. The rapidly advancing technology helps in building cooperative vehicular networks in which a variety of different ITS applications communicate with a variety of different units. This results in improving public and private transport safety, efficiency, comfort and also environmental performance (Dar *et al.* 2010). These systems serve as the backbone of smart urban transport systems and thus are a good approach for meeting future travel demands of urban populations. Figure 4.1 illustrates the broad classification of ITS applications (Chowdhury and Sadek 2003), and one of the smart urban transport systems is placed under the microscope for a thorough investigation in the following section.

Autonomous vehicles

Undoubtedly one of most advanced applications that utilises numerous ITS tools as part of a smart urban transport system is the autonomous vehicle, which can drive itself without human supervision or direct input. Fortunately, technologies that will make autonomous vehicles a reality are already emerging rapidly. The National Highway Traffic Safety Administration (NHTSA 2013) determines five automation levels of autonomous vehicle (see Table 4.1). We have already reached Level-3 automation that utilises V2V communication technology through a wireless connection, such as a mobile communications network (3G, 4G), Wi-Fi, Bluetooth or DSRC, to exchange information between vehicles (Anderson *et al.* 2014), providing the details of speed and position of surrounding vehicles, allowing them to locate each other and warn drivers about traffic hazards and immediate dangers (NHTSA 2013). Luo and Hubaux (2004) categorise the main applications of V2V technology as follows: (i) information and warning functions, provisioning road information between vehicles such as traffic congestion, incidents and road conditions; (ii) communication-based longitudinal control, utilising the exchange of vehicle information to avoid collisions and facilitate the formation of vehicle platoons; and (iii) cooperative assistance systems, assisting drivers during hazardous situations such as highway merging and blind intersections.

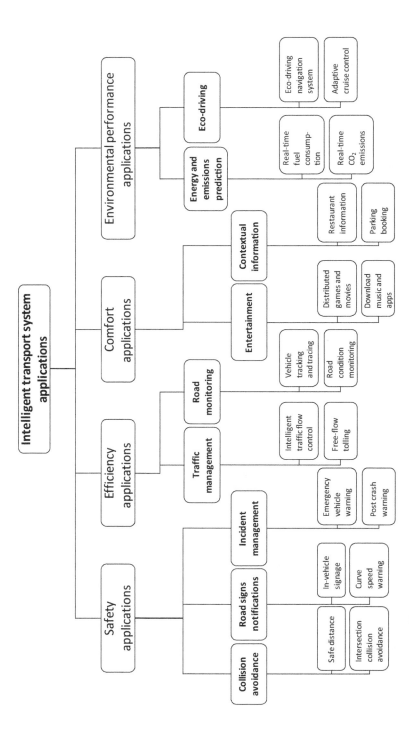

Figure 4.1 Classification of ITS applications.

Source: Dar *et al.* 2010.

Table 4.1 Level of automation

Level of automation	Description	Examples of technology
Level-0: No automation	The driver is responsible for full control and safe operation of the vehicle including acceleration, breaking, steering and monitoring the road. Vehicles that contain advanced driver assistance systems (ADAS) that do not take vehicle control away from the driver are still considered level 0.	Collision warning, lane retention warning, blind spot monitoring
Level-1: Assisted automation	Automation of one or more control functions that operate independently from one another, such as automated parallel-parking or adaptive cruise control. The automated system may assist or control, with limited authority, one of the primary functions of steering and braking/acceleration, but not both. The driver is still solely responsible for the control and safe operation of the vehicle.	Cruise control, automatic braking, lane keeping, park assist
Level-2: Partial automation	The vehicle has two or more of its primary control functions automated, which work in unison to accomplish a specific driving task, such as the use of adaptive cruise control and lane centring in highway driving. The driver is still responsible for the control and safe operation and must be ready to relinquish control at any time while the automated systems are in use.	Adaptive cruise control with lane centring
Level-3: High automation	The primary control functions are fully automated and can operate safely without any assistance from the driver, including the need to monitor external conditions. The vehicle will determine when automated control is no longer possible, giving the driver an appropriate amount of time to take control.	Platooning

(continued)

Table 4.1 (continued)

Level of automation	Description	Examples of technology
Level-4: Full automation	The vehicle can perform all primary and secondary control functions, and monitor and adapt to any changes in road conditions. The only task expected of the driver is to input destination coordinates; the vehicle is solely responsible for the control and safe operation of itself.	Autonomous vehicle

Source: NHTSA 2013.

Another emerging ITS is vehicle-to-infrastructure (V2I) communication, which involves the exchange of information from road infrastructure to vehicles and vice versa using similar wireless technology to V2V. Although V2I technology would greatly synergise with autonomous vehicles, current original equipment manufacturer (OEM) car companies are developing driverless vehicles that will operate independently from such technology (O'Toole 2014). V2I is still very much in the experimental stages of development, but potential applications of this technology have already been proposed, such as the 'road intersection assistant'. It would incorporate cameras at intersections to analyse traffic flow, pedestrians and traffic light timing and send this information to oncoming vehicles, while they would send their position and speed to the intersection so that traffic light timing can be managed more efficiently (see Prisma 2015). Another V2I application proposed by Fajardo *et al.* (2011) is the reservation idea, which presents a first-come-first-served approach for fully and highly autonomous vehicles where the vehicle calls ahead to an intersection-manager program at the incoming traffic light to reserve space-time at the intersection; the vehicle is then either granted or denied the request to go through the intersection based on the path of the vehicle and any potential conflicts.

There are numerous advantages of fully autonomous vehicles. First, when Level-4 autonomous vehicles are developed they will be able to provide a new dimension of mobility to certain demographic groups that have no access to driving including the elderly, under-aged and disabled, providing benefits, such as increased accessibility and reduced social isolation (Anderson *et al.* 2014). In particular, car-sharing services are expected to play a major role in utilising autonomous vehicles and shifting the transportation paradigm. It is estimated that cars spend only 4 per cent of their lifetime in use, while only 17 per cent of household vehicles are in use at any given time on a daily basis. This creates a potential market that could capitalise on these opportunity costs (Thrun 2010; Fagnant and Kockelman 2014). One group of thought is that the number of vehicles on the road will decrease as a result of private car-sharing services, where people will choose to rent out their cars instead of parking them while they not in use. Families may also choose to decrease their household fleet as one vehicle could serve multiple users simultaneously (Morgan Stanley 2013; Fagnant and Kockelman 2014). Others predict a surge in the use of self-driving taxis resulting in people forgoing vehicle ownership altogether. A study by Fagnant and Kockelman (2014) on the use of shared autonomous vehicles (SAV) found that one SAV can replace up to 12 privately owned vehicles. Litman (2015) also establishes that the use of self-driving taxis or SAVs as a replacement for private vehicles would be most suitable for people who drive fewer than 10,000 km per year.

Second, some of the key features of fully autonomous vehicles will include their capability to improve travel times and reduce congestion due to the expectation that they will be able to travel closer together with no danger of collision, resulting in improvements in road capacity and vehicle efficiency (Fagnant and Kockelman 2014). This has been evidenced by autonomous vehicles projects, which showed that a platoon could achieve speeds of 90 km/h with a 6 m gap, while increasing fuel economy by 10 per cent, along with the potential to reduce highway-related accidents by approximately 50 per cent (Brännström 2013). Shladover (2005) argues that the full range of benefits of road efficiency will only be achieved by providing dedicated lanes for autonomous vehicles, which will prevent any potential conflicts between autonomous and manually driven cars. Pinjari *et al.* (2013) postulate that the benefits of road efficiency will be realised as their market penetration increases, and only then will governments provide dedicated lanes. Researchers further support this view. For example, Reich (2013) illustrates that it took electronic toll collection seven years from inception and 55 per cent market penetration to be given exclusive lanes. Numerous studies highlight the benefits that can be realised by autonomous vehicles in highway driving, with some suggesting that autonomous technology could increase highway capacity by up to 273 per cent (Tientrakool 2011). Highways have been found to move between 2,000–2,500 vehicles per hour on average, but with the use of fully automated vehicles this capacity could increase by 2 to 4 times (Polzin 2013; O'Toole 2014). Other studies have found less impressive results, estimating a maximum road capacity increase of only 50 per cent and 80 per cent at a Level-4 market penetration of 80 per cent and 100 per cent respectively (Pinjari *et al.* 2013). The environmental and societal benefits have also been explored, which include increased fuel efficiency and a reduction in CO_2 emissions. Eugensson *et al.* (2013) calculate that drivers could save up to 4,300 litres of fuel and 5,000 hours of lost time collectively as a result of 30-minute traffic jams involving 7,200 vehicles caused by a highway collision, which account for 25 per cent of all congestion delays (Anderson *et al.* 2014).

Third, autonomous vehicles will prove to be a double-edged sword with regard to safety. On the one hand, they will reduce road accidents caused by human error, such as poor decision making, risky driving, inattention or distraction, while on the other, introducing a whole new range of concerns including cyber-attacks, system failure and mixed-traffic compatibility (Lin and Wang 2013). Human error is found to be the cause of over 90 per cent of traffic accidents, but autonomous vehicles will be able to remove human inefficiencies from the road, significantly reducing the amount of crashes, although not eliminating them altogether due to the additional risks they bring (Pinjari *et al.* 2013). Some predict that current levels of traffic-related fatalities could be reduced to 1 per cent (DiClemente *et al.* 2014). On the other hand, Schoettle and Sivak (2014) conversely argue that traffic collisions could potentially increase as a result of autonomous vehicles operating alongside human drivers.

Currently available driverless technologies have been implemented and tested through various public–private partnership projects, such as the Safe Road TRains for the Environment (SARTRE) and Highly Automated VEhicles for intelligent transport (HAVEit) projects. The SARTRE project has implemented the use of autonomous vehicles in platooning that are fitted with sensors, a computer interface, a V2V communication node and electronic control units (ECU), which are used to control individual vehicles and the platoon as a whole. Platooning involves a group of vehicles travelling closely together in a single line formation, led by a platoon leader that is a human-driven vehicle. The proposed benefits of a platoon are to reduce road congestion, fuel consumption and increase safety and driver/passenger convenience (Chan *et al.* 2012).

HAVEit is a system that integrates numerous advanced driver assistance systems (ADAS) to produce a highly automated car that can switch between four varying levels of autonomy, the highest of which allows the vehicle to drive by itself with the driver playing just a supervisory role. Some of the key technologies used in the HAVEit system include (Hoess 2009): (i) temporary autopilot, which incorporates a variety of features that can provide highly and semi-automated lateral (steering) and longitudinal (acceleration/braking) control, allowing for complete hands and feet-off driving on motorways; (ii) automated queue assistance, which relieves drivers of monotonous low-speed driving below 30 km/h by taking control of steering, acceleration/braking and monitoring surrounding vehicles using front and side sensors, and infrared V2V communication; and (iii) automated assistance in road works and congestion, which allows for automated driving in high-work load driving, such as navigating through temporary roads created by road works using radar sensors, a front camera and adaptive cruise control.

Apart from the existing ADAS technology that will be part of most autonomous vehicles, Google's driverless car relies on proprietary technology to facilitate its automation. Figure 4.2 illustrates an overview of the technology used by the Google Car. One of the most prominent features of the car is the light detection and ranging (LIDAR) scanner, which is a roof-mounted sensor that works by using 64 lasers to send out light in a 360-degree rotation to scan the surroundings up to a range of 120 m and calculates the time it takes for the light to return. This information is then used to create a virtual map of obstacles around the vehicle (Guizzo 2011). The surrounding distance radar sensors are used to track the distance of other vehicles in real time, while the position estimator sensor and the front mounted video camera are used to track the car's position and monitor all other static and dynamic objects to provide the vital information necessary for the

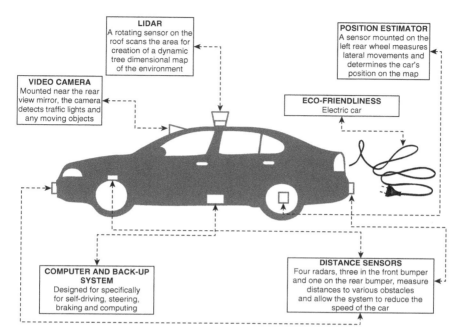

Figure 4.2 Components of Google Car.
Source: Google Self-Driving Car Project 2015.

car's computer to make navigational and safety decisions (Katkoori *et al.* 2013). As of 2014, Google's driverless vehicle fleet has logged just over one million kilometres. However, according to Moore and Lu (2011), autonomous vehicles currently experience a low mean failure distance (MFD), the amount of distance an autonomous vehicle can travel before human intervention is required, while it is suggested that they will need to reach an MFD of at least a few million kilometres travelled before they can be commercially viable. They also predict that the technology itself will take at least another decade to reach a reliable safety standard, which is supported by a survey of 200 experts at a vehicle symposium who predict that fully automated vehicles will be commercially available by 2030 (O'Toole 2014). Nonetheless, the following challenges still need to be addressed before the mass introduction of autonomous vehicles on public roads.

First, technology used in current autonomous vehicles suffers from two main issues: the capabilities of the sensors and the fusion between the incoming data and the ability of the vehicle's computer to interpret and produce an accurate real-time model of the environment (KPMG 2013). The LIDAR, for instance, has difficulties detecting surfaces with low reflectivity, such as black asphalt, while the radar sensors, which are used to track movement in real time, cannot detect non-metallic surfaces, such as pedestrians (Anderson *et al.* 2014). Additionally, the Stanford team who won the 2007 DARPA Grand Challenge noted that one of the limitations of their driverless vehicle was being able to recognise and segregate pedestrians from the environment, such as a person standing next to a pole at a crossing (Levinson *et al.* 2011). Autonomous vehicles have also yet to be tested in harsh environmental conditions, such as snow, rain or fog, with their resulting impact on the sensors, which may affect the ability to detect, recognise and locate objects. Furthermore, exacerbation could also result from age, physical damage or electrical fault (DiClemente *et al.* 2014). Katkoori *et al.* (2013) present some unexplored situations that could severely affect the performance of autonomous vehicles, such as electromagnetic interference from other electronics in the environment or even from other autonomous vehicles, which could degrade the performance of sensors in every car in the area. Other situations that need to be carefully considered include: how autonomous vehicles will handle interaction with human drivers; and how they will adapt to low-frequency and surprise events, such as road works, construction zones and repurposed lanes.

Second, several economic factors affect the deployment of highly and fully autonomous vehicles on the road, including cost, market penetration and user attitudes. The current price of the systems used in autonomous vehicles is prohibitive, with the LIDAR scanner alone costing over $70,000. However, this price will decrease with time with, for instance, the German LIDAR company, Ibeo, declaring that they will be able to produce the same product for only $250 (Priddle and Woodyard 2012). IHS automotive believes that Level-4 autonomous systems will add $5,000–$10,000 to the price of cars, but that this is expected to reduce to $3,000 in subsequent years (Tannert 2014). However, a survey conducted by KPMG (2013) indicates that the median price people were willing to pay for autonomous features was $4,500. On the other hand, a global survey by Schoettle and Sivak (2014) found that over 50 per cent of participants from Australia, UK and the United States were not willing to pay extra for Level-4 autonomous cars, with only 10 per cent of respondents stating they would pay over $5,000. Similar results have been reported by other studies, none of which has shown a positive response to the predicted price of autonomous vehicles (Casley *et al.* 2013; Morgan Stanley 2013). Thus, market penetration will be heavily dependent on the costs and user attitudes towards autonomous cars, in addition to the negative attitudes with regard to the price. A UK study found that 65 per cent of motorists would rather continue to drive manually even if they had the choice (Lloyd's 2014). This, coupled with the predicted trends that the first wave of Level-4 autonomous vehicles will be limited to full automation only on certain kinds of roads and at low speeds, while retaining manual operation at all other times (Anderson *et al.* 2014), will most likely follow the deployment trajectory proposed by Litman (2015) who argues that it could take until 2040 for Level-4 autonomous vehicles to represent at least 20 per cent of all vehicles on the road. Morgan Stanley (2013) predicts that freight transportation will adopt autonomous technology faster than the commercial market. However, they argue that full automation cannot occur while manually driven vehicles are still on the road.

Third, Level-4 automated vehicles are expected to raise a great amount of concerns for manufacturers with regards to their liability for road accidents and may further delay market saturation or even completely halt the adoption of autonomous vehicles (Villasenor 2014). Level-4 assumes that the driver is neither necessary in the operation of the vehicle nor expected to monitor the road; therefore in the case of an accident, the liability will be shifted entirely onto the manufacturer and suppliers of the automated systems (Marchant and Lindor 2012). Schellekens (2015), however, underlines that under current German road traffic law, the vehicle keeper (the registered owner) will still be liable as they are the ones who place the operational risk of the vehicle onto the road, regardless of whether they are the driver or not. Furthermore, he adds that even fully automated vehicles will shift some responsibility onto the driver who will still have to prove exoneration in the case of an accident. Similar views of traffic law are shared by some states in the United States, which imply that there is always someone who has control of the vehicle and who may therefore be responsible even if they are not driving it (Smith 2014). Douma and Palodichuk (2012) present two main concerns for policymakers, the first being the definition of the term 'operator' or 'driver', which will need to distinguish between when the vehicle is being driven by a human driver and when it is being driven by artificial intelligence (AI). Smith (2014) ascertains that according to current US legislation, autonomous vehicles could be seen as having multiple simultaneous drivers including the person who is able to directly control the vehicle physically or electronically, the person who turns on the vehicle or sends it to a location and the person who initiates or customises an automated operation, such as selecting or changing a destination or route. The variations in state legislation across the United States could inhibit the widespread commercialisation of autonomous vehicles. It is argued that the different requirements and regulations between states would make it impossible for manufacturers to create an autonomous car that could operate across multiple jurisdictions (Anderson *et al.* 2014). A possible solution to this issue would require federal intervention to standardise the terminology applicable to autonomous vehicles (DiClemente *et al.* 2014). Another concern for policymakers is the question of liability when the driver uses manual override to regain control of the vehicle; a range of scenarios could necessitate the driver having to regain control of the vehicle with or without warning, such as in the case of sudden technological malfunctions (Douma and Palodichuk 2012). Technological issues present additional legal challenges. Pinto (2012) specifically points out situations where the vehicle AI will need to make cost-benefit decisions between different collisions, such as whether it should avoid hitting a child that runs onto the street by swerving into traffic, putting the vehicle's occupants at risk. This could further escalate into multiple parties being liable due to either the camera mistaking a dog for a child or the AI being programmed to prioritise the value of different lives. Other legal liabilities exist, and they have been addressed by studies including those of Eugensson *et al.* (2013) and Villasenor (2014).

Smart urban grid systems

Electricity is critical to sustain quality of life and economic growth. The power grid delivers electricity and is a complex system as it contains an aggregation of several networks and multiple generation companies, which have different operators that use diverse levels of communication and coordination (Pereira *et al.* 2015). Therefore, the transition from traditional power grid towards smart grid is a movement of transition from astatic to flexible infrastructures with improved observability, controllability and efficiency (Vijayapriya and Kothari 2011). A reliable power grid is one of the critical infrastructure systems required for cities to function properly. However, the current traditional power system faces major challenges, such as growing demand, environmental externalities, efficiency requirements, connection of more decentralised generation and security of supply (Marques *et al.* 2014). According to Farhangi (2010), the traditional:

> [e]lectricity grid is unidirectional in nature. It converts only one-third of fuel energy into electricity, without recovering the waste heat. Almost 8% of its output is lost along its transmission lines, while 20% of its generation capacity exists to meet peak demand only (i.e. it is in use only 5% of the time). In addition to that, due to the hierarchical topology of its assets, the existing electricity grid suffers from domino effect failures.
>
> (Farhangi 2010: 9)

However, the next generation electricity grid, i.e. smart grid, has the capability to address these shortcomings and challenges. A smart urban grid system is defined as a power grid specifically designed to improve efficiency of production and distribution of electricity by collecting and using information on the behaviours of suppliers and consumers (Bulu *et al.* 2014). It implies smart generation, smart transmission, smart storage and smart sensors. In other words, it is the convergence of ICT with electricity infrastructure and power system engineering. Such a system is characterised as having the following salient features: digital, two-way communication; distributed generation; network; sensors throughout; self-monitoring; self-healing; adaptive and islanding; remote check/test; pervasive control; and many customer services (Farhangi 2014). Figure 4.3 illustrates the main components of a smart grid system.

Smart grid technology is particularly popular for its demand response, power cut management, disaster prevention and disaster recovery systems, as power cuts alone cost $80 billion annually (Miller 2009). For many (e.g. Moslehi and Kumar 2010), smart grid is a quantum leap in harnessing ICTs to enhance grid reliability and enable integration of various smart grid resources, such as renewable resources, demand response, electric storage and electric transportation. On the operational side, Fox-Penner (2014: 6) believes smart grid will bring a total transformation of the industry's operating model in the United States, and declares that this is, 'the first major architectural change since alternating current became the

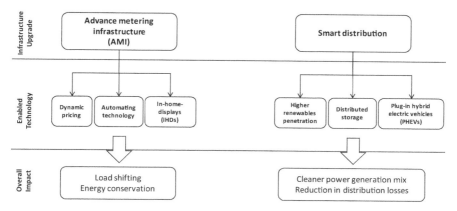

Figure 4.3 Components of a smart grid.

Source: Hledik 2009.

dominant system after the Chicago World's fair in 1893'. On the environmental side, Toft *et al.* (2014) underline that as:

> [a] response to climate change and the desire to gain independence from imported fossil fuels, there is a pressure to increase the proportion of electricity from renewable sources, which is one of the reasons why electricity grids are currently being turned into smart grids.
>
> (Toft *et al.* 2014: 392)

Therefore, in recent years, the need for a smart grid has become a growing concern in many circles including those of utilities, academics and energy/environmentally conscience customers (Pepermans 2014). Consequently, there is a large number of cities that have already managed or are in the process of transforming their grid into a smart one, such as various cities in Australia, Korea, Japan, the Netherlands, the UK and the United States. Furthermore, the 'super grid' concept is being discussed in Europe, expanding the smart grid to a supranational regional level, such as the EU (Purvins *et al.* 2011). For many other cities, however, the cost is an important barrier for the transformation of the current electricity system into a smart grid system, despite the expected decline in such costs as a result of the deployment of technology (Marques *et al.* 2014). In the next section, one of the critical components of a smart grid is explored.

Smart meters

Smart grids, and specifically smart meters, at present, are high on both the energy and urban development agendas (Guerreiro *et al.* 2015). Up until recently, the lack of effective demand response was one of the major challenges in the urban electricity system. However, driven by technological evolution (along with increasing energy needs and prices), demand response has been introduced on a large scale, and 'smart meters' played a crucial role in this evolution (Pepermans 2014). As stated by Horne *et al.* (2015: 65), smart grids', 'enhanced monitoring capabilities address problems of the old grid (such as its limited response capability), while also making it easier to incorporate renewable energy resources such as wind and solar power into the energy system'. Smart metering systems, also the term used for water and gas delivery but generally used in reference to energy, are principal components of a smart grid, and are referred to as the next generation power measurement system. Smart meters are considered a revolutionary and evolutionary regime of existing power grids. These meters could measure instantaneous parameters, such as voltage, current, power and power factor, along with billing parameters, such as kilowatt-hour (kWh), reactive power (kVArh), maximum demand and load profile (Sharma and Saini 2015). As indicated by Yute and Jeng (2006), smart meters with existing communication technologies, such as radio frequency (RF), global system for mobile communications (GSM), general packet radio service (GPRS), public switched telephone network (PSTN) and power line communication (PLC), provide consumers with value-added services. A smart meter contains eight basic metrology computation blocks: a microcontroller unit, analogue-to-digital converter, analogue-front end, interface unit, liquid crystal display driver, real-time clock, security scheme and wireless/wire-line communication protocol stack (Sharma and Saini 2015).

Smart meters are currently in use in many countries including Australia, Canada, Denmark, Finland, Italy, Japan, the Netherlands, New Zealand, Korea, Norway, Spain, Sweden, Taiwan and the UK, and have been installed in over 25 million US homes (Karlin 2012). Furthermore, many other countries, such as France, Ireland, Italy, Iran and Malta are transitioning to replace the century-old analogue electro-mechanical energy meters (introduced by Ferrari in the 1880s) with smart ones. There are two information infrastructure types for information flow in a smart meter system. The first flow is from electrical appliances and sensors to smart meters, and the second one is between smart meters and utilities' data centres (Pereira *et al.* 2015). The first data flow is accomplished by resorting to power line or wireless communications, such as ZigBee, 6LowPAN and Z-wave, among others (Güngör *et al.* 2011); and the second information data flow is realised through mobile phone technologies (3G/4G LTE) or the internet. Figure 4.4 illustrates an example of a smart meter system from Victoria, Australia. As two-way digital communication systems, these intelligent electricity meters provide information that enable users to make choices about how much energy they use by allowing them to access accurate real-time information about their consumption. Smart meters measure and record how much electricity a household or business is using in short intervals, such as every 30 minutes in Australia. These meters communicate meter readings directly to electricity distributors, eliminating the need for someone to come out and read meters, whether that is required for each bill, to change

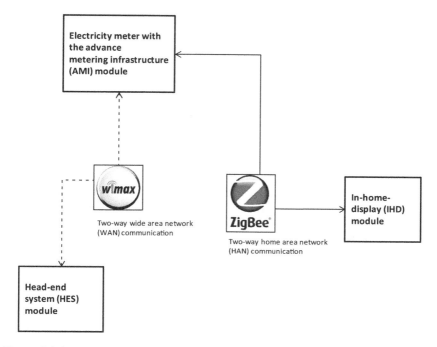

Figure 4.4 A smart meter system from Victoria, Australia.

Source: Energy Monitors 2015.

electricity retailers or to reconnect power when customers move house. This not only reduces fees but also calculates electricity bills more accurately (Victoria Government 2015).

As the user's interface with smart grids, smart meters provide several benefits. First of all, smart metering offers benefits to stakeholders in the electricity system (Carroll *et al.* 2014). For example, electricity suppliers and generators benefit from increased grid information and smoother load profiles, both of which improve the operational efficiency and stability of the system and tackle the imbalance between supply and demand on the grid (Faruqui *et al.* 2010; Toft *et al.* 2014). There are periods of the day where the demand for electricity causes a great load on the grid, such as during the day in industries and businesses, and during the early evening when households are consuming power. Obviously, during these peak periods, electricity is more expensive. There are also periods when there is not much demand, such as late at nights when most of the wind power is produced, and where electricity is less expensive in this off-peak period. Basically, smart meters provide flexible electricity pricing by connecting or disconnecting electricity, switching to a new electricity retailer and/or feeding electricity back into the grid from rooftop solar panels. In other words, smart meter technology helps households to shift some of their power consumption from peak period to off-peak automatically without any inconvenience. Another benefit of smart meters is that they improve the operational efficiency of the grid and allow for proactive maintenance (Krishnamurti *et al.* 2012). For instance, automation enabled by smart meters reduces blackout times from hours to seconds by identifying faults and compensating for them remotely (Pratt *et al.* 2010). The other benefits include users being provided with supplementary enabling technologies that respond to smart meter signals, such as central air control, direct load control and in-home displays (Ehrhardt-Martinez *et al.* 2010). Effects of smart meter technologies on energy efficiency, such as smart meter enabled communication infrastructure and devices, could decrease CO_2 emissions, which is another significantly beneficial side to the technology (Siddiqui *et al.* 2008). According to Hledik (2009), the rollout of a smart grid with smart metering and time-of-use tariffs at its core in the United States would reduce CO_2 emissions by 5 to 16 per cent. On this point, supporters of smart meters claim that having real-time energy consumption information on hand will revolutionise the way that households consume energy, with the domestic sector being responsible for about one-third of carbon emissions in most of the developed countries (Venables 2007). Nevertheless, attaining smart meter and smart grid goals surely will require consumer acceptance.

As much as there are benefits, smart meters pose some risks as well. The violation of consumer privacy is a threat. For instance, in the case of the release of detailed billing data, this information reveals when a household is at home and how they use their appliances. This may lead to being a potential target for burglary, assault or sales/telemarketing. Likewise, hackers might be able to remotely disconnect power to large areas (McDaniel and McLaughlin 2009), or obtain decrypted personal information (Anderson and Bezuidenhoudt 1996). Another concern is that these meters might be a threat to health due to the pulsed radiofrequency (RF) radiation emitted by wireless smart meters (Hess and Coley 2014). Additionally, the income of customers is a sociodemographic characteristic that may impact on the degree of price-responsiveness.

Customers in low-income groups are generally more price-inelastic in terms of their electricity consumption as opposed to high-income groups (Faruqui *et al.* 2009). That is to say, high-income groups are not as highly motivated as low-income customers to change their consumption patterns. Hence, the overall energy consumption and CO_2 emission levels may not be significantly reduced. The last concern relates to the cost of the technology to users. In particular, the investment needed to replace traditional meters with smart ones, when considering a large city, is substantial, especially as the cost would be covered by the users. Therefore, the promised savings on the utility bill will take a long time to come through (Henry 2012). As highlighted by Guerreiro *et al.* (2015), for a better understanding of what may promote the use of smart meters, it is useful to take into account both the sociopsychological factors that may influence pro-environmental behaviours, as well as those that may be associated with technology acceptance.

Smart urban water and waste systems

Water is essential for our survival to maintain our quality of life, safeguard food security, provide the modern conveniences we enjoy in our everyday life, continue the economic prosperity that we take for granted and preserve the ecosystems (Goonetilleke *et al*. 2014). In other words, increasing urban populations cannot maintain their living standards without clean and adequate water. Fortunately, most developed countries have made remarkable achievements in providing reliable supplies of safe drinking water as a result of infrastructure engineering and a welfare economic regime that ensures an affordable supply and quality standards for consumers (Goonetilleke *et al*. 2014). However, at the dawn of the climate change era, water scarcity is showing its ugly face in many parts of the world including in developed countries, e.g. California in the United States and Queensland in Australia. Much like water provision to individual homes, municipalisation of the collection, treatment and disposal of waste marked a significant moment in the evolution of our cities. However, today, rapid urbanisation and growth of urban agglomerations call for more collective approaches to better deal with management issues in the urban waste system. Not properly handling the collection, treatment and disposal of waste in cities can result in severe health and environmental hazards (Goonetilleke *et al*. 2014).

Water supply and waste collection networks, and waste treatment and disposal units, especially in large metropolitan cities, are quite complex infrastructure systems with many operational challenges, e.g. increasing system efficiency, real-time information and incident detection, minimising cost, achieving required sustainable outcomes and so on (Yigitcanlar and Dizdaroglu 2015). In order to effectively deal with the complexity and associated challenges, a number of smart infrastructure applications have been developed. For example, reliable demand forecasting is of paramount importance for making informed operational decisions (Donkor *et al*. 2014). Hence, as part of smart urban water systems, 'smart water demand forecasting' (SWDF) applications are utilised to forecast short- and medium-term demand. Real-time demand signals are captured through sensors embedded in water supply infrastructure for SWDF. These sensors are also used in the water quality area for constant monitoring. SWDF employs an evolutionary artificial neural network (EANN) to analyse the current and past demand signals for accurate estimation of future demand. The main advantage of the smart demand forecasting approach is its self-learning ability, which helps it to adapt to the ever-changing operating conditions (Romano and Kapelan 2014). Smart sensors are also used to monitor water quality, as monitoring the infrastructure using these sensors helps in saving annual operational costs by predicting the behaviour of the assets in the long run. They help in improving the safety of drinking water supplied to consumers and respond rapidly to any changes in the behaviour of the system (Mohamed *et al*. 2014).

Another exemplar application for smart waste and resource management is the use of smart labels. Binder *et al*. (2008) investigate how and to what extent RFID technology could be used to improve the waste and resource management system in the context of Switzerland. This study reveals that RFID tags provide an increased degree of precision in separating recyclables at the recycling plant

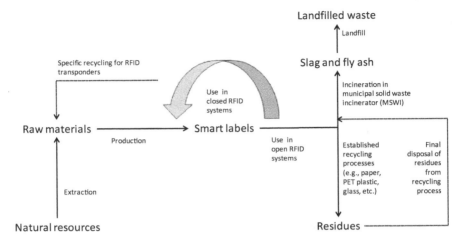

Figure 4.5 Smart label use in waste management.

Source: Wager *et al.* 2005.

(e.g. battery type or polyethylene terephthalate (PET) by colour), enabling separation of high-quality products from secondary materials, an increase in dismantling efficiency of heterogeneous long-lived goods and a design for integrated material and waste management. Furthermore, the findings suggest that, from an ecological perspective, the implementation of RFID for waste management would be desirable and would lead to an improvement in the current recycling rate. From an economic perspective, new investments would be required in the range of one to five times the current costs for maintaining the current separate collection system. From a social perspective, the utilisation of RFID tags in the waste management process was ambiguous due to perceived threats to privacy and, what is more, social responsibility (Binder *et al.* 2008). Figure 4.5 shows an example of smart label use in waste management. Closed RFID systems are systems where transponders, such as smart labels, are only used to tag objects that remain in the system for a long time, such as reusable containers. Smart labels used in open RFID systems will find their way either to municipal solid waste incinerators (MSWI) or to established recycling systems for packaging, where they become part of the residues and are then incinerated. After incineration, most of the material content of the smart labels is found in the slag or in the fly ash from the MSWI, which is ultimately landfilled (Wäger *et al.* 2005). One of the key application areas of smart urban water and waste systems is examined in the following section.

Water smart homes

As water availability and quality are closely linked to the climate system, the water environment is highly vulnerable to climate change, where climate change refers to the significant and lasting change in the statistical distribution of weather patterns (Goonetilleke *et al.* 2014). Although climate change can be influenced by natural causes, it is accelerated as a result of human activities, such as combustion of fossil fuels, industrial activities and more livestock, resulting in increased emissions of greenhouse gases into the atmosphere (Pittock 2013). As a result of climate change and urban population growth, a decrease in the availability of fresh water resources all over the world and an increase in the costs of water consumption, many local governments and water distribution companies have had to come up with water conservation strategies. These strategies included water sensitive urban design (WSUD) and climate-resilient water systems. As defined by Goonetilleke *et al.* (2014):

> WSUD is a land planning and engineering design approach that integrates the urban water cycle, including stormwater, groundwater and wastewater management and water supply into the urban design in order to minimise environmental degradation and to improve aesthetic and recreational appeal of water environments.
>
> (Goonetilleke *et al.* 2014: 47)

Climate-resilient water systems include features such as: sufficient extra water storage capacity to cope with long droughts; efficient water infrastructure, such as low leakage rates for pipe networks, water conserving fixtures or grey water systems, so as to maximise use of scarce water resources; rooftop capture and storage; design of water intakes for varying water levels and strengthening to withstand turbulent flows; construction of overflows for reservoirs to avoid failure; and greater use of groundwater resources to provide a more stable supply (WHO 2010).

For instance, the drought between 1995 and 2009 affected many parts of Australia including Brisbane. In 2010, drought conditions were eased and ended in 2012. However, the 2010–2011 floods killed 38 people in Queensland, affected at least 90 urban localities (including Brisbane), caused damage estimated at about $2.5 billion (approximately USD 1.75 billion) and a reduction in Australia's GDP of about $40 billion (approximately USD 28 billion). As a response to these extreme climate conditions, Brisbane City Council (BCC), through extensive consultation with key stakeholders across industry, business, residents and a team of experts, developed a 'water smart strategy'. This strategy aims to make Brisbane a 'water smart city' by making the best use of the available fresh water resources and supporting the liveability of their city by managing water sustainably (BCC 2010). As part of this strategy, BCC promotes 'water smart homes' in order to build a 'water smart community' (BCC 2015). The water smart homes initiative includes incentives for domestic greywater treatment plant and rainwater tank installations, provides guidelines for water use in indoor and outdoor areas and encourages the building of stormwater gardens. Technology solutions also come in handy in turning homes into water smart homes, for example, an energy-efficient smart water monitoring application using RFIDs. According to Nasir *et al.* (2014), in water smart homes:

> RFIDs integrated with pressure sensors are embedded in the pipe infrastructure. They collect pressure information and send it along with their IDs to the reader/writer destination node. From the available pressure data from the sensors, the determined usage patterns, tap events and their patterns assist the real-time control of the home water system. The information from the sensors is then run by the algorithms on the cyber system to render decisions in order to support the hardware controllers responsible for managing the water distribution parameters.
>
> (Nasir *et al.* 2014: 18354)

There are similar commercially available smart water management solutions, such as Driblet and Water Hero. Driblet is a self-powered inline water meter that tracks, stores and transmits water consumption data of each pipe where it is installed. It connects to the cloud via Wi-Fi and relays real-time water usage information through an app on smartphones (Driblet 2015). Water Hero, a Kickstarter project, measures the magnetic field from the municipal water meter to monitor home water usage and detect leakages. It has an emergency shutoff valve and needs to be plugged into a wall outlet (Water Hero 2015). A system diagram of a water smart home application is illustrated in Figure 4.6.

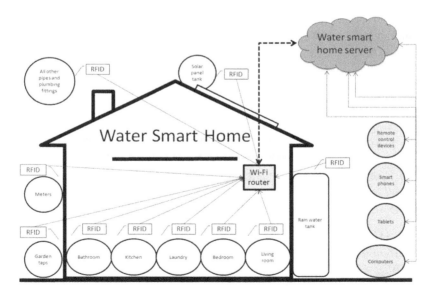

Figure 4.6 System diagram of a water smart home application.

Source: Nasir *et al.* 2014.

Smart urban emergency and safety systems

The importance and scope of emergency response systems have grown tremendously over the few years as disasters, human-made or natural, are a cause of great economic and human loss throughout the world (Uhr *et al.* 2008). The changing climate conditions of our time, especially floods, heat and water stress, fires, hurricanes, tropical cyclones, landslides, tsunamis and earthquakes, have become frequent natural disasters threatening our cities' populations and infrastructure. Adoption of early detection mechanisms, along with applications with great penetration of ICT in such emergency conditions, has been proved to be useful in minimising the impacts and casualties (Bulu *et al.* 2014). That is to say, confronted by a human-made and natural disaster, cities can use a sophisticated smart technology-embedded infrastructure with analytical capabilities to enhance and coordinate the information flow between public agencies, such as transport authorities, emergency services and energy providers, and citizens (Schmitt *et al.* 2007).

For instance, Japan's comprehensive disaster warning and recovery system, developed by the Japan Meteorological Agency, reveals a useful system structure that is helping cities to adopt smart urban emergency systems in their mitigation, preparedness, response and recovery phases. Data captured during each stage from observation systems continuously feed into data processing platforms. These platforms then quickly generate accurate information to be transmitted to both individuals and companies, while helping emergency services, such as police, rescue teams, fire brigade and hospitals, to be prepared for immediate action. This system also makes use of 'Big Data' (that is the ever-increasing possibilities of gathering, interconnecting and analysing huge amounts of data relating to a wide range of fields and domains of everyday life) in crisis response where, much like in many mobile disaster management systems (Fajardo and Oppus 2010), mobile phone technology is utilised for collecting various data. For example, in Japan, radiation levels are monitored through SIM-enabled devices located on farmlands and in parks, offices, and danger and evacuation zones, and mobile networks are used to transmit measurements of radiation back to the command centre where Big Data are carefully analysed (GSMA 2013). The system also benefits from cloud computing that allows reliable, resilient, agile and incrementally deployable and scalable operations at low cost. Table 4.2 portrays the structure of a disaster warning and recovery system. Some of the technology applications that are used for emergency response systems are also utilised for safety and security purposes. The following section focuses on the application of smart surveillance systems in the urban context.

Smart urban surveillance systems

Security incidents in urban environments span a wide range, from property crimes to violent crimes and terrorist incidents. As a consequence, security infrastructures with surveillance technologies, initially developed for military purposes,

Table 4.2 A disaster warning and recovery system structure

Mitigation & preparedness	Coordination & response	Recovery
Information gathering ① Satellite Communication System ② Terrestrial Radio System ③ Optical Transmission System	**Information Gathering** ① Satellite Communication System ② Terrestrial Radio System ③ Optical Transmission System	**Radiation Monitoring** ① SIM card based devices spread around parks, offices, farmlands, Danger and Evacuation zones to monitor radiation levels ② Advanced Data Processing (Big data, cloud services)
Data Analysis and Decision-Making ① Earthquake Early Warning System ② Disaster Information System ③ Disaster Emergency Response Centre System ④ Advanced Data Processing (Big data, cloud services)	**Data Analysis and Decision-Making** ① Earthquake Early Warning System ② Disaster Information System ③ Disaster Emergency Response Centre System ④ Advanced Data Processing (Big data, cloud services)	**Soil Desalination** ① Platform (i.e., NEC Connexive) to utilise mobile network operator's network infrastructure to monitor soil moisture, temperature and salinity ② Advanced Data Processing (Big data, cloud services)
Observation ① Ocean Bottom Observation System ② Earth Observation System ③ Land (Coast, Dam) Observation System ④ Land Observing Satellite Systems ⑤ Global navigation satellite Systems	**Announcement** ① National Early Warning System ② Municipality Disaster Prevention Radio System ③ Cell Broadcast Service System	**Web Portal** ① A site used for disseminating official communication ② Regular people to leave personal messages about their own individual status
Building Code ① Building certificates and inspections became stricter ② Introduction of the 10-Year Warranty Against Defects	**Power Grid** ① Gas disconnection ② Nuclear reactors initiate shutdown ③ Prepare for power outage	**Mobile Network Operator** ① Development of disaster resilient networks and prompt restoration methods ② Secure prompt reconnection for local relief sites ③ Secure means of information distribution after disasters ④ Provide services and solutions useful during a disaster and during recovery ⑤ Extension of payments ⑥ Support for mass transmission of community information to evacuated people
Planning ① Preparing disaster conscious urban plans ② Planning for building and retrofitting resilient urban infrastructure ③ Determining evacuation procedures and plans and training	**Smart Traffic** ① Informed by Matrix around the roads, cars pull over ② Trains receive a warning to stop	
	Emergency Coordination ① Fire Brigade and Hospitals raise the readiness level ② Police to free major roadways for rescue teams & relief goods	

Source: GSMA 2013.

are widely in use, especially in large cities, for civilian purposes, such as crime and incident prevention, emergency management and counter terrorism (Pavlidis *et al*. 2001). This technology was first used in 1968 in Olean, New York along the main business street in an effort to fight crime (Robb 1979). Today, surveillance cameras, also known as closed-circuit television (CCTV), are present and monitoring and recording 24/7 at almost every moment of our everyday lives for crime prevention, alarm and evidencing, traffic and parking monitoring, and health and safety monitoring (Ma and Qian 2009). Centralised surveillance systems are commonly installed in public arenas, e.g. urban squares, football stadiums, city parks and train stations, while in-house self-contained video surveillance systems are used in most institutions and small companies, e.g. banks, post offices, hospitals, schools, supermarkets, shops, offices and warehouses, homes, cars and even motorbikes and bicycles. The purpose of these services is to record and locate moving targets, to understand their behaviour and detect suspicious or abnormal activities for crime prevention or directing emergency services (Atrey *et al*. 2013).

Starting out as an analogue video surveillance system, and then becoming digital and now turned into network remote surveillance systems, smart surveillance systems in urban security are playing an increasingly important role. Many cities, therefore, operate a networked video surveillance system as a smart urban surveillance service that combines CCTV video feeds of government agencies installed in city buses, businesses, public schools, subway stations and housing projects, and runs computer controlled analytics and identification for video content analysis. Advantages of networked surveillance include having: (i) hierarchical architecture that benefits establishment and improves standardisation of digital video surveillance; (ii) integrated management and control that increases the quality outputs and improves the stability and security of systems; (iii) unified business interface that enhances network video monitoring systems and are operationally convenient and flexible; (iv) deployment of distributed systems that realise large-capacity smooth expansion and application of multistage cascade large-scale networks; and (v) network storage playback that helps users to access centralised searching of video resources and on-demand playback in any place (Sun *et al*. 2011).

While there are many users handling their own systems, a number of companies offer 'video surveillance as a service' (also known as VSaaS) for private users. This helps in distributing not only storage space in the cloud that is necessary for handling large amounts of video data but also infrastructures and computational power (Prati *et al*. 2013). Some of the commercial video surveillance as a service solution include Alarm.com (https://www.alarm.com/video), Brivo (http://www.brivo.com), ByRemote (http://www.byremote.net), CameraManager (http://www.cameramanager.com), Connexed (http://www.connexed.com), Dropcam (https://www.dropcam.com) and Envysion (http://www.envysion.com). These companies provide services ranging from video analytic tools to surveillance platforms to storage and central processing units (CPUs). Figure 4.7 illustrates the basic components of a cloud-based video surveillance as a service.

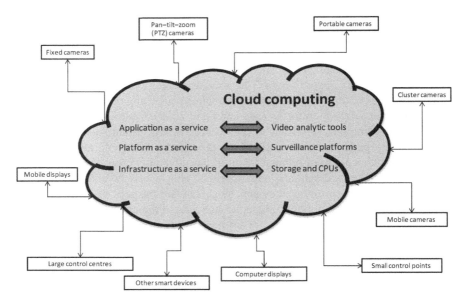

Figure 4.7 Cloud-based video surveillance as a service.

Source: Prati *et al*. 2013.

Today, digital technologies have enabled surveillance to become extended to almost all areas of our daily lives. It is not only CCTV surveillance systems but also the internet, RFID implants, targeted advertising, retail loyalty cards, ATM cards, credit cards, travel cards and ID scanning in nightlife districts that are used to monitor consumers, customers, employees, internet/telephone users and citizens' behaviours. That is to say, even though surveillance originally meant to act as a safety net for society and a way to prevent crime, it is now primarily concerned with finding new techniques, such as Big Data (Klauser and Albrechtslund 2014), of identifying and classifying groups of people rather than with individuals' safety (Van Klaveren 2015). In other words, 'Big Brother', whether it is another individual, the government or big businesses and corporations, now has a new means of watching everyone not only in public and open spaces but also in virtual spaces. According to Klauser and Albrechtslund (2014), scholars stressed that:

> a number of critical issues arising from surveillance, including the effects on privacy, social trust, human behaviour and public space; the depth of accountability and transparency; the risks associated with information sharing; the role of private interests in urban public policies; the cost-benefit and effectiveness of technological systems; and the prevalence of errors in such systems, etc.
>
> (Klauser and Albrechtslund 2014: 283)

While different forms of surveillance in cities are intertwined, it becomes a problem for individuals in terms of possible breaches in ethics of privacy and individual rights (Whitaker 1999). Martinez-Balleste *et al.* (2013) advocate the development of privacy-aware smart cities and put forward methods for existing privacy enhancing technologies to be used for preserving citizens' privacy. These include statistical disclosure control, private information retrieval, privacy-preserving data mining, location privacy, anonymity and pseudonyms, privacy in RFID and privacy in video surveillance. Martinez-Balleste *et al.* (2013) propose a five-dimensional model for citizens' privacy in smart cities. The dimensions include: identity privacy (disclosing the identity every time a user accesses a smart city service), query privacy (preserving the privacy of the queries made by users to services), location privacy (guaranteeing that the privacy of the physical location of the user is preserved), footprint privacy (control of the information that can be retrieved or inferred from micro data sets) and owner privacy (privacy-aware computation of queries across the databases from different autonomous entities). Lately, drone usage has become more widespread in some countries for surveillance beyond military or national security purposes, e.g. surveillance during major events such as a marathon. With the rise of domestic drones, we need to make sure technology does not trample all over our privacy and rights. This may require properly regulating and controlling the proliferation of drone surveillance (see Calo 2011).

Smart urban participatory decision systems

Since their emergence, ICTs have been applied in many aspects of urban planning, development and management. Just as technology has become more pervasive in society, so has the importance of public participation, though not in any simple fashion up until now. Probably one of the most exciting areas for the use of new technology is in the public participatory decision- or policy-making domain. This domain is also critical for establishing a full democracy, transparency, social trust and wider acceptance or legitimisation, and appreciation of urban policy and resulting planning decisions and their subsequent development. According to Ekenberg (2014), public participation occurs at different levels and plays diverse roles in various democracy models. For instance, Arnstein's (1969) seminal article on citizen participation in planning activities identified eight different models of participation based on power. From lowest to highest these levels of participations are: manipulation, therapy, informing, consultation, placation, partnership, delegate power and citizen control. Public participation, when done well, for urban and environmental decision making can improve the quality and legitimacy of decisions, build capacity to engage in the policy process, enhance trust and understanding of participants and lead to better results for environmental quality and social objectives (Brown *et al.* 2014). Today, we observe an increased interest, particularly in fully democratic societies, in the integration of technology and spatial information into public participation methods.

One of the main vehicles used to achieve such integration is the utilisation of online public participation geographic information systems (PPGIS), also referred as web-based PPGIS or web-PPGIS. PPGIS is a field within geographic information science that focuses on ways the public uses various forms of geospatial technologies to participate in public processes, such as mapping and decision making (Tulloch 2008), and online PPGIS is its application in the web-based environment for capturing and using non-expert spatial information. Online PPGIS enhances inputs and outputs of a decision or planning process in several ways such as: (i) providing and strengthening public access to urban and environmental information; (ii) retrieving the real picture of the public will; (iii) empowering the public by increasing the level of involvement; and (iv) providing scenario testing, negotiation and consensus building platforms to select the most suitable policies and actions to deal with the specific problem. In an online PPGIS, GIS functionality, combined with online applications to facilitate a range of dynamic functionalities (such as interactive user engagements, personalised maps), allows a deeper level of explanation and enables new relationships to emerge (Baum *et al.* 2010). Since the start of the twenty-first century, a number of online PPGIS studies have used internet technology, providing the opportunity for a 'volunteer public' to participate in the study as a contrast to the randomly sampled target population. However, according to Brown *et al.* (2014) most of these academic studies (see Brown and Kyttä (2014) for a review of these studies) did not generate enough volunteer public response for meaningful analysis. For online PPGIS examples visit the websites of Google Crisis Map (http://google.org/crisis-map/weather_and_events), Havara (https://www.eharava.fi/en), Landscape Values and PPGIS Institute (http://www.landscapevalues.org), New Orleans BlightStatus (http://blightstatus.nola.gov) and BCC (http://cityplan2014maps.brisbane.qld.gov.au/CityPlan). The lack of or limited volunteer public interest brought about the idea of bringing together online PPGIS and volunteered geographic information (VGI) systems. The second vehicle to integrate technology and spatial information into public participation methods is VGI, and it is discussed thoroughly in the next section. Table 4.3 underlines some of the key characteristics of PPGIS and VGI.

Table 4.3 Characteristics of PPGIS and volunteered geographic information

	Traditional ppgis	*Online ppgis*	*Volunteered geographic information*
Process emphasis	Community empowerment; foster social identity; build social capital	Enhance public involvement to inform urban and environmental planning and management; community empowerment	Expand spatial information using citizens as sensors; community empowerment

Sponsors	Non-governmental organisations (NGOs)	Government planning agencies	NGOs and ad hoc groups, individuals
Global context	Developing countries	Developed countries	Developed and developing countries
Place context	Rural	Urban and regional	Urban, regional and rural
Importance of mapped data quality	Secondary	Primary	Primary
Sampling approach	Active: purposive	Active: probability	Passive: voluntary
Data collection	Collective (e.g., community workshops)	Individual (e.g., online)	Individual (e.g., online)
Data ownership	People and communities that created data	Sponsors of the process	Shared (e.g., data commons licence)
Dominant mapping technology	Non-digital	Digital	Digital

Source: Brown and Kytta 2014.

VGI apps

As discussed in Chapter 3, user-generated content is a core feature of web 2.0 and web 2.0 technologies, such as application programming interfaces (APIs) allowing programmers to combine services into so-called mashups. Along with advances in GIS, this provides a foundation for an exponentially growing amount of user-generated content including geospatial information (Rinner *et al.* 2008). In recent years, especially following the introduction of Google Earth in 2004 and of Google Maps in 2006, we observe an increasing popularity of citizen VGI for the contribution of local geospatial knowledge to online community platforms. Goodchild and Li (2012: 110) define VGI as, 'a version of crowd-sourcing in which members of the general public create and contribute georeferenced facts about the Earth's surface and near-surface to websites where the facts are synthesized into databases'. VGI systems are a type of PPGIS that literally use a network of humans as sensors, where this network potentially could have over seven billion components, each an intelligent synthesiser and interpreter of local information (Goodchild 2007). Presently, VGI, also known as 'participatory sensing', through sensor-rich and internet-enabled smart mobile phones, has opened the door for monitoring and sharing the collected multimodal data streams from the surrounding urban landscape. The data contributed from multiple participant ordinary citizens are then combined to build a spatiotemporal view of the phenomenon of interest (Kanhere 2013). This approach has a number of advantages over the traditional sensor networks. For instance, as it is a volunteered system and personal mobile phones and 3G/4G or Wi-Fi communication infrastructures are used, there are no deployment costs involved. Rapidly growing diversity and functionality of smart phone apps for participatory sensing makes it widely accessible to a large population. Today, out of a world population of more than 7 billion, almost 5 billion people have access to mobile phones and about 1.75 billion to smart phones. This consequently makes it possible to observe unpredictable events more easily through VGI. Additionally, using mobile phones as sensors intrinsically affords economies of scale. Involving people in the sensing loop increases their consciousness, awareness and belongingness to the observed phenomenon and the cause, and helps in improving people's quality of life (Kanhere 2013).

The popularity of VGI has resulted in a broad range of applications, where these applications mainly focus on people-centric (such as personal health monitoring, calculating environmental impact, monitoring and documenting sport experiences, enhancing social media and price auditing) and environment-centric issues (such as air quality monitoring, monitoring noise and ambiance, monitoring road and traffic conditions and monitoring crime, natural disaster and emergency conditions). Starting with online maps and georeferenced image sets, such as Google Maps, Bing Maps, Yahoo Maps and Apple Maps, today there are a number of successful initiatives counting on the perspective of user collaboration in the creation and/or maintenance of a niche geographic dataset. For instance, WikiMapia (http://wikimapia.org) is one of the first examples of VGI systems that combines Google Maps and Wiki (this combination is also referred as Geo-Wiki), where any user can add a place mark to any location and provide information, and users can vote for or against other users' contributions as a means of data trust (Bugs *et al.* 2010). Similarly, OpenStreetMap (https://www.openstreetmap.org) is a public-domain street map of the entire world developed through volunteer efforts to create map data that is free to use and editable. In the OpenStreetMap platform, each contributor develops a map of their local streets using GPS tracking, and individual contributions are then assembled and reconciled into a single patchwork (Haklay 2010). In addition, Flickr (https://www.flickr.com) contains several hundred million user georeferenced photographs; Geonames (http://www.geonames.org) provides geographic access to Wikipedia (Elwood *et al.* 2012); Ushahidi (http://www.ushahidi.com) makes smart decisions with a data management system that rapidly collects data from the crowd and visualises what happened, when and where, and is an application that was developed specifically to monitor election violence in Kenya in 2008; and Map Kibera (http://mapkibera.org) recruits residents to monitor the progress of infrastructure projects in Nairobi, Kenya. Furthermore, GIS Cloud Mobile Data Collection, MapItFast, OsmAnd, Fieldtrip GB, Field Traces, Fulcrum, Mappt, OruxMaps, Geopaparazzi, Locus, pcMapper, OpenPaths, EpiCollect, WolfGIS, Maps 3D, GIS Pro, Integrity GIS, Explorer for ArcGIS and GIS2go are among the popular GIS apps available for smart phones, iOS and/or Android. Although not all of them are equipped with VGI capabilities, the increasing number of apps in the GIS domain is an indication of a possible expansion in user-generated content/maps and public

Table 4.4 Aspects of a volunteered geographic information system

	Map mashup	Contributory platform	Collaborative platform
Objectives	Inform people; receive information from people	To collect relevant data to support decision making	To produce and update base maps and data
Technologies and features	Map mashups; web services (API); visualisation (videos, photos, base maps, layers); aggregation tools	Contribution platforms (Ushahidi); web services (API); crowdsource platform; filtering tools	Collaborative platforms (OSM, Google Map Maker, wiki, geoCMS . . .)
Data	Authoritative and non-authoritative data (videos, photos, points, lines, zones and base maps)	Non-authoritative data (videos, photos, points)	Authoritative and nonauthoritative data (videos, photos, points, lines, zones and base maps)
Strengths	Interoperability of systems; cross-checking of data sources; flexibility of platforms; variety of contents (multimedia); simplicity; ergonomy of interfaces	Real-time data (deployment timelines); triangulation of sources (cross checking); communication supports	Crowdsourcing; mass effect; emulation; cost saving; collective intelligence
Weaknesses	Non-homogeneous sources; map interface; poor and non-homogeneous legends; graphic semiology	Reliability of contributory data; complexity of the validation and qualification mechanisms; inferring user context and activities; dealing with incomplete information	Reliability of contributory data; complexity of the validation and qualification mechanisms; preserving user privacy; trustworthiness of data
Opportunities	Providing faster information to those in need; more communication media (mobile applications)	Building a culture of participation and contribution; people's science (citizen sensors); local knowledge acquisition; maintenance of the social bond (mobile application)	Improving citizens' spatial skills and spatial reasoning; developing alternative ways to update geospatial databases
Constraints	Information flow; visualisation; understanding the message; reliability	Temporal emergency; data accessibility; fragmented data aggregation; trust; reliability	Data quality; interoperability; licenced data; liability; preserving user privacy; trustworthiness of data

Source: Roche *et al.* 2013.

participatory and collaborative decision making. Table 4.4 highlights some of the key aspects of a VGI system. In 2015, Periscope, a live video streaming app for iOS and Android, was launched by Twitter Inc. The app allows users to record and share events happening in their surroundings and also to explore the world through someone else's eyes, whether it is an activist movement protest or an accident, crime, environmental catastrophe or a live gig.

Summary

The provision of good quality electricity, water, waste, transportation, emergency, safety, telecommunication and other critical urban infrastructures and services not only form a vital underpinning to urban development but also to sustainable and knowledge-based development, human well-being and quality of life and place. Following on from the current technology development and take-up trends, we can say that exciting and yet challenging times lie ahead. In the developed world and rapidly emerging economies in particular, urban infrastructures and systems are undergoing a swift transformation with great prospects and at the same time great challenges. Today, smart wireless sensor technology, with increased reliability, low-cost, low power and fast deployment characteristics, provides a new way of managing infrastructure. This Chapter, therefore, introduced and examined a number of technology applications to provide a clearer understanding of smart urban system utilisation, its benefits and also challenges of the relevant technology system applications. Investigating key urban infrastructural and decision systems and their exemplar applications only constitutes a small portion of the wider use of smart technology in urban infrastructure. For instance, at present, smart sensor technologies are being used in many other diverse areas including in structural health monitoring to emergency medical care, from wildlife monitoring and protection to robotics, and from smart homes to smart kindergartens. These systems and technologies are showcasing a rapid evolution towards forming the 'internet-of-things', in which everyday objects have network connectivity, allowing them to send and receive data and gain smartness. The prospects and constraints analyses presented in this Chapter also produced some useful insights particularly into highlighting critical issues in cost, technology acceptance, adoption and risks and gives us hope for the construction of truly smart cities in the foreseeable future.

References

Anderson, JM, Kalra, N, Stanley, KD, Sorensen, P, Samaras, C, Oluwatola, OA 2014, *Autonomous Vehicle Technology: A Guide for Policymakers*, accessed on 7 July 2015 from http://www.rand.org/content/dam/rand/pubs/research_reports/RR400/RR443–1/ RAND_RR443–1.pdf

Anderson, RJ, Bezuidenhoudt, SJ 1996, 'On the reliability of electronic payment systems', *IEEE Transactions on Software Engineering*, vol. 22, no. 1, pp. 294–301.

Arnstein, S 1969, 'A ladder of citizen participation', *Journal of American Institute of Planners*, vol. 35, no. 7, pp. 216–224.

Atrey, PK, Cavallaro, A, Kankanhalli, MS (eds) 2013, *Intelligent Multimedia Surveillance*, Springer, Berlin, Germany.

Baum, S, Kendall, E, Muenchberger, H, Gudes, O, Yigitcanlar, T 2010, 'Geographical information systems: An effective planning and decision-making platform for community health coalitions in Australia?', *Health Information Management Journal*, vol. 39, no. 3, pp. 28–33,

BCC 2010, *Water Smart Strategy*, accessed on 16 July 2015 from http://www.brisbane.qld.gov.au/sites/default/files/20150501-watersmart_strategy.pdf

BCC 2015, *Water Smart Homes*, accessed on 16 July 2015 from http://www.brisbane.qld.gov.au/environment-waste/water/water-smart-homes

Binder, CR, Quirici, R, Domnitcheva, S, Stäubli, B 2008, 'Smart labels for waste and resource management', *Journal of Industrial Ecology*, vol. 12, no. 2, pp. 207–228.

BIS (Department for Business Innovation and Skills) 2013, *Smart Cities: Background Paper*, accessed on 8 July 2015 from https://www.gov.uk/government/uploads/system/uploads/attachment_data/file/246019/bis-13-1209-smart-cities-background-paper-digital.pdf

Brännström, M 2013, *Commercial Viability: SARTRE, Volvo Car Corporation*, accessed on 8 July 2015 from http://www.sartre-project.eu/en/publications/Documents/SARTRE_5_001_PU.pdf

Brown, G, Kyttä, M 2014, 'Key issues and research priorities for public participation GIS (PPGIS): A synthesis based on empirical research', *Applied Geography*, vol. 46, no. 1, pp. 122–136.

Brown, G, Kelly, M, Whitall, D 2014, 'Which "public"? Sampling effects in public participation GIS (PPGIS) and volunteered geographic information (VGI) systems for public lands management', *Journal of Environmental Planning and Management*, vol. 57, no. 2, pp. 190–214.

Bugs, G, Granell, C, Fonts, O, Huerta, J, Painho, M 2010, 'An assessment of public participation GIS and web 2.0 technologies in urban planning practice in Canela, Brazil', *Cities*, vol. 27, no. 3, pp. 172–181.

Bulu, M, Önder, MA, Aksakalli, V 2014, 'Algorithm-embedded IT applications for an emerging knowledge city: Istanbul, Turkey', *Expert Systems with Applications*, vol. 41, no. 12, pp. 5625–5635.

Calo, R 2011, 'The drone as privacy catalyst', *Stanford Law Review Online*, vol. 64, no. 1, pp. 29–33.

Carroll, J, Lyons, S, Denny, E 2014, 'Reducing household electricity demand through smart metering: The role of improved information about energy saving', *Energy Economics*, vol. 45, no. 1, pp. 234–243.

Casley, S, Jardim, A, Quartulli, A 2013, *A Study of Public Acceptance of Autonomous Cars*, accessed on 8 July 2015 from http://www.wpi.edu/Pubs/E-project/Available/E-project-043013-155601/unrestricted/A_Study_of_Public_Acceptance_of_Autonomous_Cars.pdf

Chan, E, Gilhead, P, Jelínek, P, Krejčí, P, Robinson, T 2012, *Cooperative Control of SARTRE Automated Platoon Vehicles*, accessed on 7 July 2015 from http://www.sartre-project.eu/en/publications/Documents/ITSWC_2012_control.pdf

Chowdhury, MA, Sadek, AW 2003, *Fundamentals of Intelligent Transportation Systems Planning*, Artech House, Norwood, MA.

Dar, K, Bakhouya, M, Gaber, J, Wack, M, Lorenz, P 2010, 'Wireless communication technologies for ITS applications', *Communications Magazine IEEE*, vol. 48, no. 5, pp. 156–162.

DiClemente, J, Mogos, S, Wang, R 2014, *Autonomous Car Policy Report*, accessed on 8 July 2015 from http://www.cmu.edu/epp/people/faculty/course-reports/Autonomous%20 Car%20Final%20Report.pdf

Donkor, E, Mazzuchi, T, Soyer, R, Roberson, AJ 2014, 'Urban water demand forecasting: Review of methods and models', *Journal of Water Resources Planning and Management*, vol. 140, no. 2, pp. 146–159.

Douma, F, Palodichuk, SA 2012, 'Criminal liability issues created by autonomous vehicles', *Santa Clara Law Review*, vol. 52, no. 1, pp. 1157–1170.

Driblet 2015, *Your Smart Water Management Solution*, accessed on 14 July 2015 from http://driblet.io/#features

Ehrhardt-Martinez, K, Donnelly, K, Laitner, J 2010, Advanced metering initiatives and residential feedback programs: A meta-review for household electricity-savings opportunities. *Report no. E105*, American Council for an Energy Efficient Economy, Washington, DC.

Ekenberg, L 2014, 'Public participatory decision making', in Fujita, H, Selamat, A (eds) *Intelligent Software Methodologies, Tools and Techniques*, Springer, New York, pp. 3–12.

Elwood, S, Goodchild, MF, Sui, DZ 2012, 'Researching volunteered geographic information: Spatial data, geographic research, and new social practice', *Annals of the Association of American Geographers*, vol. 102, no. 3, pp. 571–590.

Energy Monitors 2015, *Smart Meter In-Home Display*, accessed on 14 July 2015 from http://energymonitors.com.au/oc/index.php?route=product/productandproduct_id=53

Eugensson, A, Brannstrom, M, Frasher, D, Rothoff, M 2013, *Environmental, Safety, Legal and Societal Implications of Autonomous Driving Systems*, accessed on 8 July 2015 from http://www-nrd.nhtsa.dot.gov/pdf/esv/esv23/23ESV-000467.PDF

Fagnant, D, Kockelman, K 2014, 'The travel and environmental implications of shared autonomous vehicles, using agent-based model scenarios', *Transportation Research Part C: Emerging Technologies*, vol. 40, no. 1, pp. 1–13.

Fajardo, D, Au, T, Waller, S, Stone, P, Yang, D 2011, 'Automated intersection control', *Transportation Research Record*, vol. 2259, no. 1, pp. 223–232.

Fajardo, JTB, Oppus, CM 2010, 'A mobile disaster management system using the android technology', *WSEAS Transactions on Communications*, vol. 9, no. 6, pp. 343–353.

Farhangi, H 2010, 'The path of the smart grid', *IEEE Power and Energy Magazine*, vol. 8, no. 1, pp. 18–28.

Farhangi, H 2014, 'A road map to integration: Perspectives on smart grid development', *IEEE Power and Energy Magazine*, vol. 12, no. 3, pp. 52–66.

Faruqui, A, Hledik, R, Sergici, S 2009, 'Piloting the smart grid', *The Electricity Journal*, vol. 22, no. 7, pp. 55–69.

Faruqui, A, Sergici, S, Sharif, A 2010, 'The impact of informational feedback on energy consumption: A survey of the experimental evidence', *Energy*, vol. 35, no. 1, pp. 1598–1608.

Fox-Penner, P 2014, *Smart Power Anniversary Edition: Climate Change, the Smart Grid, and the Future of Electric Utilities*, Island Press, Washington, DC.

Goh, K 2015, 'Who's smart? Whose city? The sociopolitics of urban intelligence', in Geertman, S, Ferreira, J, Goodspeed, R, Stillwell, J (eds) *Planning Support Systems and Smart Cities*, Springer, New York, pp. 169–187.

Goodchild, MF 2007, 'Citizens as sensors: The world of volunteered geography', *GeoJournal*, vol. 69, no. 4, pp. 211–221.

Goodchild, MF, Li, L 2012, 'Assuring the quality of volunteered geographic information', *Spatial Statistics*, vol. 1, no. 1, pp. 110–120.

Google Self-Driving Car Project 2015, *What's in a Self-Driving Car*, accessed on 7 July 2015 from http://www.google.com/selfdrivingcar/how

Goonetilleke, A, Yigitcanlar, T, Ayoko, G, Egodawatta, P 2014, *Sustainable Urban Water Environment: Climate, Pollution and Adaptation*, Edward Elgar, Cheltenham, UK.

GSMA (Groupe Speciale Mobile Association) 2013, *Smart City Resilience: Learning from Emergency Response and Coordination in Japan*, accessed on 22 July 2015 from http://www.gsma.com/connectedliving/wp-content/uploads/2013/02/cl_SmartCities_emer_01_131.pdf

Guerreiro, S, Batel, S, Lima, ML, Moreira, S 2015, 'Making energy visible: Sociopsychological aspects associated with the use of smart meters', *Energy Efficiency*, vol. 8, no. 6, pp. 1149–1167.

Guizzo, E 2011, *How Google's Self-Driving Car Works*, accessed on 7 July 2015 from http://spectrum.ieee.org/automaton/robotics/artificial-intelligence/how-google-self-driving-car-works

Güngör, VC, Sahin, D, Kocak, T, Ergüt, S, Buccella, C, Cecati, C, Hancke, GP 2011, 'Smart grid technologies: Communication technologies and standards', *IEEE Transactions on Industrial Informatics*, vol. 7, no. 4, pp. 529–539.

Haklay, M 2010, 'How good is volunteered geographical information? A comparative study of OpenStreetMap and ordnance survey datasets', *Environment and Planning B*, vol. 37, no. 4, pp. 682–703.

Hasan, SF, Siddique, N, Chakraborty, S 2012, *Intelligent Transport Systems: 802.11-Based Roadside-To-Vehicle Communications*, Springer Science and Business, New York.

Henry, M 2012, *Smart Meters + Uninformed Consumers = Huge Corporate Profits*, accessed on 12 July 2015 from http://www.dpl-surveillance-equipment.com/articles/article_66.html

Hess, DJ, Coley, JS 2014, 'Wireless smart meters and public acceptance: The environment, limited choices, and precautionary politics', *Public Understanding of Science*, vol. 23, no. 6, pp. 688–702.

Hledik, R 2009, 'How green is the smart grid?', *The Electricity Journal*, vol. 22, no. 1, pp. 29–41.

Hoess, A 2009, *Highly Automated Vehicles for Intelligent Transport*, accessed on 7 July 2015 from http://haveit-eu.org/LH2Uploads/ItemsContent/26/2009–07–02-HAVEit.pdf

Horne, C, Darras, B, Bean, E, Srivastava, A, Frickel, S 2015, Privacy, technology, and norms: The case of smart meters', *Social Science Research*, vol. 51, no. 1, pp. 64–76.

Kanhere, SS 2013, 'Participatory sensing: crowdsourcing data from mobile smartphones in urban spaces', in Hota, C, Srimani, PK (eds) *Distributed Computing and Internet Technology*, Springer, Berlin, Germany, pp. 19–26.

Karlin, B 2012, 'Public acceptance of smart meters: Integrating psychology and practice', in *Proceedings of the 2012 ACEEE Summer Study on Energy Efficiency in Buildings*, 12–17 August 2012, Pacific Grove, CA, pp. 102–113.

Katkoori, S, Barbeau, S, Lin, P, Bittner, J 2013, *Technology Barriers to Deployment of Automated Vehicles in Urban Environments*, accessed on 7 July 2015 from http://www.usfav.com/pdf/TAVI_3-TechnologyBarriersKatkoori.pdf

Klauser, FR, Albrechtslund, A 2014, 'From self-tracking to smart urban infrastructures: Towards an interdisciplinary research agenda on big data', *Surveillance and Society*, vol. 12, no. 2, pp. 273–286.

KPMG 2013, *Self-driving Cars: Are We Ready?*, accessed on 8 July 2015 from http://www.kpmg.com/US/en/IssuesAndInsights/ArticlesPublications/Documents/self-driving-cars-are-we-ready.pdf

Krishnamurti, T, Schwartz, D, Davis, A, Fischhoff, B, De Bruin, WB, Lave, L, Wang, J 2012, 'Preparing for smart grid technologies: A behavioral decision research approach to understanding consumer expectations about smart meters', *Energy Policy*, vol. 41, no. 1, pp. 790–797.

Levinson, J, Askeland, J, Becker, J, Dolson, J, Held, D, Kammel, S, Kolter, JZ, Langer, D, Pink, O, Pratt, V, Sokolsky, M, Stanek, G, Stavens, D, Teichman, A, Werling, M, Thrun, S 2011, *Towards Fully Autonomous Driving: Systems and Algorithms*, accessed on 8 July 2015 from http://ieeexplore.ieee.org/stamp/stamp.jsp?tp=andarnumber=5940562

Lin, P, Wang, Z 2013, *Impact of Automated Vehicles on Highway Safety and Operations*, accessed on 8 July 2015 from http://www.usfav.com/pdf/TAVI_7-SafetyLinWang.pdf

Litman, T 2015, 'Autonomous vehicle implementation predictions: Implications for transport planning', in *Proceedings of the Transportation Research Board 94th Annual Meeting (No. 15–3326)*.

Lloyd's 2014, *Autonomous Vehicles Handing over Control: Opportunities and RISKS for Insurance*, accessed on 7 July 2015 from https://www.lloyds.com/~/media/lloyds/reports/emerging per cent20risk per cent20reports/autonomous per cent20vehicles per cent20final.pdf

Luo, J, Hubaux, J 2004, *A Survey of Inter-Vehicle Communication*, accessed on 7 July 2015 from http://infoscience.epfl.ch/record/28039/files/IC_TECH_REPORT_200424.pdf

Ma, Y, Qian, G (eds) 2009, *Intelligent Video Surveillance: Systems and Technology*, CRC Press, New York.

Marchant, GE, Lindor, RA 2012, 'The coming collision between autonomous vehicles and the liability system', *Santa Clara Law Review*, vol. 52, no. 4, pp. 1321–1340.

Marques, V, Bento, N, Costa, PM 2014, 'The "smart paradox": Stimulate the deployment of smart grids with effective regulatory instruments', *Energy*, vol. 69, no. 1, pp. 96–103.

Martinez-Balleste, A, Perez-Martinez, P, Solanas, A 2013, 'The pursuit of citizens' privacy: A privacy-aware smart city is possible', *IEEE Communications Magazine*, vol. 51, no. 6, pp. 136–141.

McDaniel, P, McLaughlin, S 2009, 'Security and privacy challenges in the smart grid', *IEEE Security and Privacy*, vol. 3, no. 1, pp. 75–77.

Miller, E 2009, 'Renewables and the smart grid', *Renewable Energy Focus*, vol. 10, no. 2, pp. 67–69.

Mohamed, MIM, Wu, W, Moniri, M 2014, 'Data reduction methods for wireless smart sensors in monitoring water distribution systems', *Procedia Engineering*, vol. 70, no. 1, pp. 1166–1172.

Moore, M, Lu, B 2011, *Autonomous Vehicles for Personal Transport: A Technology Assessment*, accessed on 8 July 2015 from http://papers.ssrn.com/sol3/papers.cfm?abstract_id=1865047

Morgan Stanley 2013, *Autonomous Cars: Self-Driving the New Auto Industry Paradigm*, accessed on 8 July 2015 from http://www.wisburg.com/wp-content/uploads/2014/09/%EF%BC%88109-pages-2014%EF%BC%89MORGAN-STANLEY-BLUE-PAPER-AUTONOMOUS-CARS%EF%BC%9A-SELF-DRIVING-THE-NEW-AUTO-INDUSTRY-PARADIGM.pdf

Moslehi, K, Kumar, R 2010, 'A reliability perspective of the smart grid', *IEEE Transactions on Smart Grid*, vol. 1, no. 1, pp. 57–64.

Nasir, A, Hussain, SI, Soong, BH, Qaraqe, K 2014, 'Energy efficient cooperation in underlay RFID cognitive networks for a water smart home', *Sensors*, vol. 14, no. 10, pp. 18353–18369.

NHTSA (National Highway Traffic Safety Association) 2013, *U.S. Department of Transportation Releases Policy on Automated Vehicle Development*, accessed on 7 July 2015 from http://www.nhtsa.gov/About+NHTSA/Press+Releases/U.S.+Department+of+Transportation+Releases+Policy+on+Automated+Vehicle+Development

O'Toole, R 2014, *Policy Implications of Autonomous Vehicles*, accessed on 7 July 2015 from http://object.cato.org/sites/cato.org/files/pubs/pdf/pa758_1.pdf

Pavlidis, I, Morellas, V, Tsiamyrtzis, P, Harp, S 2001, 'Urban surveillance systems: From the laboratory to the commercial world', *Proceedings of the IEEE*, vol. 89, no. 10, pp. 1478–1497.

Pepermans, G 2014, 'Valuing smart meters', *Energy Economics*, vol. 45, no. 1, pp. 280–294.

Pereira, R, Figueiredo, J, Melicio, R, Mendes, VMF, Martins, J, Quadrado, JC 2015, 'Consumer energy management system with integration of smart meters', *Energy Reports*, vol. 1, no. 1, pp. 22–29.

Pinjari, AR, Augustin, B, Menon, N. 2013, *Highway Capacity Impacts of Autonomous Vehicles: An Assessment*, accessed on 7 July 2015 from http://www.usfav.com/pdf/TAVI_8-CapacityPinjari.pdf

Pinto, C 2012, 'How autonomous vehicle policy in California and Nevada addresses technological and non-technological liabilities', *Intersect: The Stanford Journal of Science, Technology and Society*, vol. 5, no. 1, pp. 1–16.

Pittock, AB 2013, *Climate Change: The Science, Impacts and Solutions*, Routledge, New York.

Polzin, S, 2013, *Implications to Public Transportation of Automated or Connected Vehicles*, accessed on 8 July 2015 from http://www.usfav.com/pdf/TAVI_1-PublicTransitPolzin.pdf

Prati, A, Vezzani, R, Fornaciari, M, Cucchiara, R 2013, 'Intelligent video surveillance as a service', in Atrey, PK, Cavallaro, A, Kankanhalli, MS (eds) *Intelligent Multimedia Surveillance*, Springer, Berlin, Germany, pp. 1–16.

Pratt, RG, Balducci, P, Gerkensmeyer, C, Katipamula, S, Kintner-Meyer, MCW, Sanquist, TF, Schneider, KP, Secrets, TJ 2010, 'The smart grid: An estimation of the energy and CO_2 benefits', The U.S. Department of Energy by Pacific Northwest National Laboratory, *Research Report no. PNNL-19112*.

Priddle, A, Woodyard, C 2012, *Google Discloses Costs of Its Driverless Car Tests*, Accessed on 8 July 2015 from http://content.usatoday.com/communities/driveon/post/2012/06/google-discloses-costs-of-its-driverless-car-tests/1#.UapgNWRgaBy

Prisma 2015, *Road Intersection Assistant*, accessed on 7 July 2015 from http://www.prisma-solutions.at/index.php/en/solutions/road-intersection-assistant

Purvins, A, Wilkening, H, Fulli, G, Tzimas, E, Celli, G, Mocci, S, Tedde, S 2011, 'A European supergrid for renewable energy: Local impacts and far-reaching challenges', *Journal of Cleaner Production*, vol. 19, no. 17, pp. 1909–1916.

Reich, S 2013, *Automated and Autonomous Vehicles and Managed Lanes*, accessed on 8 July 2015 from http://www.usfav.com/pdf/TAVI_5-ManagedLanesReich.pdf

Rinner, C, Keßler, C, Andrulis, S 2008, 'The use of web 2.0 concepts to support deliberation in spatial decision-making', *Computers, Environment and Urban Systems*, vol. 32, no. 5, pp. 386–395.

Robb, GC 1979, 'Police use of CCTV surveillance: Constitutional implications and proposed regulations', *Journal of Law Reform*, vol. 13, no. 3, pp. 571–602.

Roche, S, Propeck-Zimmermann, E, Mericskay, B 2013, 'GeoWeb and crisis management: Issues and perspectives of volunteered geographic information', *GeoJournal*, vol. 78, no. 1, pp. 21–40.

Romano, M, Kapelan, Z 2014, 'Adaptive water demand forecasting for near real-time management of smart water distribution systems', *Environmental Modelling and Software*, vol. 60, no. 1, pp. 265–276.

Schellekens, M 2015, 'Self-driving cars and the chilling effect of liability law', *Computer Law and Security Review*, vol. 31, no. 4, pp. 506–517.

Schmitt, T, Eisenberg, J, Rao, RR (eds.) 2007 *Improving Disaster Management: The Role of It in Mitigation, Preparedness, Response, and Recovery*, National Academies Press, Washington, DC.

Schoettle, B, Sivak, M 2014, *A Survey of Public Opinion about Autonomous and Self-Driving Vehicles in the U.S., the U.K., and Australia*, accessed on 8 July 2015 from http://deepblue.lib.umich.edu/bitstream/handle/2027.42/108384/103024.pdf

Sharma, K, Saini, LM 2015, 'Performance analysis of smart metering for smart grid: An overview', *Renewable and Sustainable Energy Reviews*, vol. 49, no. 1, pp. 720–735.

Shladover, S, 2005, 'Automated vehicles for highway operations: Automated highway systems', *Journal of Systems and Control Engineering*, vol. 219, no. 1, pp. 53–75.

Siddiqui, O, Hurtado, P, Parmenter, K 2008, 'The green grid energy savings and carbon emissions reductions enabled by a smart grid', *Report no. 1016905*, Electric Power Research Institute, Palo Alto, CA.

Smith, BW 2014, *Automated Vehicles Are Probably Legal in the United States*, accessed on 8 July 2015 from http://papers.ssrn.com/sol3/papers.cfm?abstract_id=2303904

Sun, T, Xia, Y, Gan, Y 2011, 'Discussion on integration of urban video surveillance system', *Procedia Engineering*, vol. 15, no. 1, pp. 3255–3259.

Sussman, JS 2008, *Perspectives on Intelligent Transportation Systems (ITS)*, Springer Science and Business Media, New York.

Tannert, C 2014, *Will You Ever Be Able to Afford a Self-Driving Car?*, accessed on 14 August 2015 from http://www.fastcompany.com/3025722/will-you-ever-be-able-to-afford-a-self-driving-car

Thrun, S 2010, 'Toward robotic cars', *Communications of the ACM*, vol. 53, no. 4, pp. 99–106.

Tientrakool, P 2011, *Highway Capacity Benefits from Using Vehicle-To-Vehicle Communication and Sensors for Collision Avoidance*, accessed on 8 July 2015 from http://safevehicle.ee.columbia.edu/docs/Tientrakool11.pdf

Toft, MB, Schuitema, G, Thøgersen, J 2014, 'Responsible technology acceptance: Model development and application to consumer acceptance of smart grid technology', *Applied Energy*, vol. 134, no. 1, pp. 392–400.

Tulloch, D 2008, 'Public participation GIS (PPGIS)', in Kemp, K (ed.) *Encyclopedia of Geographic Information Science*, SAGE Publications, Thousand Oaks, CA, pp. 352–355.

Uhr, C, Johansson, H, Fredholm, L 2008, 'Analysing emergency response systems', *Journal of Contingencies and Crisis Management*, vol. 16, no. 2, pp. 80–90.

Van Klaveren, C 2015, *8 Things You Should Know About Surveillance in the City*, accessed on 23 July 2015 from https://urbantimes.co/2014/06/city-surveillance

Venables, M 2007, 'Smart meters make smart consumers: Analysis', *Engineering and Technology*, vol. 2, no. 4, pp. 23–24.

Victoria Government 2015, *About Smart Meters*, accessed on 14 July 2015 from http://www.smartmeters.vic.gov.au/about-smart-meters

Vijayapriya, T, Kothari, DP 2011 'Smart grid: An overview', *Smart Grid and Renewable Energy*, vol. 2, no. 1, pp. 305–311.

Villasenor, J 2014, *Products, Liability, and Driverless Cars: Issues and Guiding Principles For Legislation*, accessed on 8 July 2015 from http://www.brookings.edu/research/papers/2014/04/products-liability-driverless-cars-villasenor

Wäger, PA, Eugster, M, Hilty, LM, Som, C 2005, 'Smart labels in municipal solid waste: A case for the precautionary principle?', *Environmental Impact Assessment Review*, vol. 25, no. 5, pp. 567–586.

Water Hero 2015, *Protect Your Home From Costly Water Damage*, accessed on 16 July 2015 from http://www.waterheroinc.com

Whitaker, R 1999, *The End of Privacy: How Total Surveillance is becoming a Reality*, The New Press, New York.

WHO (World Health Organization) 2010, *Vision 2030: The resilience of water supply and Sanitation in the Face of Climate Change: Summary and Policy Implications*, WHO, Geneva, Switzerland.

Yigitcanlar, T, Dizdaroglu, D, 2015, 'Ecological approaches in planning for sustainable cities: A review of the literature', *Global Journal of Environmental Science and Management*, vol. 1, no. 2, pp. 71–94.

Yute C, Jeng HK 2006, 'A reliable energy information system for promoting voluntary energy conservation benefits', *IEEE Transactions on Power Delivery*, vol. 21, no. 1, pp. 102–107.

Part III

Applications

Part III of the book provides a thorough review of comprehensive application attempts of smart urban technology and systems in the contemporary cities by looking into emerging practices across the globe and demonstrating the pioneering smart city best practices. This part, using the case study investigation approach, creates an instrumental platform for broadening the understanding of how smart urban information technologies and smart urban systems are being implemented in differing city contexts. Chapter 5 illustrates successful smart city practices from the: (i) South East Asian context, including Incheon and Tianjin; (ii) European context, including Amsterdam and Barcelona; (iii) Middle Eastern context, including Abu Dhabi and Istanbul; (iv) North and South American context, including Rio de Janeiro and San Francisco; and (v) Oceanian context, including Auckland and Brisbane. This part of the book aims to determine and share smart urban technology and system experiences of successful cities across the globe. By doing so, it addresses the second research question of the book, i.e. How can smart urban technologies and systems be adopted in the planning, development and management processes of cities to provide desired urban futures?

5   Smart cities in practice

Cities that lack the capacity to design their own smart solutions will fall behind.
(Anthony M Townsend, author of *Smart Cities*)

Introduction

Since the mid-2000s, smart urban technologies have begun to blanket our cities, forming the backbone of a large and intelligent infrastructure network. Along with this, dissemination of the sustainability ideology has had a significant imprint on the planning, development and management of our cities. Accordingly, the concept of smart cities, evolved from intelligent cities (see Komninos 2008), has become a popular topic particularly for scholars, urban planners, urban administrations, urban development and real estate companies, and corporate technology firms.

There are numerous perspectives on what constitutes a smart city. These range from the purely ecological (Lim and Liu 2010) to technological (Townsend 2013), and from economic (Kourtit *et al*. 2012) to organisational (Hollands 2015) and societal views (Deakin and Al Waer 2011, 2012). Moreover, for Kitchin (2015), smart city symbolises a new kind of technology-led urban utopia. Utopia or not, in all these perspectives the vision of technology and innovation is a common ground to shape our cities into a form that we want to leave to our descendants. In this Chapter, the smart cities concept is viewed as a vision, manifesto or provocation encompassing all techno-economic, techno-societal, techno-spatial and techno-organisational dimensions, aiming to constitute the ideal twenty-first century city form. Presently, there are no fully-fledged smart cities. As stated by Glasmeier and Christopherson (2015: 4), 'the global smart city market will be valued at $1.6 trillion in 2020. Over 26 global cities are expected to be smart cities in 2025, with more than 50% of these smart cities from Europe and North America'. At the moment, with the building of these cities underway in a number of places around the world, smart city examples abound in both the popular media and in academic discussions. This provides us with the ability to place these cities under the microscope, even though they are not developed as a fully functioning smart cities, in order to evaluate their prospects and constraints. Building on the reviewed technologies and systems in Chapters 3 and 4, this Chapter aims to examine the promising smart city initiatives and assess their challenges and opportunities in becoming a role model for the cities of the twenty-first century. The smart city initiatives selected for examination in the Chapter include: (i) Incheon and Tianjin from the South East Asian context; (ii) Amsterdam and Barcelona from the European context; (iii) Abu Dhabi and Istanbul from the Middle Eastern context; (iv) Rio de Janeiro and San Francisco from the North and South American context; and (v) Auckland and Brisbane from the Oceanian context.

Smart city initiatives from South East Asia

Rapid urbanisation across the globe is expected to see about five billion people located in cities by the late 2020s, with South East Asia hosting a significant proportion of their population in its megacities (UN 2015). The challenges ahead in combatting potential problems associated with this trend laid the foundations for the 'smart cities movement' in the region (Cohen 2015). Today, South East Asia is one of the trendsetting contexts when it gets to large-scale and ambitious smart city projects (IBM 2015a). In this region of the world, different countries, due to their local developmental characteristics and conditions, market their smart cities with diverse urban brands. For instance, Malaysia focuses on establishing smart cities under the banner of 'knowledge cities', which include the cities of Cyberjaya and Iskandar (see Yigitcanlar and Sarimin 2011, 2015). In Korea, smart cities are gathered under the 'ubiquitous cities' brand and total some 64 cities. The most well-known of these are Gwanggyo Ekonhill, Incheon, Songdo, Magok/Seoul and Sejong, with 21 of them mostly completed, 12 under construction and 31 at the design stage (see Shwayri 2013; Yigitcanlar and Lee 2014). In Japan, they are branded as 'ecological cities' or 'eco-cities' and total 26 projects including Chiyoda, Iida, Kitakyushu, Kyoto, Minamata, Miyakojima, Obihiro, Sakai, Shimokawa, Toyama, Toyota, Yokohama and Yusuhara (see Low 2013). In China, the brand is also eco-cities and examples include Dongtan, Sino-Singapore Tianjin, Sino-Singapore Nanjing, Caofeidian, Huangbaiyu and Kunming Shibo (see Cheng and Hu 2010; De Jong *et al*. 2013). Likewise, other smart city initiatives are also rapidly emerging from the region's major cities including Singapore, Hong Kong and Taipei and many others, such as Bangkok and Ho Chi Minh City, are also getting ready to jump on the smart city bandwagon. Among the many promising initiatives from the region, the next section explores Incheon from Korea and Tianjin from China.

Incheon, Korea

Korea trademarks its smart cities under the brand of 'ubiquitous cities' or 'ubiquitous eco-cities' and most recently as 'compact and smart cities'. In Korea, these cities are basically an ICT and eco-technology (EcoT) embedded smart and sustainable city model, where people can access both digital and eco-services based on the technology convergence between ICTs and EcoTs. These cities also lay an emphasis on the connection between technological innovation, behavioural change and education driven by local community involvement, e.g. in the areas of waste management (waste-to-energy), public transport use, water management and so on. Through the processes of sociotechnological innovation and political and socioeconomic governance, these cities have developed and evolved to provide citizens with a higher level of sustainable living and democratic governance (Yigitcanlar and Lee 2014). One of the most renowned ubiquitous cities in Korea is Incheon's New Songdo City, also known as Songdo International City or Songdo Smart City, a smart city being developed from scratch.

Planned as a global business hub, Songdo, a district of Incheon, is divided into land-use zones including a high-tech industrial cluster, a prominent knowledge and information complex, a new port logistics complex and an international business district (Shwayri 2013). Initially inspired by Dubai, New Songdo City is a master-planned international business centre, which is being developed on 53.4 km^2 of sea-reclaimed land in the Yellow Sea along Incheon's waterfront (roughly 60 per cent the size of Manhattan), 35 km south of Seoul and connected to the new Incheon international airport by a 12 km highway via Incheon's 2nd bridge. The development forms the heart of the region, to be completed in 2020, and will house about 65,000 people and 300,000 workers in what developers claim to be the greenest and most wired smart city in the world. New Songdo City is the outcome of joint work between real estate developers, corporate technology companies, and national and local level governments to build an urban centre from scratch that is filled with technologically enhanced infrastructure and services. In Songdo, high-rise towers meet strict standards for green buildings, neighbourhoods are smartly laid out, an urban oasis is created modelled on New York City's Central Park, a robust public transit network and a state-of-the-art water recycling system are put in place, and the entire city is wired with ubiquitous broadband internet connections (Strickland 2011). Planned as the largest smart city project in the world, Songdo is presented as a smart living space where wireless, context-aware, computer-driven ICTs imbue nearly all aspects of urban life (Kim 2010).

Being in an economic zone (Incheon Free Economic Zone) and in addition to tax cuts and other financial incentives to attract foreign business, large sums of money are being channelled to fund the science, technology and innovation efforts of Korean companies and many R&D institutes relocating and investing in Songdo. The city was originally conceived as a weapon for fighting trade wars, and the idea was to entice multinationals to set up Asian operations at Songdo with lower taxes and less regulation (Townsend 2013). The city aims to excel particularly in bio, nano, information and communication, and ubiquitous commuting technologies and to become a global hub for innovation (Carvalho 2012). Currently, many leading technology companies, such as Samsung, Cisco and IBM have located their R&D facilities in the city. According to Townsend (2013), this investment is going to turn Songdo into a test bed for RFID and a centre for R&D in its crucial smart urban technologies. The city is still under construction; nevertheless, most of the infrastructure is in place, as are its major landmarks, providing clues as to its future form (Kim 2010). As stated by Shwayri (2013), Songdo's master plan is based on a combination of sustainable design principles, such as sustainable modes of transport, and a mix of open and green spaces. It received the Sustainable City Award in 2008, which was sponsored by the Financial Times and the Urban Land Institute. However, the city is located on sea-reclaimed land and caused the destruction of precious wetlands, home to some of the rarest species on the planet. The development of ubiquitous urban environments is in rapid progress. Smart city technologies, coupled with sustainable design principles, are targeting the creation of a unique city type, a smart city for a utopian future. Nevertheless, with high-cost investment the smart city can only serve those who can afford it, and it will become a city solely for the affluent class.

Yigitcanlar and Lee (2014) offer the following comprehensive appraisal of Korean ubiquitous cities, which also applies to Songdo, from an economic, societal, spatial and governance perspective. First of all, these cities, due to top-down development strategy, are typically prone to problems related to the lack of social infrastructure, market restrictions, political quagmires and vested financial interests. Such cities have been built from the perspective of technical computing with an emphasis on supply-side technology, which has put in place advance technologies with impressive budgets. However, through such a computer-driven approach, social and cultural aspects have been neglected and are absent from discussions about the design of ubiquitous cities, which have emphasised physical aspects and industry portfolios and veered away from the idea of a knowledge culture.

Second, as technology only becomes cheaper as it becomes more widespread, in the case of ubiquitous cities this creates a chicken and egg causality dilemma. Examples of Korean ubiquitous cities are largely based on 'supply-push' instead of 'demand-driven'. These government initiated projects supply technology in the space where it is embedded, i.e. cities, however, the lack of demand for such expensive places keeps technology prices higher. Additionally, the technology and services seem to be lacking focus on the social infrastructures and needs of the communities. Therefore, further efforts are needed to create a market for the better utilisation of the technology and building the partnership with society to establish the required social infrastructures. Public participation can support these cities to be shaped by a mix of technological, social, cultural, economic, political and organisational processes. Moreover, planners and designers should undertake due diligence to develop an environment that best matches their image of prospective users and shape a sociotechnical environment in which social and technological aspects are intimately related to, and define and redefine, each other. Additionally, the retrofitting of the ubiquitous cities concept should also be considered, as it is not always possible to construct such cities from scratch everywhere.

Third, Korean ubiquitous city projects are perceived as national growth engines, especially when national governments and large technology corporations are partners in the development of these projects. The development and application of smart urban technologies by these large corporations help them to keep the innovative cutting edge and contribute to the competitiveness of the national economy. However, in the glocalised, global and local, world of the twenty-first century, local economies have become as important as the national economies. Therefore, the ability of new smart urban technologies and projects to regenerate local economies from the bottom up is definitely seen as important. However, so far this has been completely absent in the Korean cases.

Last, current ambitious initiatives from Korea are somehow providing a positive outlook and progress in forming the smart and sustainable cities of the twenty-first century. In particular, the success of high-tech use in the planning, development, monitoring and management of various urban services gives us hope for the formation of a truly smart and sustainable urban form. In its infancy, it is very early to refer to ubiquitous cities as having a smart and sustainable urban form. However, Korean initiatives, including Songdo, are determining a new development path and setting the benchmark high for the next generation of cities in this century. This is surely giving us some hope for future developments, while still keeping all of the criticisms and skepticisms in mind, and someday realising the idea of living in harmony with each other and the environment.

Tianjin, China

China's adoption of the smart cities framework in its urban development practice is a central tenet of its grand urban plan (Poole 2014). Being the world's largest carbon emitter, China has started to concentrate on promoting low carbon, ecological, human settlement development as a solution to addressing national and also global environmental challenges. As a result of government policy in this direction, a number of smart cities, branded as eco-cities, have started to be planned and developed since the beginning of the 2000s. As part of the government financial support in 2012, eight initiatives were awarded 50 million yuan (about $7.8 million). These eco-cities are: Sino-Singapore Tianjin Eco-city, Tangshan Bay Eco-city, Shenzhen Guangming New District, Wuxi Taihu New Town, Meixihu New Town, Chongqing Yuelai Eco-city, Kunming Chenggong New District and Guiyang Future Ark Eco-city (Yu 2014). This section provides an analysis of the Sino-Singapore Tianjin Eco-city, a smart city being developed from scratch.

The Sino-Singapore Tianjin Eco-city project, positioned in one of the fastest growing regions in China, represents the Chinese and Singaporean governments' joint attempt at building a sustainable and smart urban model from scratch. The project embodies a socially harmonious, environmentally friendly and resource-conserving smart city. Prior to its development, the site comprised mainly salt-pans, barren land and polluted water-bodies, including a large wastewater pond (Tianjin Eco-city 2015). Located 150 km south-east of Beijing and 40 km east of Tianjin, the 31.2 km^2 Sino-Singapore Tianjin Eco-city project was commenced in 2007 and is currently under construction. The first phase of the project developed the start-up area that covers 8 km^2, which will and house a projected population of 85,000 residents, 30,000 of them have already moved in. When fully developed in 2020, Sino-Singapore Tianjin Eco-city will be home to about 350,000 permanent and 60,000 temporary residents. The master plan, developed in 2008, adopts a holistic approach towards creating and designing a liveable, efficient and compact smart city. As stated by Pow and Neo (2013: 2266), planning principles are, 'centred on a set of 26 key performance indicators (KPIs). These KPIs are divided into four groups comprising: a good natural environment; a healthy balance in the manmade environment; good lifestyle habits; and developing a dynamic and efficient economy'. These KPIs are listed in Table 5.1. One of the major reasons for adopting quantifiable indicators was to enhance the ease of replicability of the city building model from one place to another. This approach resulted in the development of the Sino-Singapore Nanjing Eco High-tech Island project, located in the Changjiang River, which is based on the experiences gained in master planning, design, development and the latest green technology use from the Tianjin project.

At the heart of this eco-city project lies the successful marriage of numerous EcoTs with good urban and architectural design and engineering so as to create a sustainable and attractive quality living environment. For instance, the Low Carbon Living Lab located in Tianjin Eco-city showcases best practices in the development of sustainable design strategies and green building technologies, including climate oriented design, natural day lighting, high-performance envelope, energy efficient mechanical and electrical services, renewable energy systems, intelligent building management systems, green building operations, air purification technologies, vertical greenery systems, water saving measures, use of environmentally friendly materials, and ubiquitous and sensing technologies (Tianjin Eco-city 2015).

Although the project received attention for its environmental sustainability and EcoTs, Tianjin Eco-city receives criticism due to its design and the lack of recognition of the complex web of sociocultural and economic processes, which link the lived environment of the city to its environmental characteristics. On that very point, Wong (2011) argues that the city lacks a human scale, as each block is about four times the size of a typical block in Manhattan and therefore makes pedestrian and bike journeys cumbersome. As for Caprotti (2014), one of the critical issues in Tianjin is the internal social resilience and the emergence of new communities. Moreover, Caprotti (2014) highlights that the project needs to consider not only the high-tech, new urban environments in smart cities but also the production and reproduction of large, often transient populations of low-paid workers that build the city and who form the 'new urban poor', forming 'workers' cities' on the edges of flagship smart and sustainable urban projects. Yu (2014) emphasises that Tianjin Eco-city overly focuses on the application of green and ecological technologies to minimise the use of energy and natural resources, where social equality and environmental protection have not been fully considered in the process of low carbon smart city development. Yu (2014) underlines that even though 10 per cent of the building stock is planned as affordable housing:

> [i]t is not clear who the beneficiaries of this affordable housing will be, as typically it is also regulated that the renters must be working in the eco-city, and the proposed industries within the eco-city are mainly specified as high-tech, creative industries, e.g. animation, film making, culture industries.
>
> (Yu 2014: 108)

Table 5.1 Key performance indicators of Sino-Singapore Tianjin eco-city

Good Natural Environment	Healthy Balance in the Built Environment	Good Lifestyle Habits	Developing a Dynamic and Efficient Economy	Qualitative Key Performance Indicators
Ambient air quality: The air quality in the city should meet China's National Ambient Air Quality Grade II Standard for at least 310 days. The SO_2 and NOx content in the ambient air should not exceed the limits stipulated for China's National Ambient Air Quality Grade 1 standard for at least 155 days.	*Proportion of green buildings description:* All buildings in the city should meet green building standards.	*Per capita daily water consumption description:* The daily water consumption per day for each person should not exceed 120 litres by 2013.	*Usage of renewable energy description:* The proportion of energy utilised in the city which will be in the form of renewable energy, such as solar and geothermal energy, should be at least 20% by 2020.	Maintain a safe and healthy ecology through green consumption and low-carbon operations.
Quality of water bodies within the city: Water bodies in the city should meet Grade IV of China's latest national standards by 2020.	*Native vegetation index description:* At least 70% of the plant varieties in the city should be native plants/vegetation.	*Per capita daily domestic waste generation description:* The amount of domestic waste generated by each person should not exceed 0.8 kg by 2013.	*Usage of water from non-traditional sources description:* At least 50% of the city's water supply will be from non-traditional sources such as desalination and recycled water by 2020.	Adopt innovative policies that will promote regional collaboration and improve the environment of the surrounding regions.

(continued)

Table 5.1 (continued)

Good Natural Environment	Healthy Balance in the Built Environment	Good Lifestyle Habits	Developing a Dynamic and Efficient Economy	Qualitative Key Performance Indicators
Quality of water from taps: Water from all taps should be potable.	*Per capita public green space description:* The public green space should be at least 12 square metres per person by 2013.	*Proportion of green trips description:* At least 90% of trips within the city should be in the form of green trips by 2020. Green trips refer to non-motorised transport, i.e. cycling and walking, as well as trips on public transport.	*Proportion of R&D scientists and engineers in the city workforce description:* There should be at least 50 R&D scientists and engineers per 10,000 workforce in the city by 2020.	Give prominence to the river estuarine culture to preserve history and cultural heritage, and show its uniqueness.
Noise pollution levels: Noise pollution levels must satisfy the stipulated standards for different functional zones.		*Overall recycling rate description:* At least 60% of total waste should be recycled by 2013.	*Employment-housing equilibrium index description:* At least 50% of the employable residents in the city should be employed in the city by 2013.	Complement the development of recycling industries and promote the orderly development of the surrounding regions.
Carbon emission per unit GDP description: The carbon emission per unit GDP in the city should not exceed 150 tonne-C per US$1 million.		*Access to free recreational and sports amenities description:* All residential areas in the city should have access to free recreational and sports amenities within a walking distance of 500m by 2013.		

Net loss of natural wetlands description: There should be no net loss of natural wetlands in the city.

Waste treatment description: All hazardous and domestic waste in the city should be rendered non-toxic through treatment.

Barrier-free accessibility description: The city should have 100% barrier-free access.

Services network coverage description: The entire city will have access to key infrastructure services, such as recycled water, gas, broadband, electricity and heating by 2013.

Proportion of affordable public housing description: At least 20% of housing in the city will be in the form of subsidised public housing by 2013.

Source: Tianjin Eco-city 2015.

As well as over-emphasising technology and economic development, or city building, he underlines that a smart city requires innovation not only in relevant technologies but also in institutional and community development, pointing out the unsuitable government performance assessment mechanism and the limited community engagement. The observations from Tianjin are in line with the view of Lombardi *et al.* (2012) that emphasise the role of human capital and education, social and relational capital, and environmental interests among the important drivers of smart city growth. Much like in Korea, according to De Jong *et al.* (2013), smart cities in China:

> [a]re not sold by motivated citizens to their peers and governments as major contributions to sustainable production and consumption, but by local governments to future developers, high-tech corporations, and highly educated inhabitants as attractive green areas where they can generate extra GDP, produce new technologies, and live comfortably and safely.
>
> (De Jong *et al.* 2013: 110)

Furthermore, the 2015 Tianjin explosions, a series of explosions that occurred at a container storage station at the Port of Tianjin between 12 and 15 August 2015 and causing over a hundred deaths and hundreds of injured, is an indication of poor industrial, environmental, and health and safety regulations. Therefore, achievement of the goal of successfully building truly sustainable and smart cities is highly questionable for a country with such low standards and corruption scandals that surface frequently.

Smart city initiatives from Europe

The smart and sustainable city movement originated from Europe in the 1990s with cities including Almere (Amsterdam/the Netherlands), Eko-Viikki (Helsinki/Finland), Freiburg (Germany), Linz (Austria) and Växjö (Sweden). Since the start of the twenty-first century, a few more European cities have adopted smart and sustainable city frameworks. Leading examples include Ecociudad Logroño (Montecorvo/Spain), PlanIT Valley (Porto/Portugal), Brøset (Trondheim/Norway), Clonburris (Dublin), Hamburg-Harburg (Germany), Hammarby Sjöstad (Stockholm/Sweden), Barcelona Trinita Nova (Barcelona/Spain) and Thames Gateway (London/UK), see Joss *et al.* (2013). Furthermore, in recent years, the EU has devoted a constant effort to devise strategies for achieving urban growth in a smart way, under the brand of smart cities (Caragliu *et al.* 2011). As the birthplace of the concept of smart cities, Europe showcases the most vibrant examples of the smart cities initiatives.

Cities from European context that are specifically branded as smart cities include Amsterdam (the Netherlands), Barcelona (Spain), Bristol (UK), Copenhagen (Denmark), Florence/Prato, Venice (Italy), Frankfurt (Germany), Issy-les-Moulineaux, Lyons (France), Malmo (Sweden), Manchester (UK), Riga (Latvia), Tallinn (Estonia), Vilnius (Lithuania) and Zagreb (Croatia).

Different from the large-scale South East Asian greenfield or brownfield smart cities developed from scratch, European smart cities were mainly constructed by retrofitting smart urban technology solutions in existing cities. Among the large number of initiatives from the region, this section explores Amsterdam from the Netherlands and Barcelona from Spain.

Amsterdam, the Netherlands

The City of Amsterdam, Amsterdam Economic Board (formerly Amsterdam Innovation Motor), internet operator Liander and telecom provider KPN jointly initiated the Smart City Amsterdam project in 2009, an existing city evolving towards becoming a smart city. Smart City Amsterdam aims to turn itself into a more sustainable city by working with two principles to: (i) enable partners to apply innovative technologies; and (ii) stimulate behavioural change with end users (Sauer 2012). The starting point for the project, therefore, was not merely to provide technical solutions but also to achieve the collaboration, co-creation and partnership between stakeholders within the city to move towards sustainable and smart solutions. The project, therefore, was developed in a quadruple-helix partnership model between businesses, authorities, research institutions and citizens. The operational aim of the project was to help achieve ambitious sustainability targets set in Europe 2020, Amsterdam Structural Vision 2040 and the Amsterdam Energy Strategy 2040 (Manville *et al.* 2014). Local planners expect to bolster the economy through public and private investment, as well as cut emissions by 40 per cent by 2025 by converting Amsterdam into a smart city (Dameri 2014). The Amsterdam smart city project maintained strong linkages with a number of other European smart city initiatives, including NiCE, Citadel, Digital cities, Open cities and Common4EU. The NiCE project aims to decrease ICT's direct carbon footprint by 30 per cent. The Citadel project aims to enable the public to create apps from open data, therefore capitalising on talent and contributing to R&D. The Digital cities project intends to ensure 100 per cent access to fast broadband, thereby connecting citizens to the ICT-related resources available, thus making their lives smarter. The Open cities project works towards validating how to approach open and user-driven innovation methodologies in the public sector in a scenario of future internet services for smart cities. The Common4EU project aims to create digital services for citizens to access (Manville *et al.* 2014).

In 2013, this smart city platform of Amsterdam has grown into a partnership with over 70 partners that are engaged in 38 different smart city projects. These projects deal with a variety of topics including a smart grid development across five different themes, including smart living, smart working, smart mobility, smart public space and open data themes. The 'smart living' theme of the smart city project concentrates on determining technologies and methods that are the most effective for various projects. These range from renovating old canal-side buildings for higher energy efficiency to installing smart meters for improved consumer energy conservation behaviour, e.g. more efficient use of household devices, switching off and lowering heating, substitution of household devices and consumers producing their own energy through solar panels and household wind turbines. The 'smart working' theme of the project focuses on determining technologies and methods that are the most effective to enable smart working for various projects in new and existing building stock, including Amsterdam's historic seventeenth-century townhouses. These projects aim to support sustainable real estate development, company energy consumption improvement and employee awareness to work in a smarter manner, e.g. installing smart plugs, submetering per floor, insulation, energy and management scans, LED lighting and other smart building solutions. The 'smart mobility' theme determines technologies, concepts, approaches and forms of cooperation that are most successful for various mobility projects. These projects focus on sustainable modes of transport and the infrastructure, e.g. implementing new logistic concepts, dynamic traffic management, quick charging electrical vehicle batteries (20 min) and a network of recharging points for electric scooters throughout the city. 'Smart public space' focuses on determining technologies, concepts, approaches and forms of cooperation that are most successful to make public facilities more sustainable on a large scale and organised in a smarter manner. These projects include smart schools, hospitals, sport areas, libraries, streets and so on providing a number of energy efficient smart solutions and approaches, e.g. waste collection with electric vehicles, dimming public lighting, energy scans, smart plugs, sustainable tram stops, awareness programs at schools and performance comparison through an online portal. The 'open data' theme deals with publicly available data that can be used and combined to provide citizens with new insights, knowledge and the chance to make decisions based upon actual facts and figures (Manville *et al.* 2014). In the Smart City Amsterdam project, such information is summarised and shared through the city's dashboard, which is an instrument that displays the operation of the smart city in real time (see Batty 2015).

The following initiatives that have deployed solutions in the Smart City Amsterdam are worth pointing out: climate street, ship-to-grid, smart building management systems and health lab. The climate street project is a holistic concept for shopping streets with a focus on a number of different aspects, i.e. public space, logistics and entrepreneurial spaces. The project aims to: (i) create a sustainable platform in a city centre environment; (ii) record user insights, as well as insights into collaboration and implementation processes; and (iii) stimulate sustainable entrepreneurship among SMEs (Sauer 2012). This project combines physical and logistical initiatives in the public space, as well as sustainable initiatives within present businesses. The main objectives of the project include the reduction of CO_2 emissions and energy consumption in the neighbourhood. This is to be achieved through a combination of sustainability initiatives including sustainable waste logistics, energy displays, LED lighting, smart meters and energy management systems, and the related changes in user behaviour (Manville *et al.* 2014).

The ship-to-grid project, also known as green energy project, is a result of the Port of Amsterdam's ambition to become one of the most sustainable harbours in Europe by 2020 with the help of the ship-to-grid electricity project. This project allows inland ships in the harbour of Amsterdam to use green energy from the grid instead of their own stationary diesel generators. This reduces CO_2 emissions and leads to less noise and air pollution. The ICT component of this project is that ship owners can pay via a telephone payment system. In total, 195 ship-to-grid connection points were installed in the Amsterdam harbour for the project (Manville *et al.* 2014).

The smart building management system project was aimed at reducing energy use and operating costs for office buildings. This pilot project ran in the ITO Tower, the head office of Accenture in the Netherlands, where various smart energy management solutions were deployed. The main objective of the project was to reduce energy consumption by collecting, analysing and visualising data about the amount of energy consumed and applying energy saving strategies based on this information. The smart building management system pilot project consisted of the installation of smart plugs and LED lightning. Smart plugs can measure energy use within an outlet and switch off electronic devices automatically. Around 360 smart plugs where installed in the office floors. The second part (less 'smart' but an effective measure for office buildings) was the installation of LED lighting on office floors (Manville *et al.* 2014).

The health lab project is a network of living labs in the Amsterdam region bringing together researchers, government, practitioners and healthcare users in the fields of ICT technologies and innovative healthcare solutions. The Amsterdam Economic Board and various research, business and governmental partners initiated this project. The project focuses on increasing the efficiency of technological innovation in the health sector and circulates around scientists, practitioners and entrepreneurs. End users play a central role and ICT is considered the most important enabler. The three goals of the health lab are to: (i) create a platform, where all those involved can meet, discuss and share developments in and implementation of new solutions in care; (ii) support and stimulate the setting up of several living lab locations, where new solutions can be tested and improved, together with users; and (iii) create new curricula focusing on the implementation of these solutions in educational settings (Manville *et al.* 2014).

As in most of the European smart city projects. Amsterdam also adopted a retrofitting approach in its efforts to develop the Amsterdam Metropolitan Area into a flourishing smart city. It has successfully integrated both environmental and societal goals with economic and technological ones. This smart city development managed to embed all kinds of digital infrastructure and networks, devices, sensors and actuators, as a result of which the volume of data produced has grown exponentially. Smart city data mangers need to pay special attention to this issue, as stated by Kitchin (2014), because it may create concerns about the data quality, fidelity, security, management and validity of analytics that can be interpreted and acted upon. Furthermore, as underlined by Townsend (2013), even though Amsterdam is widely recognised as a global leader in smart solutions for sustainable urban outcomes, emissions generated from the city are still rising at 1 per cent annually.

Barcelona, Spain

The smart city initiative, previously coined 'knowledge city', of Barcelona, is the final step of its urban transformation that dates back to the early 1980s. The 1992 Olympic Games provided the city with better infrastructure, and the strategic development plan in the 1990s aimed at achieving Barcelona's transformation into a smart one. The conceptualisation of the Barcelona perspective on smart cities is comprehensive and places ICT as a core element in the city's approach to becoming a smart city. According to Bakici *et al.* (2013) the development perspective:

> [i]mplies a high-tech intensive and an advanced city that connects people, information and city elements using new technologies in order to create a sustainable, greener city, competitive and innovative commerce and a recuperating life quality with a straightforward administration and a good maintenance system. [Moreover, it] is a collaborative movement among its corporations (retail), academic institutions, government authorities and the residents of Barcelona, aimed at becoming a reference programme for economic engines and urban development.
>
> (Bakici *et al.* 2013: 139)

Barcelona received the City Climate Leadership award, European Capital of Innovation prize of Europe and Bloomberg Mayor's Challenge award in 2014 in recognition of its smart city progress (Capdevila and Zarlenga 2015). The smart city strategy of Barcelona aims to build productive urban districts that are constructed by following the sustainable urban development principles and wired with cutting-edge technologies.The key objectives of the strategy are: (i) a new organisation targeted at smart city principles and objectives; (ii) a legal framework for public–private-partnership (PPP) to flourish; (iii) an urban area for PPP to settle and grow; (iv) to feed the urban innovation ecosystem; (v) to create a living lab, a development of a community of citizen developers; (vi) to provide facilities for SME experimentation; (vii) the opening of new opportunities for citizens to be more active and participative; and (viii) strong international linkages (Barcelona City Hall 2012).

Barcelona, especially with various initiatives in the industrial area 22@ Barcelona district, also called a 'smart city campus' or 'innovation district', is considered a success story in smart city development across Europe and is an existing city, which is evolving towards becoming a smart city. The Barcelona Smart City initiative aims to actively generate smart ideas in an open environment through fostering clusters, open data or developing living labs, while directly involving citizens in the co-creation process of products or services (Bakici *et al.* 2013). At present, smart district 22@Barcelona is the city's internationally renowned innovation district, around 200 hectares of redeveloped brownfield site located at the heart of Barcelona and formerly used as an old industrial zone (Leon 2008). This smart district supports the formation of urban research and facilitates a new working space between city administration, companies and research institutes. Moreover, it intends to foster research activities about the smart management of the urban space and e-services. The success of this development model comes from it having been based on discussions about territory, economy and society, creating its own unique model, which puts universities, companies and the administration at the heart of economic and technological transformations. The accomplishments of 22@Barcelona model have made it a benchmark of urban, economic and social transformation for cities such as Rio de Janeiro, Boston, Istanbul and Cape Town. This model is studied and followed by smart cities and knowledge and innovation districts around the world (Pareja-Eastaway and Piqué 2011).

Similar to Amsterdam, the Barcelona Smart City project also maintained strong linkages with a number of other European smart city initiatives, including NiCE, Citadel, iCity, CitySDK, Open cities and Common4EU. The following initiatives deployed solutions in the Smart City Barcelona project: zero energy blocks, energy efficiency in buildings, smart parking, the orthogonal network of public transport, pay per lighting, rain water management, new tools for a new waste management, situation room, service delivery platform and a new generation network for the municipality.

The suburb of Sant Cugat built the first smart street in Catalonia to incorporate innovative ICT solutions through urban, environmental and mobility management services. The solutions deployed are: (i) a sensor network monitoring system in the parking areas and outdoor area of business management and unloaders; (ii) a mobility sensorised system for vehicles to achieve efficiency and avoid traffic jams; (iii) solar energy, which allows automatic compaction to reduce the volume of waste to a fifth and volume sensors allow efficient garbage collection; (iv) environmental sensors (temperature, humidity and pollution), which give added information on waste collection and management of the irrigation system for intelligent urban green areas; and (v) presence sensors to control lighting and regulation of the intensity in pedestrian areas, based on the design, schedule and so on (see http://smartcity.santcugat.cat/?lang=en).

The control of lighting zones is important to tackle the problem of public street lighting being used inefficiently in a way that is harmful to the environment. The approach undertaken to overcome the problem in Barcelona is as follows. First, street lamps are equipped with LED technology, which needs much less energy than usual light bulbs. Then, the lamps are equipped with sensors to receive information on the environment (e.g. humidity, temperature, wind velocity, sunlight, atmospheric pressure and pollution) as well as noise and the presence of people. The lights communicate with a central unit in the street, which also manages other services such as fibre-optic cabling to the home, Wi-Fi or electrical vehicle recharging stations. The information is then sent to the central control centre. This centre monitors all activities and services taking place at a certain location, receives alerts and manages them from a distance. Sensors automatically adjust lighting depending on the time of day and the presence of approaching people (Manville *et al.* 2014).

Worldsensing piloted a smart parking system called Fastprk by installing parking sensors in the 22@Barcelona district. This smart parking application tracks parking through wireless sensors, indicating to drivers the location of vacant parking places and enabling them to find available spots and pay for them (MIT Technology Review 2014). The system works by real-time parking information being sent from the sensor in the parking lots to the data centre, which makes this information available through an app that drivers' smart phones can receive. In this way, the system guides the driver to the nearest vacant parking spot. This application helps not only to ease the city traffic but also decreases fuel use and CO_2 emissions (Manville *et al.* 2014).

Barcelona is also advanced in smart building design. An example is the Media-tic building located at 22@Barcelona. It is a 40-metre high transparent cube, clad in a warped mesh of steel cables and ethylene-tetrafluoroethylene (ETFE) bubbles (Australian Design Review 2010). The building hosts companies and institutions in the ICT, media and audio-visual sectors. It was designed as a communication hub and meeting point for these businesses with the ambitious architecture of Barcelona. The façade of the building is striking and at the same time functional. The translucent and innovative covering material, ETFE, acts as an external covering and a mobile sunscreen. The use of ETFE not only lends the building a quality of transparency but also serves as the basis for two very unique environmental controls that are perhaps the project's most remarkable features. The covering is activated using pneumatic mechanisms. These 'luxometer sensors' regulate levels of sunlight and temperature automatically and independently (Manville *et al.* 2014).

Smart grid and smart metering projects are focused on upgrading the power supply system in Barcelona, where they have rolled out a cutting-edge smart grid offering greater savings and more efficient and sustainable management. Additionally, sensor technology has been implemented in the irrigation system in Parc del Centre de Poblenou, where real-time data are transmitted to gardening crews about the level of water required for the plants. Moreover, Barcelona is the first European city to have a solar thermal ordinance, making it compulsory to use solar energy to supply 60 per cent of running hot water in all new private and public buildings, renovated buildings or buildings changing their use.

Even though numerous successful applications of smart urban technology and systems in Barcelona make many to point the city out as a successful smart city practice, the city needs to be cautious not to 'ghetto-ise' the smart city into some prestigious districts (Poole 2014). That is to say, the administrators of the City of Barcelona should find ways of expanding smart city and its applications beyond 22@Barcelona. So far, as a world famous innovation district, 22@Barcelona has served its purpose to showcase smart city applications. Now it is time to see the implementation of these applications in much less affluent neighbourhoods, leading to a reversal of the 'ghettoisation' and 'elitisation' processes. In other words, technology should be the vehicle used to deliver a truly smart city that is a low carbon city, or a city that is easy to move around, or a balanced city with jobs and housing for all, perhaps developed with a joined-up approach, a mixture of top-down and bottom-up or citizen-led approaches.

Smart city initiatives from the Middle East

The Middle East is another colourful region of the world when it comes to smart city development. The region is fuelled by increasing diffusion of global knowledge-based economic activities and green-consciousness, which have resulted in investment in smart city formation efforts. Being conscious of increasingly scarce natural resources, governments and regulators of Dubai (UAE), and followed by cities including Abu Dhabi (UAE), Doha (Qatar), Amman (Jordan), Istanbul (Turkey), Tehran (Iran), Abu Rawash (Egypt) and Mecca (Saudi Arabia), started to look at the options of becoming smarter in energy, technology and urban development investments, thus making a move towards forming smart cities. Similar to South East Asian smart cities, most of the Middle Eastern smart cities are constructed from scratch as new developments, although retrofitting practices are not uncommon, particularly in Turkey and Iran. Among a number of promising initiatives from the region, this section explores Abu Dhabi from the UAE and Istanbul from Turkey.

Abu Dhabi, UAE

Abu Dhabi is part of the UAE and is the largest of seven semi-autonomous emirates forming a federation located in the Arabian Peninsula, where the land is largely hot and dry desert. Abu Dhabi's Masdar City is a planned smart city project situated in a desert location 17 km southeast of Abu Dhabi. Masdar Smart City, a $22 billion state funded project of almost 6 km^2 in size, was launched in 2006 as a living laboratory for sustainable urban technologies. It is one of the first projects in the Middle East aimed at a master-planned, zero-carbon, sustainable and smart settlement (Cugurullo 2013). As part of the government of Abu Dhabi's long-term development agenda of Vision 2030, targeting a move from petro-urbanism to urban sustainability, Abu Dhabi created the Abu Dhabi Future Energy Company (commonly known as Masdar) in 2006 and took its first steps in the multifaceted world of sustainable development, with Masdar smart city development being the core initiative. Construction began in 2008 and the first stage of development was completed in 2011. Soon after, Masdar claimed to be the largest planned development in the world intending to rely on renewable energy sources for its entire energy balance. Today, the city is seen as an emerging global clean technology cluster located on one of the world's most challenging geographies and fighting for a sustainable urban development powered by renewable energy. According to Sgouridis and Kennedy (2010), when the city is completed in 2025 the energy needs of its 50,000 residents, 1,500 clean-tech companies, start-ups staffed by 10,000 new employees, research university (Masdar Institute of Science and Technology, MIST) and 60,000 daily commuting workers will be generated on site through a portfolio of energy sources, including rooftop photovoltaics (PV), concentrated solar thermal power plants (CSP), evacuated tube solar thermal collectors, geothermal sources, the world's largest hydrogen plant and a waste-to-energy facility. Moreover, according to the plans, residents will rely on an electrified mass transit system (i.e. light rail transit) for intercity connections and a combination of walking, cycling and automated electric taxis (i.e. personal rapid transit) for intra-city connectivity. As stated by Kingsley (2013), Masdar is powered by a 22-hectare field of 87,777 solar panels with more on the roofs of the buildings. Cars are planned to be replaced by a series of driverless electric vehicles. The design of the walls of the buildings reduces demand for air conditioning by 55 per cent. Buildings have no light switches or taps, just movement sensors that cut electricity consumption by 51 per cent and water usage by 55 per cent. Through this project, Abu Dhabi aims to gain a foothold in the global alternative energy industry and transition Abu Dhabi from technology consumer to technology producer, while positioning itself as an alternative energy thought leader along the way (Hopwood 2010).

Although most of these ideas to develop Masdar into a truly smart and sustainable city were innovative and ambitious, not so many of them could find an application at the city scale. For instance, the automated personal rapid transit, which is the flagship feature of Masdar's car-free strategy, has been discarded due to technology not being able to meet the city's transport needs. There are also delays in the development of the planned light rail network and metro system. Additionally, the planners realised that construction of large solar panels would be less effective than anticipated due to local dust storms, which are reducing solar power output by at least 40 per cent (Crot 2013). Similarly, the hydrogen power plant project, a joint venture of BP Alternative Energy and Rio Tinto, was placed on hold in Abu Dhabi due to a lack of resources and a change in the project's priorities (CCST 2015). These downgrades, due either to technology miscalculations or the economic downturn, pushed the city administration to change the city brand from 'zero-carbon' to 'carbon-neutral'. Perhaps in the midst of these disappointments, MIST (also known as Masdar Institute) can be introduced as one of the most promising initiatives of the Masdar smart city project.

As much as building a smart city that is more sustainable and more energy efficient, the idea behind Masdar was to investigate the future of sustainable living and look at the science behind it. For that reason, it was crucial to establish a world-class research institute in Masdar. Developed in cooperation with the Massachusetts Institute of Technology (MIT) in 2009, the MIST is a postgraduate-level research university focused on the science and engineering of advanced renewable energy, environmental technologies and sustainability. MIST is the nucleus of the R&D activities in Masdar and plays a major role in developing and trailing technology solutions for the smart city. Designed by Fosters + Partners, MIST's green building is a test bed for technologies that will help Masdar achieve its carbon-neutral, zero waste and clean-power goals. The building uses 70 per cent less electricity and potable water than conventional buildings of its size. It is wired throughout with an energy metering system that monitors energy consumption and produces data that are easily accessible to students and researchers for use as a research tool (Mezher *et al.* 2011). The faculty is engaged in over 300 joint projects with academia, private enterprises and government agencies on renewable energy, smart grids and smart buildings, energy policy and planning, water use, environmental engineering and electronics research to address clean and affordable energy, equitable access to water, a robust and healthy environment, and sustainable economic development challenges for the city (Masdar Institute 2015).

So far, Masdar has performed best in the environmental domain of sustainable development. As well as smart urban technology use, another reason for the success was replicating the traditional Arabic urban form, such as the city's shape, orientation of its streets, wind catcher, courtyard, the pattern of streets, and density and mixed use. In a recently published research article, Hassan *et al.* (2015) compare urban form attributes of the medieval Cairo with the modern Masdar. The study reveals that the success of Masdar lies in pursuing, learning and including the key characteristics of traditional Arab city form and the historic urban experience, developed over centuries in the region. Unlike the skyscrapers of the region's other cities, e.g. Dubai and Doha, Masdar does not have any high-rise buildings. However, as stated by Cugurullo (2015: 13), 'the way sustainability is expressed in Masdar City associates environmentalism with consumerism'. Although Masdar is one of the first attempts at constructing carbon-neutral cities, it creates hope for the development of an environmentally sustainable smart city. However, the Masdar project is not economically feasible. The project is initiated and continuously supported by funding from the Emirate hoping that by developing, integrating and commercialising clean technologies, the project will capitalise on environmental concerns to generate profit (Cugurullo 2015). Nevertheless, the project has not been able to attract as many innovative industries as had been hoped for following the impacts of the global financial crisis. This has forced Masdar to scale back its budget and ambitions (Kingsley 2013). Even though the project is scaled back, the leadership of Abu Dhabi still remains convinced that building a knowledge-based economy in renewable energy is the right trajectory (Mezher *et al.* 2010).

At the conception stage of the Masdar project, challenges were mostly economy-driven meaning that the focus of Masdar was too much on the economic aspects of sustainability. However, today these challenges are expanded to include: natural resource depletion, population growth, climate change and the Arab Spring (Cugurullo 2015). Similarly to the exemplar cases investigated from South East Asia, Masdar does not currently have any affordable housing, meaning that the city is for the affluent to live in, and most of the city's workforce drive to their jobs. Additionally, the economic targets of Masdar are shaped to the advantage of a small group of already privileged people in Abu Dhabi. In the urban plan of the Masdar City, only 20 per cent of the accommodation areas are assigned to low-income workers due to the council's planning code requirements. Despite the frequent presence in the vision of the concepts of social justice and equity, along with social sustainability, the city only reserves a small area for underprivileged groups. This indicates that the project is not as socially sustainable as it is claimed to be (Cugurullo 2013). Furthermore, Mezher *et al.* (2010) suggest that in order to ensure social prosperity in Abu Dhabi, all stakeholders (i.e. government institutions, private sectors, NGOs, public and universities) must be engaged in direct coordination and collaboration to develop the right energy policies and incentives to invest in projects, ensure the funding is available for R&D, put in place the needed market mechanisms for diffusing renewable energy technologies and build public awareness.

Istanbul, Turkey

Istanbul is literally a bridging city between two continents, i.e. Europe and Asia. This unique geographic position has impacted the cultural features of both the city and its residents. The city is widely considered as a European city. However, due to the urban and infrastructure development model adopted and followed by the city administration since 1990s, particularly envying Dubai (Colak 2012; Yigitcanlar and Bulu 2015), the city showcases smart city initiatives similar to those of the Middle East and the emerging economies of the world. For this reason, the city is investigated under the smart city initiatives of the Middle East.

Since the 1980s in particular, the metropolitan city of Istanbul has been struggling to meet the steeply rising demand for urban services, due to an increasing population, which today stands at over 15 million. This vast population has generated serious problems, including deficiencies in the city's amenities (i.e. inefficient waste and sewage collection, and telecommunication and water distribution services), dilapidation of historic neighbourhoods, sprawl-related environmental degradation (i.e. air-water-soil pollution and deforestation) and traffic congestion and accidents due to heavy motor vehicle dependency (Kocabas 2006; Baz et al. 2009; Gunay and Dokmeci 2012; Yalçintaş et al. 2015). After the 1999 earthquake, which caused the deaths of about 30,000 people in the region, Istanbul has decided to face the challenge of better managing the city through implementing smart city concepts in its metropolitan area. As part of the smart city agenda, since the 1990s new urban policies have been introduced aimed at addressing major infrastructural issues, initiating productivity-increasing measures and total quality management frameworks, and providing incentives to industries and businesses (Yigitcanlar and Bulu 2015). Local councils in Istanbul started to use urban information systems effectively for urban development control and monitoring of Istanbul's acute pollution, sewage, water and waste collection problems (Bulu et al. 2014). Although, Istanbul has been investing in most of the abovementioned problematic areas through smart urban technology use, so far the most promising smart city initiatives focus on transport and safety applications.

Istanbul has one of the largest public transport systems in the world and the biggest in Europe. The system is heavily bus-oriented due to the relatively lower cost of bus infrastructure development, although there is an expanding train, metro/subway and ferry network in the city. About four million passengers daily make use of over 5,500 city buses for their transport needs, whether it is for commuting, leisure, shopping or education purposes. According to Bulu et al. (2014):

[d]espite each bus line having a fixed time schedule, it is virtually impossible for bus drivers to adhere to these schedules due to unpredictable traffic congestion as well as weather conditions . . . Significant deviations from planned arrival times at bus stops cause tremendous frustration and dissatisfaction for passengers.

(Bulu *et al.* 2014: 5631)

This issue has led to the development of a public transport travel time prediction system, generating short-term predictions of the arrival of a bus at down-stream stops based on historical and current traffic data. As part of this project, some of the more than 10,000 bus stops in Istanbul are equipped with LCD screens displaying predicted arrival times of buses in real time. So-called 'smart bus stops', these also include functions such as LED lighting that saves energy of up to 75 per cent and mobile phone integration to provide simultaneous information regarding routes and bus schedules (Ozdemir 2015).

A fully adaptive traffic control system is another smart city application for Istanbul. In the city, there are over 1,600 signalised intersections that are connected to a traffic management centre and remotely controlled. In this system, traffic light durations are determined dynamically in real time by optimising the intersections' green/amber/red signal times based on parameters such as traffic volume and queue in order to minimise the average delays and number of stops. According to Bulu *et al.* (2014), this system decreases vehicular delay by up to 30 per cent and saves $400 in fuel cost per hour at signalised intersections. It also helps in reducing total travel times on the traffic road network and traffic jams, resulting in increased driving comfort.

Since 2012, IBM, which claims to be a knowledge base that spans over 2,000 smart cities projects (Townsend 2013), has been working in partnership with Istanbul transportation authority and Vodafone to build an understanding of where public transportation is required, using the privacy protected data collected from the mobile phone network. The project is entitled 'Istanbul in Motion'. The purpose of the project is to generate required analytics to provide new insights to city administrators, helping them to better understand how people move throughout the city and enabling them to more effectively improve city infrastructure, and private and public transportation systems. In other words, the goal of the project is to lay out bus routes to move people closer to where they actually want to be. This will eventually improve traffic flow, public safety decisions, fuel conservation and cost effectiveness, resulting in healthier living conditions for residents and an attractive location for businesses (IBM 2015b).

Due to the dramatic 1999 earthquake, the city prioritised earthquake-related smart projects. Istanbul Gas Distribution Company, in collaboration with the Turkish Scientific and Technological Research Council, developed a smart city safety application. This application is designed to diagnose real-time seismic activities using about 120 earthquake sensors located in and around the city and act in the case of an earthquake hazard. The system acquires earth movement data as well as corresponding movements in seabed and temperature change in seawater as input parameters. The application processes collected real-time information with an embedded rule-based algorithm, and this expert system determines when it is necessary to shut off the gas distribution to a district or the entire city. This sensor-based system for emergency shut off of natural gas during an earthquake provides significant benefits in emergency situations in earthquake-prone cities, such as Istanbul (Bulu *et al.* 2014).

Istanbul, so far, has tried to address its two major problems, traffic and earthquake hazards, through several smart city initiatives. Although the city has progressed in developing and adopting useful smart urban applications, the smart city concept has only been seen as technology tools to prevent or ease some of the limited urban problems. A broader perception of the concept is needed among the city administration to also look at the societal, environmental and also economic dimensions of the smart city formation. Considering Istanbul is following in the footsteps of Dubai to create an urban revolution by constructing mega projects, such as the under and over Istanbul Channel crossings, building Europe's largest airport, and urban renewal and transformation and new town development projects, the limited application of smart technologies to provide sustainable solutions for the city and citizens is a major disappointment. Furthermore, a magnificent city with a millennia-long history could offer its over 10 million tourists annually, smart solutions that could help them navigate their way in and around the historical quarters of the city, while obtaining information on the colourful past of Istanbul through, for instance, mobile augmented reality technology.

Furthermore, the city should consider investing in suitable smart technologies that encourage citizens to engage in local planning and environmental debates, and create awareness on the critical issues, e.g. sustainable practices (Townsend 2013). For instance, the city could develop city or neighbourhood dashboards accessible via computers, smart phones and public displays located in urban squares. It could also further develop the aforementioned smart public transport stops, or vehicles could be linked to these dashboards. In this regard, Istanbul could adopt successful initiatives from Amsterdam, Boston, Chicago and Seoul.

Smart city initiatives from North and South America

The regional context of North and South America provide a vibrant setting for the smart cities initiatives with their old and new cities embracing technology, ubiquitous transit, green infrastructure and support for entrepreneurial ecosystems (Cohen 2012; Reis 2014). A number of cities and their districts in this region have already adopted smart urban technologies, infrastructures and services, with the aim of becoming a smart city or society and maintaining a scientific-technological position of excellence via ensuring and expanding economic competitiveness to transform and modernise their societies and cities (Yigitcanlar and Lee 2014). Successful examples come from Boston, Chattanooga, Chicago, New York, Portland, San Francisco, San Jose, Seattle, Washington DC (United States); Montreal, Toronto, Vancouver (Canada); Monterrey (Mexico); Santiago (Chile); Bogota, Medellin (Colombia); Buenos Aires (Argentina); and Curitiba, Rio de

Janeiro and Sao Paulo (Brazil). Similar to European smart cities, most of the abovementioned cities in this region have adopted urban retrofitting as the main approach in the transformation of their cities into smart and sustainable ones. Among the many initiatives from the region, this section explores Rio de Janeiro from Brazil and San Francisco from the United States.

Rio de Janeiro, Brazil

Brazilian cities have experienced chaos, dissent and grassroots improvisation as a result of a century-long struggle to deal with their cruel social and economic problems (Townsend 2013). Like most other Brazilian cities, Rio de Janeiro also faces many major economic (e.g. income inequality and high poverty), societal (e.g. slums called favelas and high crime rates), environmental (e.g. sudden rain and massive landslides) and governance issues (e.g. mismanagement and corruption cases). However, Rio de Janeiro has chosen to adopt the smart cities model as a way of dealing with them appropriately (Singer 2012). As part of this model, the Rio de Janeiro local government opened its Intelligent Operations Center in 2010, with the centre's system having been designed by IBM. The centre has an overall vision of promoting effective and efficient policies through the use of technology and connectivity to deal with the city's major challenges. The centre developed most of its projects in partnership with international technology companies IBM, Cisco and Samsung and Brazil's largest telecommunication company, Oi (formerly known as Telemar). Rio de Janeiro was fortunate enough to use a substantial monetary investment resulting from the city's selection to host the 2014 World Cup and the 2016 Summer Olympics to embark on an ambitious program to connect multiple systems to improve the city's acute infrastructure problems.

The centre's first task was the development of 'safety and emergency response system', a crime control system and a custom flood forecast system, with real-time automated command-and-control of safety and emergency responses. This city-wide safety and emergency response system integrates data from over 30 public agencies, serving primarily safety and transport functions, and uses integrated business analytics and intelligence with predictive trend analysis. These systems provide city authorities with access to data and information from most of the urban amenities and services, such as traffic and public transport, municipal and utility services, emergency services, weather feeds and the power grid. The centre receives video feeds from over 500 surveillance cameras installed in and around the city. The centre also collects dynamic data from weather sensors, video surveillance and field personnel, overlaid on a comprehensive GIS, and relevant departments from the local government access this information simultaneously. According to Kitchin (2014), at the centre:

> [a]lgorithms and a team of analysts process, visualise, analyse and monitor a vast amount of live service data, alongside data aggregated over time and huge volumes of administration data that are released on a more periodic

basis, often mashing the datasets together to investigate particular aspects of city life and change over time, and to build predictive models with respect to everyday city development and management and disaster situations such as flooding.

(Kitchin 2014: 6)

Moreover, as these systems evolve, researchers can integrate data from transportation systems, buildings and possibly energy, water and other subsystems into the centre to create a true closed-loop system (Naphade *et al.* 2011). In consequence, through the use of these systems, policymakers of Rio de Janeiro are now able to make more coordinated, intelligent, informed and prompt decisions (Angelidou 2015). These decisions and planned actions result in increased health and safety outcomes. For instance, in 2012, during the months of heavy rainfall, actions coordinated by the centre helped ensure zero casualties related to floods or landslides. Reports from that year also indicate that the interchange of intelligence between the city's departments resulted in a 25 per cent decrease in the time taken to respond to traffic accidents (Innovation Norway 2015). Furthermore, it is predicted that Rio de Janeiro's smart platforms will soon be able to gather data on all incidents and events occurring in the city. This means that operators of the centre will soon be given access to an unblinking eye monitoring the city, so that governmental and public employees can anticipate events in time to provide efficient responses (IBM 2010).

Another smart city service example from Rio de Janeiro was developed by the city's electricity distributor, Ampla. In 2003, Ampla began to roll out smart meters as part of a pilot, so-called Rede DAT. These smart meters communicated consumption by households to the utility over a mobile network, and users received the consumption figures to their mobile phone. This pilot application proved the usefulness of smart meter systems as losses from energy theft reduced by more than 50 per cent, the number of supply interruptions decreased by over 40 per cent and it resulted in lower operational costs. After the success of the pilot, a wider rollout took place in Rio de Janeiro (CAICT 2016). Most recently, Rio de Janeiro has made an agreement with Landis+Gyr to expand the smart meter systems of the city, which provide a two-way flow of data between customer meters and utility back-end systems.

The city of Rio de Janeiro has showcased the promising impact of data and system integration along with new technology using smart meters to push towards a smart city vision. At present, the Intelligent Operations Center has about a dozen different control centres managing the city's critical infrastructure, i.e. electricity, water, oil, gas, public transportation, urban traffic, air quality and airports (Salunkhe 2015). Although so far smart city applications have proved useful for the city, the critical question in the case of Rio de Janeiro, which also applies to the previously investigated case of Istanbul, is whether the smart city model that has proved successful in a few applications can be expanded to work in most of the city's infrastructure, amenity and service operations in this large and highly problematic city.

San Francisco, United States

The San Francisco Bay Area in general, including the major cities and metropolitan areas of San Francisco, Oakland and San Jose, and San Francisco in particular, are renowned among global trendsetters when it comes to smart urban technology initiatives. San Francisco sees smart city strategies as an important method to build its sustainable urban future. Primarily, San Francisco's high concentration of talent base, strong entrepreneurial culture and close proximity to the world's most innovative technology cluster, i.e. Silicon Valley, all contribute to the establishment of an urban ecosystem in the city that accelerates smart and sustainable urban outcomes. Since the start of the twenty-first century, many Silicon Valley-based companies have made a move to base their headquarters in San Francisco, due to the high quality of life and place offerings to companies' talented staff, along with affordability and tax benefits available. Today, the city is home to a large number of internet-based companies, e.g. Twitter, Dropbox, Uber and Yammer (Maleady 2015). San Francisco provides its residents with a large number of free Wi-Fi hotspots in various public locations, funded by Google. For example, on a main road downtown, Market Street, there is about a five kilometre-long free Wi-Fi zone. The main goal of this free Wi-Fi project is to support the broader vision of establishing connectivity for the city as a whole, bridging the digital divide and ensuring that diverse communities have access to innovation (Steinmetz 2014).

San Francisco is widely acknowledged as a leader in embracing sustainability and smart urban development, as the city excels in green and sustainability initiatives. The city has an ambitious goal of achieving zero waste by 2020, sending nothing to landfill. San Francisco's recycling program mandates residents to separate their garbage into recycling, compost and landfill wastes. In order to reduce waste and increase access to recycling and composting, the city introduced a number of smart city initiatives. The first of these initiatives is called 'RecycleWhere', an open source software and an open data model to provide localised and accurate results. This online tool provides residents with the latest and most convenient recycling, reuse and disposal options for plastics, batteries, fluorescent lights, televisions, couches and so on. The second one is the 'Zero Waster Signmaker'. With this online tool, residents and business owners can make their own compost, recycling and landfill signs for their homes or businesses. As a result of the policy and initiatives, the city has reached an 80 per cent waste diversion rate (SF Environment 2012).

San Francisco's other ambitious goal is reducing greenhouse gas emissions by 25 per cent from 1990 levels by 2017 and becoming a carbon-free city by 2030. The city has implemented a number of incentive programs to improve the performance of new and existing buildings. The following are among the smart technology applications used to achieve this goal. 'SF Energy Map' is a tool that tracks the solar and wind installations across the city. With this application, residents and businesses can check the solar potential of their own roof and also access various rebates provided by the government. The 'Energy Use Challenge' application is a vehicle for residents to submit their ideas to encourage other residents to share their energy bill data, where this data can be used to enhance programs and policies that promote energy efficiency. 'Honest Buildings' is a software platform that focuses on buildings to help them save energy. This online portal informs property owners, managers and tenants about their building's sustainability performance and provides the most effective energy efficiency strategies to help them reduce utility costs. 'SFpark' is an application to improve parking in San Francisco by collecting and distributing real-time information about where parking is available, so drivers can quickly find open spaces. In this way, traffic congestion can be avoided or eased, less energy is consumed and therefore fewer pollutants are released into the atmosphere. 'ChargePoint' is an application to help track the usage and functional status of electric vehicle charging stations. It provides the real-time status of the chargers, generates long-term reports, helps the city to establish a charger demand mechanism and determines where chargers should be located in the future (SF Environment 2012). As a result of the policies and applications, San Francisco is 41 per cent renewable energy powered, and the city houses over 300 Leadership in Energy and Environmental Design (LEED) certified buildings (Cohen 2013). In addition, citizens are encouraged to participate in energy conservation with mobile and web access to precise and near real-time energy use data. They also receive advice on how they can save money and support the environment. Moreover, with over 100 charging stations, the city promotes the use of hybrid and electric cars and brings down the motor vehicle-related pollution and greenhouse gas emissions (Reis 2014).

Another important development that supports the smart city formation of San Francisco is the open data legislation that was passed in 2009. This pioneering legislation has made all city departments provide public access to all non-confidential datasets through the city's e-government portal, namely DataSF (https://data.sfgov.org). A number of apps use the open data source provided through DataSF. For instance, the 'Metro San Francisco' app is used to inform travellers of the location of their bus or train in San Francisco; the 'Transit Bay' app assists blind or visually impaired travellers to navigate the city's transit systems; and the 'Walkonomics' app rates and maps the pedestrian-friendliness of streets and urban areas of San Francisco (SF Environment 2012).

Today, San Francisco is considered one of the greenest cities and the clean technology capital of North America. The city has various smart city support mechanisms for its clean technology and innovation firms that eventually contribute to the city's economic development, neighbourhood revitalisation and sustainable operations. For example, the 'Living Innovation Zones' project helps businesses transform prototypes into products and services by designating permanent and temporary zones throughout the city where businesses can use city assets to demonstrate new and emerging technologies. Furthermore, 'smart grid' and 'LED streetlight conversion' projects help the city save energy and use lighting more efficiently (SF Environment 2012).

A critical evaluation of the functions and effectiveness of the smart city framework of San Francisco by Lee *et al.* (2014) indicate the following key characteristics and issues of the city's twist on smart urban technology utilisation:

- *Urban openness*: most services are location-based (GPS) combined with conventional services; few participatory services run on innovation platform; most are unidirectional (79.4 per cent); services analyse civic issues, identifying and resolving problems (e.g. Improve SF); participation and engagement levels are very high; entrepreneurial community is strongly motivated to join in; cultural features mean participants 'self-incentivise'; there is open transparency and user-sourced innovation; a wider range of open APIs including in location services, ethics, public administration and finance (top three domains by data usage); an open data platform, 'DataSF'; agencies willing to share data with public thanks to open access movement; and the city supports demands for greater data accessibility;
- *Service innovation*: services offered mostly in restricted domains (transportation, crime and disaster prevention, and tourism and leisure); transportation has highest number of services since transport agency is recognised as early adopter of open data; bottom-up approach using open APIs means some service duplication; 75 per cent of services run on a single service platform; and integration in same domains (transportation), integrated single entry point for over 300 services is an opportunity;
- *Partnership formation*: private sector develops services based on open data (50 per cent services); efficient market-oriented/organic approach involves direct implementation of approved technology (e.g. AMI); and innovation mechanisms target creation of self-sustaining service ecosystem;
- *Urban pro-activeness*: dominant intelligent technology based on GPS; most services sense user's location based on such sensors (55 per cent services); intelligent analytical tools based on real-time and integrated transportation services, such as Routesy SF (real-time prediction), SFPark (demand responsive pricing) and Cycle Track (Big Data); no significant investment in intelligent infrastructure; 44 per cent of services have green impacts (relate to sustainability); services mash up data with GIS mapping to promote public awareness on solar and wind energy (e.g. urban eco-map); implementing AMI for electricity, gas and water for energy monitoring; and reach over 4,000 businesses saving them an average of $4,500 per annum, resulting in 40,000 tons of local carbon reduction;
- *Smart city infrastructure integration*: high multiple platform accessibility (47 per cent of services), dominant single platform IOS (63 per cent); city's network currently under-utilised despite 10Gbps availability; and facility, equipment and staff consolidation plans ongoing, as yet no budgetary approval;
- *Smart city governance*: leadership decentralised, different agencies promote smart development and recent expansion in city hall team; recently appointed chief innovation officer in the office of civic innovation; currently defining smart strategy, dedicated org. team will take over from IT division currently responsible for internal IT resource management; currently providing non-mandatory guidance for each city agency; and decentralised agency-based decision making for smart initiatives allows for organic growth.

Finally, on 14 September 2015, the Obama Administration announced a new 'Smart Cities Initiative' to invest over $160 million in federal research and leverage more than 25 new technology collaborations to help local communities tackle key challenges, such as reducing traffic congestion, fighting crime, fostering economic growth, managing the effects of the changing climate and improving the delivery of city services (The White House 2015). This federal-level investment underlines the importance of the smart cities movement and will most likely result in many other successful initiatives from the United States.

Smart city initiatives from Oceania

The Oceania is another region with various interests and applications in smart city initiatives. Cities of Australia and New Zealand from this region generally offer a very high quality of life and place. However, these cities in general provide poor access to quality, efficient and green public transit options and are often highly contained with sprawling development. As a remedy to these problems, some promising smart city initiatives from this geographical context are underway. Leading examples include Auckland, Dunedin, Wellington (New Zealand); and Adelaide, Brisbane, Parramatta, Perth and Townsville (Australia). Similar to European smart cities, most of the cities of this region have adopted urban retrofitting as the main approach in the transformation of their cities into smart and sustainable ones. However, particularly in Australia, due to the 2008 global financial crisis and the end of the mining and energy boom, local governments have been overly cautious about whether the financial commitment to technology infrastructure is worthwhile, considering their possible short- to medium-term returns. Furthermore, the lengthy political and industry debates that lasted for a number of years delayed the start of the development and thus the completion of the national broadband network (NBN) project, offering up to 100 Mbps download and 40 Mbps upload speeds. At present, the coverage of the NBN project is very limited; this service is only available to small parts of the capital cities, and the remainder are served with ADSL2+, which at best provides up to 24 Mbps download and 1.4 Mbps upload speeds. At the current rate of NBN rollout, the project may take more than 20 years to cover the whole country (Tucker and Branch 2013). This would cause a major disadvantage to Australia's competitiveness in the digital economy (Bowles and Wilson 2012) and, in particular, will also leave the regional or rural parts of the country behind, potentially resulting in the widening of the digital divide in the nation. Among a number of smart city initiatives from the region, this section explores Auckland from New Zealand and Brisbane from Australia.

Auckland, New Zealand

In spite of its remoteness from anywhere else on the globe besides Australia, Auckland's high quality urban and natural environments, social inclusion and low crime rates make the city one of the world's most liveable urban localities.

In the 2015 Mercer Quality of Living Rankings, Auckland took third place. However, international and domestic migration is causing rapid population growth and turning Auckland into a sprawling city like Los Angeles. The city's current population is about 1.4 million and is expected to reach over 2 million by the 2030s (Zovanyi 2004). Such growth has created serious concerns about urban sustainability and its possible reflections on the quality of life and place, and the liveability achievements of the city. These concerns have pushed city officials to search for innovative solutions. Consequently, during the last few years, Auckland decided to develop effective smart growth strategies and invest in smart urban technologies. Different from many other previously investigated cities, i.e. Istanbul and Rio de Janeiro, Auckland has linked its smart city agenda to the innovation system portfolio (Chen 2012; Auckland Council 2014b).

In order to deal with the growth-related challenges, the overall idea was to turn the city into an internationally recognised, reputable innovation hub. Under the wings of innovation and smart city agendas, the city has recently launched the 'CityNext platform' for Auckland in partnership with Microsoft. The platform offers to transform the municipal government and support innovation through the use of smart urban technologies, cloud and Big Data in a number of areas including transportation, energy and buildings. The CityNext platform has so far produced a large number of initiatives. For instance, in the transport area these initiatives range from smart bridges to new bike lanes to massive rail tunnels to improve transportation infrastructure and transit services for current and future Aucklanders. The project costs and affordability of these services were among the major considerations, in particularly for these projects not to become a big burden for tax payers. They also needed to ensure high take-up/patronage/user rates.

Besides the CityNext platform, the City of Auckland has also developed other plans and smart urban technology applications to become a thriving smart and sustainable city by capitalising on five areas of intervention in particular, i.e. energy, transport, waste, built environment (roads, buildings and parks among others) and food, agriculture and natural carbon sink (Auckland Council 2014a).

In terms of smart transport applications, a good example is the Auckland Transport Authority's new transportation service applications, such as reporting potholes from a smartphone and providing information and feedback to transit system employees that help them work more productively (Jones 2015). Another is the Auckland Integrated Fares System project (Auckland Council 2014b). This project creates an integrated smartcard ticketing system for Auckland that can be used on all modes of Auckland's public transport system. Auckland's smartcards can also be used to pay for lots of everyday items, such as a coffee at selected participating retail outlets (see www.athop.co.nz). Furthermore, smart parking applications in Auckland, such as SmartGuide, SmartRep and SmartEye, help overcome the difficulties faced by drivers looking for a vacant parking space in the city's busiest car parks in the central business district, the civic, downtown and Victoria Street (see http://www.smartparking.com).

As for waste treatment systems, Watercare, Auckland Council's water provider, produces biogas by treating biosolids removed in the wastewater treatment process separately. The recycling process in turn provides about 60 per cent of the plant's energy needs, which also helps the city to meet its environmental sustainability targets. Additionally, the latest developments in laser scanning allow Watercare to accurately measure the internal diameter of the pipes in Auckland's networks. Watercare uses this data to assess corrosion and plan maintenance and asset/infrastructure replacement programs, and efficiently prioritise capital expenditure (Auckland Council 2014b).

In terms of public health and food safety, the Auckland-based company, AsureQuality's, innovative initiative 'inSight' lets consumers use their smartphone to scan QR codes (quick response code) on food product labels to view independently verified information and thus make buying decisions based on attributes important to them. The information includes origin, nutrition data, social, ethical and environmental claims and what they mean, and the safety and quality systems used in production (see www.asurequality.com). Another example is an animated 3D game called SPARX funded by the New Zealand Ministry of Health and developed by Metia Interactive to help teenagers deal with depression (Auckland Council 2014b). Users of the game learn real-life skills by solving challenges to rid a fantasy world of gloom and negativity (see https://www.sparx.org.nz).

As for digital learning and skills development, the Manaiakalani Education Trust was set up in 2011 to improve learning outcomes across schools in the region. The trust has enabled access and equipped over 3,000 students with the tools needed to become digital citizens, ready for employment in tomorrow's digital workplace (Auckland Council 2014b). In this program, 2,500 devices are being used daily in 120 digital education classes, and a community wireless infrastructure was also set up for 3,000 homes so that children can use their devices at home (see www.manaiakalani.org).

The strength of Auckland's smart city program comes from establishing a strong linkage between the different portfolios of the city, such as planning and development, and innovation and industries. Additionally, the city aims to utilise smart urban technologies not only for accommodating the service needs of the increasing population by considering and minimising their environmental impacts but also (i) incorporating these technology solutions for skill development; (ii) promoting technology as a cross-sector enabler of innovation; (iii) growing Auckland's base of innovation-led enterprise; and (iv) stepping into the knowledge economy with its businesses and people. The sensitivity and the efforts on cost and benefit balance for the society, are also noteworthy. Nevertheless, the compact city direction for Auckland has its risks and challenges ahead as well. For instance, although it is generally considered a more sustainable urban form than sprawling development, the compact city direction guarantees congestion, reduces green space, increases property prices dramatically, causes affordability issues and concentrates urban pollution. Perhaps a middle way would be to also have a planned and controlled medium-density suburban development, i.e. smart suburbs or satellite smart cities. After all, a smart city is a holistic blend of planning unique to that place, which is underpinned by people and smart technologies in order to protect and grow an urban ecosystem with balanced and well-governed economic, societal and environmental priorities.

Brisbane, Australia

There are a number of successful initiatives from Australia aimed at establishing globally leading smart cities through the creation of innovation hubs to test technology that would enhance the city's transport, healthcare, education and utility services. For instance, Adelaide City Council, the South Australian Government and Cisco are in partnership to develop smart city applications in Adelaide (Hall 2014). Similarly, IBM provided a grant for Townsville to meet the smart cities' challenge through sustainability projects and activities in partnerships between Ergon Energy, consortium/business partners, the city council and IBM (Townsville City Council 2015). Additionally, Sydney, Melbourne and Perth are progressing well on their smart and sustainable city initiatives. However, the earliest and most comprehensive smart city initiative of Australia comes from Brisbane. The smart city journey of the 'Down Under's' subtropical city, Brisbane, was initiated with the enactment of the Smart State Strategy in 2005. During his tenure as the 36th Premier of Queensland, Peter Beattie drove a government investment ideology centred on a vision for a diversified state knowledge economy, Smart Queensland. The cornerstone for the Smart State vision was the 'Smart Queensland: Smart State Strategy 2005–2015', which was founded on three ideals, i.e. capitalising on Queensland's unique strengths, establishing collaborations and promoting knowledge, creativity and innovation (DET 2005). The Smart State Strategy, over time, effectively leveraged the State's growth and demand for significant knowledge-based urban and infrastructure development to create future domestic capability and interregional comparative advantage. Since 2005, the Smart State Strategy generated several spin-off knowledge-based urban development (KBUD) policy and plan initiatives, including 'Smart Cities Policy' in 2007, 'Smart Communities Pilot Guide' in 2009, 'Herston Health Precinct Smart Community' and 'Dutton Park Knowledge Precinct Plans' in 2012.

The smart cities policy was an applied economic development and land-use macro plan for Brisbane, the capital city of Queensland, as the nucleus for Smart State. Prepared in 2007 by a working group, the so-called 'Smart State Council' chaired by Michael Rayner, Director of Cox Rayner Architects, the smart cities policy was in essence an innovative sub-regional scaled development strategy for what subsequently became branded as 'Brisbane's Knowledge Corridor'. This was a collective spine of tertiary campuses, research precincts and cultural/creative facilities within Brisbane's inner city (DPC 2007). The smart cities policy was a deliberate exercise conducted by the Smart State Council to leverage the state's significant investment in knowledge infrastructure by outlining an urban development framework to focus land-use planning around economic centres of knowledge activity. Consistent with the best practice KBUD principles, the smart cities policy draws on key themes of smart city-building principles, i.e. the development of world-class transport, diversity of housing choices, high amenity inner city precincts and, most importantly, filling a gap in city planning and local area planning.

The smart cities policy recommends eight 'smart city strategies' to catalyse Brisbane as a globally recognised and significant smart city: (i) creating a legible structure plan; (ii) uniting disparate precincts; (iii) creating definitive pedestrian spines; (iv) linking the city centre by mass transit; (v) defining a knowledge corridor; (vi) investing in sustainability; (vii) developing effective planning processes; and (viii) developing a smart city model. Constituting a mix of marketing, transport planning, community engagement and land-use planning activities, these strategies were sufficient to inspire Brisbane's resident knowledge corridor institutions and policymakers to begin to understand deliberate KBUD-related panning activities (DPC 2007).

Taking their remit from Smart State Strategy, the Smart State Council embodied exemplary elements of governance theory for knowledge economies. This forum of multidisciplinary volunteers ensured altruism governed policy development. Prioritisation of initiatives, which were presented as case studies, further cross-germinated a knowledge economy discourse in Queensland's influential industry leaders. It is important to note that the smart cities policy was a strategy only and not attached to any investment funds or statutory plans. This made the policy quite unusable. However, its benefits lay in the awareness and discussion it brought about regarding land-use planning and integrating Brisbane's four super knowledge precincts, i.e. Woolloongabba, Herston, South Brisbane and City West (Yigitcanlar and Velibeyoglu 2008). Under the Planning Act, Queensland's university, hospital and other significant centres of community infrastructure are legislated by schedule as 'community infrastructure designations'. These designations are significant state infrastructure precincts that are effectively removed from local area planning schemes. They are regulated by a shareholding minister for the purpose of ensuring that state interests are protected and development assessment and approval are controlled. While this ensures significant investment in institutions, such as hospitals, can be facilitated expeditiously, traditionally it has led to poor urban planning outcomes on these sites, particularly in Brisbane, as insular campus style development frameworks are adopted rather than best practice city precinct planning with inviting and interactive edges.

The smart cities policy was the first instance in Queensland's short planning history in which a strategic plan sought to re-interrogate the *raison d'être* style of thinking for development at its knowledge centres and also more importantly connect them into a unified corridor. It is important to contextualise the significance of this assertion. Brisbane's Knowledge Corridor encompasses about a dozen distinct knowledge precincts, hubs of smart urban technology development and utilisation featuring over 60 individual institutes, with the northern and southern anchors being the Royal Brisbane and Women's Hospital and the Princess Alexandra Hospital, and tertiary campuses alone hosting over 25,000 knowledge workers. Precincts of this scale, even in isolation, generate cyclical serendipities and aggregate a critical mass of internationally significant leaders. Today, the knowledge corridor is highly active, and Brisbane's knowledge community precincts are gaining international recognition, turning the city into a world-class smart city (Yigitcanlar *et al.* 2016).

Following the success of the smart cities policy, in 2009 Brisbane City Council launched 'CitySmart' (see www.citysmart.com.au) to help make Brisbane Australia's most sustainable city. Unlike the previous policy, CitySmart is financially supported to deliver projects. Over $300 million (approximately USD 210 million) is designated to contribute to Brisbane's economic growth and make the city smarter and more sustainable. Major CitySmart projects include: Australia's first district cooling energy system to provide cheaper/more efficient air conditioning for CBD buildings; 'Reduce Your Juice', an energy efficiency program tailored specifically for our city's low-income young adults; 'Queensland Watt Savers', which supplies more than 300 SMEs with easy-to-use tools and expertise to reduce energy consumption and related expenses; 'EzyGreen', a residential energy reduction program, which engaged 61,000 Brisbane households to save over $10 million (approximately USD 7 million) in annual energy costs; and the city's first electric vehicle charging station (CitySmart 2015). The city invested in improving its road infrastructure, as well as its public transport system, by developing a number of tunnels to ease rush-hour traffic congestion. In these projects, smart traffic systems are utilised including digital message signs, CCTV cameras and Bluetooth sensor devices to deliver notifications to motorists and improve road intelligence. Brisbane also adopted Sydney's Coordinated Adaptive Transport System (SCATS) to manage traffic signals and installed pedestrian countdown timers. Additionally, Brisbane has installed numerous way-finding devices for people with visual impairment. Furthermore, free Wi-Fi systems are installed in the major city parks and libraries (BCC 2015).

As evidenced by the aforementioned strategies and current practice, today Brisbane pursues an effective smart city vision, with its sustainable brand of smart urbanism aimed at addressing and promoting information access, life-long learning, the digital divide, social inclusion and economic development (Hollands 2008). Brisbane is among the limited number of cities that committed to economic growth and environment sustainability simultaneously. For example, Brisbane has utilised the smart label in conjunction with notions of the 'sustainable city' with regards to its smart water, water recycling, draught combatting measures, resilient infrastructure and subtropical building design programs. The city has gone a long way towards sustainable urbanism, but in terms of smart urban technology development, adoption and deployment the city is still behind most of the other cities around the world that claim the smart city title. Brisbane is capable of collecting and analysing real-time data to improve liveability, but the city needs to put more effort into investing in technological architecture and collaborating with businesses to realise its potential. At the moment, Brisbane is following in the footsteps of Barcelona and Rio de Janeiro by adopting a city-wide 'dashboard' to enable residents, businesses and councils to monitor data, such as energy consumption and traffic flow (AAP 2015). As mentioned above, due to their cautiousness over the financial commitment to technology infrastructure and technology skepticism, the delivery of Brisbane's smart city agenda has thus far been delayed. However, strong policy support since 2005 and recent developments indicate the city administration's willingness to jump on the smart city bandwagon.

Summary

The concept of smart cities is currently a very hot topic. This Chapter revealed that, in line with the views of Vanolo (2012), there are some underlying issues that are associated with smart cities, as they are increasingly becoming an idealised development model without proper critical discussion and political will. The Chapter highlighted different approaches taken in different parts of the world in the conceptualisation and application of the smart cities movement. For instance, in Korea smart cities are used to create a national identity and form the engines of economic growth (see Stimmel 2016), whereas in China they are used as a model city form to deal with the urbanisation ills of the megacities along with forming spaces of innovation (see Yu 2014). In Turkey and Brazil, the smart cities model is seen as an opportunity for the development of effective early warning and emergency services for natural disasters, along with transportation planning. In the UAE, it was mainly an economic exercise to diversify the petroleum-based economy of the country, and in the North American and Oceanian cases, the smart cities model is mostly adopted to improve the quality of life and place, and for the establishment of sustainable urban futures and outcomes.

The Chapter also showed that, as the smart city concept has not yet reached maturation nor produced any comprehensive smart city spaces, at this stage it is not possible to claim that they constitute the ideal twenty-first-century city form. However, all the investigated attempts, particularly those taking place in South East Asia on a large scale, will help us to clearly understand within the next few years whether smart and sustainable urban development can be produced via ambitious smart city projects, or whether they will come to the verge of bankruptcy as in the case of Middle Eastern development fantasies, i.e. Dubai. If the smart city model proves successful, this may change the reserved attitude towards smart city development in Western countries, particularly due to the large investment risks and not knowing how to deal with this new kind of urban formation with its limited understanding of social implications. As identified by Yigitcanlar and Lee (2014), current failures in the development of smart cities will help us to learn from the mistakes, plan much better and develop the next generation of cities, e.g. truly smart cities, by adopting a more balanced development approach. Perhaps a future smart city model would have a better chance of becoming a true role model for the cities of the twenty-first century if it were seeking balance and sustainability on all fronts. In other words, in line with the views of Ratti and Townsend (2011), rather than smart systems that improve efficiency in the city, what is needed is to make the city 'smart'. Furthermore, today there are a number of self-claimed smart cities (see Hollands 2008) based only on the fact that they are using ICTs and EcoTs. However, intense technology use alone in an urban environment does not equip this locality with the functionality of smart cities.

Thus, it would be useful to underline what Caragliu *et al.* (2011) highlight as the key characteristics of smart cities: (i) the utilisation of networked infrastructure to improve economic and political efficiency and enable social, cultural and urban development; (ii) an underlying emphasis on business-led urban development; (iii) a strong focus on the aim of achieving the social inclusion of various urban residents in public services; (iv) a stress on the crucial role of high-tech and creative industries in long-term urban growth; (v) profound attention to the role of social and relational capital in urban development; and (vi) social and environmental sustainability as a major strategic component for smart cities.

References

AAP (Aam Aadmi Party) 2015, *Brisbane on Track As a Smart City*, accessed on 30 September 2015 from http://www.sbs.com.au/news/article/2015/08/17/brisbane-track-smart-city

Angelidou, M 2015, *Smart City Strategy: Rio de Janeiro (Brazil)*, accessed on 24 September 2015 from http://www.urenio.org/2015/03/23/smart-city-strategy-rio-de-janeiro-brazil

Auckland Council 2014a, *Auckland Energy Resilience and Low Carbon Action Plan*, accessed on 29 September 2015 from http://www.aucklandcouncil.govt.nz/en/plans policiesprojects/plansstrategies/theaucklandplan/energyresiliencelowcarbonaction plan/Pages/home.aspx

Auckland Council 2014b, *Auckland Innovation Plan*, accessed on 29 September 2015 from http://businessaucklandnz.com/resources/innovation-plan.pdf

Australian Design Review 2010, *The Ambitious Architecture of Barcelona*, accessed on 26 August 2015 from http://www.australiandesignreview.com/architecture/1538-media-tic

Bakici, T, Almirall, E, Wareham, J 2013, 'A smart city initiative: The case of Barcelona', *Journal of the Knowledge Economy*, vol. 4, no. 2, pp. 135–148.

Barcelona City Hall 2012, *Barcelona Smart City*, accessed on 26 August 2015 from https://www.dropbox.com/s/h2vxzfd7g5oa5fs/helsinki2012_barcelona.pdf

Batty, M 2015, 'A perspective on city dashboards', *Regional Studies, Regional Science*, vol. 2, no. 1, pp. 29–32.

Baz, I, Geymen, I, Er, S 2009, 'Development and application of GIS-based analysis/ synthesis modeling techniques for urban planning of Istanbul Metropolitan Area', *Advances in Engineering Software*, vol. 40, no. 1, pp. 128–140.

BCC (Brisbane City Council) 2015, *Brisbane City Council Annual Report 2014–2015*, accessed on 3 November 2015 from http://www.brisbane.qld.gov.au/sites/default/ files/20150922-annual_report_2014-15_final_tagged_-_22_september_2015.pdf

Bowles, M, Wilson, P 2012, 'The NBN and Australia's race to compete in the digital economy', *Australian Quarterly*, vol. 83, no. 1, pp. 11–19.

Bulu, M, Önder, M, Aksakallı, V 2014, 'Algorithm-embedded IT applications for an emerging knowledge city: Algorithm-embedded IT applications for an emerging knowledge city', *Expert Systems with Applications*, vol. 41, no. 1, pp. 5625–5635.

CAICT (China Academy of Information and Communication Technology) 2016, *Comparative Study of Smart Cities in Europe and China 2014*, Springer, New York.

Capdevila, I, Zarlenga, MI 2015, 'Smart city or smart citizens? The Barcelona case', *Journal of Strategy and Management*, vol. 8, no. 3, pp. 266–282.

Caprotti, F 2014, 'Critical research on eco-cities? A walk through the Sino-Singapore Tianjin Eco-City, China', *Cities*, vol. 36, no. 1, pp. 10–17.

Caragliu, A, Del Bo, C, Nijkamp, P 2011, 'Smart cities in Europe', *Journal of Urban Technology*, vol. 18, no. 2, pp. 65–82.

Carvalho, L 2012, 'Urban competitiveness, u-city strategies and the development of technological niches in Songdo, South Korea', in Bulu, M (ed.) *City Competitiveness and Improving Urban Subsystems: Technologies and Applications: Technologies and Applications*, IGI Global, Hershey, PA, pp. 197–216.

CCST (Carbon Capture and Sequestration Technologies @ MIT) 2015, *Hydrogen Power Abu Dhabi Project Fact Sheet: Carbon Dioxide Capture and Storage Project*, accessed on 27 August 2015 from https://sequestration.mit.edu/tools/projects/hydrogen_power_abu_dhabi.html

Chen EM 2012, *Innovation and the City: Review of the Auckland Regional Innovation System*, Ministry of Economic Development, Auckland, New Zealand.

Cheng, H, Hu, Y 2010, 'Planning for sustainability in China's urban development: Status and challenges for Dongtan eco-city project', *Journal of Environmental Monitoring*, vol. 12, no. 1, pp. 119–126.

CitySmart 2015, *CitySmart Projects*, accessed on 30 September 2015 from http://www.citysmart.com.au/projects

Cohen, B 2012, *Filling South America with Smart Cities*, accessed on 23 September 2015 from http://www.fastcoexist.com/1680388/filling-south-america-with-smart-cities

Cohen, B 2013, *The 10 Smartest Cities in North America*, accessed on 23 September 2015 from http://www.fastcoexist.com/3021592/the-10-smartest-cities-in-north-america

Cohen, B 2015, *The 10 Smartest Asia/Pacific Cities*, accessed on 27 August 2015 from http://www.fastcoexist.com/3021911/the-10-smartest-asia-pacific-cities

Colak, E 2012, 'Istanbul, a rebelling city under construction', in Mathivet, C (ed.) *Housing in Europe: Time to Evict the Crisis*, AITEC (International Organisation of Engineers, Experts and Researchers), Paris, France, pp. 34–40.

Crot, L 2013, 'Planning for sustainability in non-democratic polities: The case of Masdar City', *Urban Studies*, vol. 50, no. 13, pp. 2809–2825.

Cugurullo, F 2013, 'How to build a sandcastle: An analysis of the genesis and development of Masdar City', *Journal of Urban Technology*, vol. 20, no. 1, pp. 23–37.

Cugurullo, F 2015, 'Urban eco-modernisation and the policy context of new eco-city projects: Where Masdar City fails and why', *Urban Studies*, DOI: 10.1177/0042098015588727.

Dameri, RP 2014, 'Comparing smart and digital city: Initiatives and strategies in Amsterdam and Genoa: Are they digital and/or smart?', in Dameri, RP, Rosenthal-Sabroux, C (eds) *Smart City*, Springer, Berlin, Germany, pp. 45–88.

De Jong, M, Wang, D, Yu, C 2013, 'Exploring the relevance of the eco-city concept in China: The case of Shenzhen Sino-Dutch low carbon city', *Journal of Urban Technology*, vol. 20, no. 1, pp. 95–113.

Deakin, M, Al Waer, H 2011, 'From intelligent to smart cities', *Intelligent Buildings International*, vol. 3, no. 3, pp. 140–152.

Deakin, M, Al Waer, H 2012, *From Intelligent to Smart Cities*, Routledge, New York.

DET (Department of Employment and Training) 2005, *Smart Queensland: Smart State Strategy 2005–2015*, Queensland Government, Brisbane, Australia.

DPC (Department of Premier and Cabinet) 2007, *Smart Cities: Rethinking the City Centre*, accessed on 30 September 2015 from http://www.chiefscientist.qld.gov.au/images/documents/chiefscientist/reports/smart-cities.pdf

Glasmeier, A, Christopherson, S 2015, 'Thinking about smart cities', *Cambridge Journal of Regions, Economy and Society*, vol. 8, no. 1, pp. 3–12.

Gunay, Z, Dokmeci, V 2012, 'Culture-led regeneration of Istanbul waterfront: Goldenhorn Cultural Valley Project', *Cities*, vol. 29, no. 1, pp. 213–222.

Hall, M 2014, *Australian Cities in No Hurry to Become Smart*, accessed on 29 September 2015 from http://www.smh.com.au/it-pro/government-it/australian-cities-in-no-hurry-to-become-smart-20141027–11cbnt.html

Hassan, AM, Lee, H, Yoo, U 2015, 'From medieval Cairo to modern Masdar City: Lessons learned through a comparative study', Architectural *Science Review*, vol. 59, no. 1, pp. 39–52.

Hollands, RG 2008, 'Will the real smart city please stand up?', *City: Analysis of Urban Trends, Culture, Theory, Policy, Action*, vol. 12, no. 3, pp. 303–320.

Hollands, RG 2015, 'Critical interventions into the corporate smart city', *Cambridge Journal of Regions, Economy and Society*, vol. 8, no. 1, pp. 61–77.

Hopwood, D 2010, 'Abu Dhabi's Masdar plan takes shape', *Renewable Energy Focus*, vol. 11, no. 1, pp. 18–23.

IBM 2010, *City Government and IBM Close Partnership to Make Rio de Janeiro a Smarter City*, accessed on 24 September 2015 from http://www-03.ibm.com/press/us/en/press release/33303.wss

IBM 2015a, *Smarter Cities*, accessed on 11 August 2015 from http://www.ibm.com/smarterplanet/us/en/smarter_cities/overview

IBM 2015b, *Fact Sheet: IBM Smarter Cities*, accessed on 22 September 2015 from http://www-03.ibm.com/press/uk/en/attachment/41078.wss?fileId=ATTACH_FILE2andfileName=IBM %2520Smarter%2520Cities%2520Fact%2520Sheet%2520Final.doc

Innovation Norway 2015, *Smart City Projects in Brazil*, accessed on 23 September 2015 from https://innovationhouserio.wordpress.com/2015/05/26/smart-city-projects-in-brazil

Jones, R 2015, *Award-Winning Solution Keeps Auckland Ahead of the Growth Curve*, accessed on 29 September 2015 from http://www.microsoft.com/en-us/citynext/blogs/award-winning-solution-keeps-auckland-ahead-of-the-growth-curve/default.aspx

Joss, S, Cowley, R, Tomozeiu, D 2013, 'Towards the "ubiquitous eco-city": An analysis of the internationalisation of eco-city policy and practice', *Urban Research and Practice*, vol. 6, no. 1, pp. 54–74

Kim, C 2010, 'Place promotion and symbolic characterization of new Songdo City, South Korea', *Cities*, vol. 27, no. 1, pp. 13–19.

Kingsley, P 2013, *Masdar: The Shifting Goalposts of Abu Dhabi's Ambitious Eco-City*, accessed on 27 August 2015 from http://www.wired.co.uk/magazine/archive/2013/12/features/reality-hits-masdar

Kitchin, R 2014, 'The real-time city? Big data and smart urbanism', *Geo Journal*, vol. 79, no. 1, pp. 1–14.

Kitchin, R 2015, 'Making sense of smart cities: Addressing present shortcomings', *Cambridge Journal of Regions, Economy and Society*, vol. 8, no. 1, pp. 131–136.

Kocabas, A 2006, 'Urban conservation in Istanbul', *Habitat International*, vol. 30, no. 1, 107–126.

Komninos, N 2008, *Intelligent Cities and Globalisation of Innovation Networks*, Routledge, New York.

Kourtit, K, Nijkamp, P, Arribas, D 2012, 'Smart cities in perspective: A comparative European study by means of self-organizing maps', *Innovation: The European Journal of Social Science Research*, vol. 25, no. 2, pp. 229–246.

Lee, JH, Hancock, MG, Hu, MC 2014, 'Towards an effective framework for building smart cities: lessons from Seoul and San Francisco', *Technological Forecasting and Social Change*, vol. 89, no. 1, pp. 80–99.

Leon, N 2008, 'Attract and connect: The 22@ Barcelona innovation district and the internationalisation of Barcelona business', *Innovation*, vol. 10, no. 2–3, pp. 235–246.

Lim, CJ, Liu, E 2010, *Smartcities and Eco-Warriors*, Routledge, New York.

Lombardi, P, Giordano, S, Farouh, H, Yousef, W 2012, 'Modeling the smart city performance', *Innovation: The European Journal of Social Science Research*, vol. 25, no. 2, pp. 137–149.

Low, M 2013, 'Eco-cities in Japan: Past and future', *Journal of Urban Technology*, vol. 20, no. 1, pp. 7–22.

Maleady, R 2015, *Move over Silicon Valley: San Francisco Pulls Ahead as a Leader in Tech*, accessed on 23 September 2015 from http://www.stackoverflowcareers.com/blog/move-over-silicon-valley-%E2%80%93-san-francisco-pulls-ahead-as-a-leader-in-tech

Manville, C, Cochrane, G, Cave, J, Millard, J, Pederson, JK, Thaarup, RK, Kotterink, B 2014, *Mapping Smart Cities in the EU*, EU, Brussels, Belgium.

Masdar Institute 2015, *Research at Masdar Institute*, accessed on 27 August 2015 from http://www.masdar.ac.ae/research

Mezher, T, Tabbara, S, Al-Hosany, N 2010, 'An overview of CSR in the renewable energy sector: Examples from the Masdar Initiative in Abu Dhabi', *Management of Environmental Quality: An International Journal*, vol. 21, no. 6, pp. 744–760.

Mezher, T, Goldsmith, D, Choucri, N 2011, 'Renewable energy in Abu Dhabi: Opportunities and challenges', *Journal of Energy Engineering*, vol. 137, no. 4, pp. 169–176.

MIT Technology Review 2014, *Barcelona's Smart City Ecosystem*, accessed on 26 August 2015 from http://www.technologyreview.com/news/532511/barcelonas-smart-city-ecosystem

Naphade, M, Banavar, G, Harrison, C, Paraszczak, J, Morris, R 2011, 'Smarter cities and their innovation challenges', *Computer*, vol. 44, no. 6, pp. 32–39.

Ozdemir, F 2015, Istanbul'un akilli durak sistemleri (Smart Bus Stop Systems of Istanbul), accessed on 22 September 2015 from http://www.fozdemir.com/istanbul-akilli-durak-sistemi

Pareja-Eastaway, M, Piqué, JM 2011, 'Urban regeneration and the creative knowledge economy: The case of 22@ in Barcelona', *Journal of Urban Regeneration and Renewal*, vol. 4, no. 4, pp. 319–327.

Poole, S 2014, *The Truth about Smart Cities: In the End, They Will Destroy Democracy*, accessed on 26 August 2015 from http://www.theguardian.com/cities/2014/dec/17/truth-smart-city-destroy-democracy-urban-thinkers-buzzphrase

Pow, CP, Neo, H 2013, 'Seeing red over green: Contesting urban sustainabilities in China', *Urban Studies*, vol. 50, no. 11, pp. 2256–2274.

Ratti, C, Townsend, A 2011, 'The social nexus', *Scientific American*, vol. 305, no. 3, pp. 42–48.

Reis, M 2014, *Five U.S. Cities Using Technology to Become Smart and Connected*, accessed on 23 September 2015 from http://www.forbes.com/sites/ptc/2014/08/15/5-u-s-cities-using-technology-to-become-smart-and-connected

Salunkhe, U 2015, *Realising Smart Cities Dream: A Few Lessons from Rio de Janeiro*, accessed on 23 September 2015 from http://www.firstpost.com/business/realising-smart-cities-dream-lessons-rio-de-janeiro-2349680.html

Sauer, S 2012, 'Do smart cities produce smart entrepreneurs?', *Journal of Theoretical and Applied Electronic Commerce Research*, vol. 7, no. 3, pp. 63–73.

SF Environment 2012, *Designing a Smarter, More Sustainable San Francisco*, accessed on 23 September 2015 from http://www.sfenvironment.org/news/update/designing-a-smarter-and-more-sustainable-san-francisco

Sgouridis, S, Kennedy, S 2010, 'Tangible and fungible energy: Hybrid energy market and currency system for total energy management: a Masdar City case study', *Energy Policy*, vol. 38, no. 4, pp. 1749–1758.

Shwayri, ST 2013, 'A model Korean ubiquitous eco-city? The politics of making Songdo', *Journal of Urban Technology*, vol. 20, no. 1, pp. 39–55.

Singer, N 2012, *Mission Control, Built for Cities: IBM Takes 'Smarter Cities' Concept to Rio de Janeiro*, accessed on 23 September 2015 from http://www.nytimes.com/2012/03/04/business/ibm-takes-smarter-cities-concept-to-rio-de-janeiro.html?_r=0

Steinmetz, K 2014, *Google Gives San Francisco Free Wi-Fi in Public Places*, accessed on 23 September 2015 from http://time.com/3453871/google-gives-san-francisco-free-wi-fi-in-public-places

Stimmel, C 2016, *Building Smart Cities: Analytics, ICT, and Design Thinking*, CRC Press, New York.

Strickland, E 2011, 'Cisco bets on South Korean smart city', *Spectrum, IEEE*, vol. 48, no. 8, pp. 11–12.

The White House 2015, *Fact Sheet: Administration Announces New 'Smart Cities' Initiative to Help Communities Tackle Local Challenges and Improve City Services*, accessed on 23 September 2015 from https://www.whitehouse.gov/the-press-office/2015/09/14/fact-sheet-administration-announces-new-smart-cities-initiative-help

Tianjin Eco-city 2015, *Sino-Singapore Tianjin Eco-city: A Model for Sustainable Development*, accessed on 13 August 2015 from http://www.tianjinecocity.gov.sg

Townsend, AM 2013, *Smart Cities: Big Data, Civic Hackers, and the Quest for a New Utopia*, WW Norton and Company, New York.

Townsville City Council 2015, *IBM Smarter Cities Challenge*, accessed on 1 October 2015 from http://www.townsville.qld.gov.au/community/sustainability/Pages/IBM.aspx

Tucker, R, Branch, P 2013, *Fact Check: Will the NBN Take Another 20 years to Complete?*, accessed on 29 September 2015 from http://theconversation.com/factcheck-will-the-nbn-take-another-20-years-to-complete-16962

UN (United Nations) 2015, *World Population Prospects: Key Findings and Advance Tables*, United Nations, New York.

Vanolo, A 2012, 'Smart mentality: The smart city as disciplinary strategy', *Urban Studies*, vol. 51, no. 5, pp. 883–898.

Wong, TC 2011, 'Eco-cities in China: Pearls in the sea of degrading urban environments', in Wong, TC, Yuen, B (eds) *Eco-City Planning: Policies, Practice and Design*, Springer, New York, pp. 131–150.

Yalçıntaş, M, Bulu, M, Küçükvar, M, Samadi, H 2015, 'A framework for sustainable urban water management through demand and supply forecasting: The case of Istanbul', *Sustainability*, vol. 7, no. 8, pp. 11050–11067.

Yigitcanlar, T, Velibeyoglu, K 2008, 'Knowledge-based urban development: The local economic development path of Brisbane, Australia', *Local Economy*, vol. 23, no. 3, pp. 195–207.

Yigitcanlar, T, Sarimin, M 2011, 'The role of universities in building prosperous knowledge cities: the Malaysian experience', *Built Environment*, vol. 37, no. 3, pp. 260–280.

Yigitcanlar, T, Lee, S 2014, 'Korean ubiquitous-eco-city: A smart-sustainable urban form or a branding hoax?', *Technological Forecasting and Social Change*, vol. 89, no. 1, pp. 100–114.

Yigitcanlar, T, Bulu, M 2015, 'Dubaization of Istanbul: Insights from the knowledge-based urban development journey of an emerging local economy', *Environment and Planning A*, vol. 47, no. 1, pp. 89–107.

Yigitcanlar, T, Sarimin, M 2015, 'Multimedia Super Corridor, Malaysia: Knowledge-based urban development lessons from an emerging economy', *VINE: The Journal of Information and Knowledge Management*, vol. 45, no. 1, pp. 126–147.

Yigitcanlar, T, Guaralda, M, Taboada, M, Pancholi, S 2016, 'Place making for knowledge generation and innovation: planning and branding Brisbane's knowledge community precincts', *Journal of Urban Technology*, DOI: 10.1080/10630732.2015.1090198.

Yu, L 2014, 'Low carbon eco-city: New approach for Chinese urbanisation', *Habitat International*, vol. 44, no. 1, pp. 102–110.

Zovanyi, G 2004, 'A growth-management strategy for the Auckland region of New Zealand: pursuit of sustainability or mere growth accommodation?', *International Journal of Sustainable Development*, vol. 7, no. 2, pp. 121–145.

Part IV

Implications

Part IV of the book provides a concluding base by examining the magnitudes and prospects of smart urban technology and systems for cities. Chapter 6 discusses the consequences of smart urban technologies and systems on: (i) economic development in smart cities; (ii) sociocultural development in smart cities; (iii) spatial development in smart cities; and (iv) institutional development in smart cities. Chapter 7 then speculates about the prospects of smart urban technology and systems with a mid-term perspective to the mid-twenty-first century and a long-term perspective to the beginning of the twenty-second century by focusing on: (i) the future of life on planet Earth; (ii) the future of smart technologies such as computers, artificial intelligence, nanotechnology, medicine, energy, media, entertainment, shopping, business and travel; and (iii) the future of smart cities. The Chapter pinpoints new technology directions for smart cities to further benefit in providing desired smart and sustainable urban futures. This part of the book also highlights the connections between past, present and future developments in the space of technology and the city.

6 Magnitudes of smart technology applications for cities

Globalization, as defined by rich people like us, is a very nice thing . . . you are talking about the Internet, you are talking about cell phones, you are talking about computers. This doesn't affect two-thirds of the people of the world.

(Jimmy Carter, the 39th president of the United States)

Introduction

Not surprisingly, the twenty-first century is being promoted as the 'century of cities', because by 2050, 75 per cent of the world's population will be living in urban areas, and the figure will reach over 80 per cent by the end of the century (Hardoy *et al.* 2013). Today, some of the developed nations have already exceeded this urbanisation figure. For instance, in Australia, over 80 per cent of the population is already residing in the metropolitan urban areas, and the country is often referred as an urban nation. While the vast majority of Australians live in cities and towns, it is arguably more accurate to say that Australia is a suburban nation; on average over 75 per cent of Australia's urban population is suburban. This rapid urbanisation (or suburbanisation) rate and its associated problems have made smart cities a hot topic of research and practice globally.

This city brand is used for many different purposes, for ecological, technological, economic and management purposes (Yigitcanlar 2015). Three key dimensions of smart cities are worth highlighting. The first of them is the technology basis. Infrastructural information technologies, i.e. World Wide Web, broadband and mobile broadband are required as the basis for technology delivery. Locational and sensing technologies, i.e. geographic information science technologies, RFID, ubiquitous sensor networks and context-aware computing are crucial to the development of context-aware applications and spaces. Ubiquitous computing and augmented reality technologies, i.e. mobile and built ubiquitous computing environments and mobile augmented reality technologies are essential to construct interactive urban spaces in these cities. Convergence technologies, that is the convergence of internet, media, marketing and telecommunications, as well as the convergence of aforementioned technologies with the objects around us, e.g. fridges, washing machines, walls, doors, cars, homes and so on, form the 'internet-of-things' or 'internet-of-everything'. The second area is the infrastructure that makes cities work efficiently, both hard and soft infrastructure systems. For example, Google Car, a driverless car, is on the streets, and it is a promising technology. The State of Victoria is a leader in Australia in the smart meter, for example. With wastewater in smart homes, there are a number of examples around the world where it is applied beyond homes and into an urban infrastructure, for example, Korean smart cities. With emergency and safety concerns, we are all surrounded by CCTV cameras. We no longer have just CCTV cameras; now we also have surveillance drones. Many cities are investing in their emergency services to cope better with, e.g. earthquakes, natural disasters, bushfires and so on. Urban infrastructure is something that government builds, develops, regulates and maintains. However, there is much that individuals can do as well. It is called volunteered geographic information. Where 'Big Brother' is out of reach, individuals (people as sensors) can take pictures or videos through apps and upload this information with their comments to an online platform for others to see and (if need be) government to act on. That could be related to an environmental hazard, or a health and safety issue or something fun or entertaining.

The last area is the city itself becoming truly smart. However, the critical question is how a smart city could be constructed. Around the world, there are two main approaches. One of them is the Eastern model to build a city from scratch with all cutting-edge smart urban technologies. The second one is the Western approach of retrofitting our cities with cutting-edge smart urban technologies. While the first model seems to be more comprehensive and likely to deliver a wider number of smart functions, the latter one seems to be more incremental and a safer approach from the investment risks point of view. However, both models have their opportunities, challenges and also consequences for cities, societies and the environment. This Chapter aims to elaborate and discuss these challenges and consequences, and provide recommendations. The rest of the Chapter is structured as follows: (i) economic development in smart cities; (ii) sociocultural development in smart cities; (iii) spatial development in smart cities; and (iii) institutional development in smart cities.

Economic development in smart cities

We need to give our cities the capability of developing their technologies unique to their own developmental problems and needs. This in turn contributes to the establishment of a local innovation economy and prosperity that is a central element of smart cities.

First of all, smart cities projects in some of the cities we investigated earlier, such as Abu Dhabi, Incheon and Tianjin, were developed particularly as economic growth engines that were jointly driven by the technology and construction industries supported by national and local governments. For instance, the smart cities concept was introduced in Korea after the 1997 Asian financial crisis and then again with some amendments after the 2008 global financial crisis. These city models are seen as not only a solution to urbanisation problems but also, and mainly, to national economic development issues (Shwayri 2013). Songdo, Incheon was designed as a testbed for an RFID-focused industrial park by Korea's national economic planners. Smart cities projects are basically considered as flagship projects for the Korean national government to combine ecological and economic development. However, the observed economic development approach in the Korean context is rather based on increased technology consumerism than production. In other words, the technology developed for smart cities is used for public consumption rather than providing citizens with an employment opportunity to contribute to the knowledge generation and/or local economic activities. This begs the question in economic terms of who is benefitting most from smart city formation? According to Anttiroiko (2013), the Korean cases show that construction companies and technology firms reap the most financial benefit, while public sector carries the major risks through their support schemes and public investment, and people are made to adjust to a new technologically mediated mode of urban life without much room for choices of their own.

Second, Townsend (2013: 15) defines smart cities as, 'places where information technology is combined with infrastructure, architecture, everyday objects, and even our bodies to address social, economic, and environmental problems'. From this definition it sounds like it is a very much locally driven agenda. While this is correct in some parts of the world, such as in the West, in the Eastern context, however, smart cities projects are a national development that is prioritised over local or regional developments, even though local governments are among the key stakeholders of these projects (Yigitcanlar and Lee 2014). This is indicative of a top-down planning approach and prioritisation of the national economic development agenda over the local economic development needs and characteristics.

Third, although the concept of smart cities is a highly useful and popular one, it is important to know who the main developers and promoters are of the smart urban technologies and services. Since the mid-1990s, globalisation has accelerated the number of large multinational corporations that are focused on smart urban technology and engineering solutions. IBM, Cisco, Samsung, LG, ARUP and a few national telecommunications companies have led the expansion of the smart cities movement and technology deployment across global cities. These technology companies are involved in most of the smart city projects. For example, IBM claims a knowledge base that spans over 2,000 smart cities projects across 170 countries (IBM 2009).

Finally, while involvement of large technology corporations is an opportunity for these companies to transfer their knowledge, experience and learnings from one city to another, this also causes a problem with the cookie-cutter approach to smart city development. This results in the development of similar-looking places without many unique characteristics. As for economic development, this restricts local economic and technology development. Cities that lack the capacity to design their own smart urban systems are destined to fall behind. Therefore, it is critical for cities to invest in and foster their endogenous technology and innovation ecosystems. Otherwise, smart city technology dependence on overseas is inevitable. Furthermore, not supporting endogenous technology development will likely result in missed local solution generation and knowledge-based economic development opportunities.

Sociocultural development in smart cities

We need to develop our cities wired with smart urban technologies not only exclusive to urban elites but also inclusive of those who are less fortunate. This in turn helps in establishing socioeconomic equality that is an essential element of smart cities.

First, in most of the smart cities projects a crucial part of the solution is missing, that is public participation and citizen involvement. In other words, we humans are the main reason for the problems the world is facing today, and thus without the involvement of everyone, there can be no viable solution to any of these problems. The Arab Spring, Istanbul Gezi Park and Occupy Wall Street uprisings are among some of the grassroots activist movements that were organised by using social media by people seeking a better future, and showcased the power of smart technologies to bring people together for a good cause. The smart cities movement needs to find a way to somehow engage all citizens collectively for a better cause for their cities and the planet. Only our collective determination will help us create effective remedies.

Second, the practice of smart cities has particular challenges for societies, hence, it is imperative that the societal compatibility of smart urban technologies, infrastructures and services should be carefully planned. In particular, autonomy, privacy, trust, affordability, access to and participation in the advantages of these technologies, infrastructures and services are as important in this context as issues of their management, e.g. integration, system dependency, the possibility of avoiding loss of control, monitoring and normalisation of behaviour (Bohn *et al.* 2005).

Third, as advocated by Rotondo (2012), smart city projects should be a driver for change in urban planning public participation processes, which provides opportunities to establish a true e-democracy. However, current practices, at least in the South East Asian and Middle Eastern contexts, do not provide such avenues for participation and e-democracy, or for user-generated content applications.

Fourth, these smart urban technology applications and systems are mainly infrastructure-based innovations and require high-level initial financial investment. Thus, not only governments but also taxpayers have to be convinced of the feasibility and socioeconomic and environmental benefits of these large-scale and highly costly projects, i.e. carefully weighing up the triple-bottom-line costs and benefits.

Last, the techo-economic polarisation that these cities produce leads to a duality in the city, i.e. the dual city phenomenon (see Marcuse 1989). This raises an important question of whether smart cities in their fragmented mode are a new way of building functionally sophisticated sustainable enclaves into society, mainly serving high-income groups. Keeping in mind that there is currently no major change in public policy in China, Korea and the UAE since the introduction of smart cities, these cities will most likely increase social polarisation and urban segregation (Yigitcanlar and Lee 2014). If we do not want to create enclaves of high quality life and place exclusively for urban elites, we need to find ways to put technology in the hands and also neighbourhoods of the poor and disadvantaged populations.

Spatial development in smart cities

We need to reform our cities by adopting sustainable urban development principles, e.g. minimising the urban footprint, limiting emissions, establishing urban farms and so on. This in turn helps in generating ecological sustainability that is a critical element of smart cities.

First of all, the spatial dimension of smart cities includes both natural and built environments, and in the context of smart and sustainable urban development, they need to be planned to co-exist without causing harm to one another. In terms of natural environments, smart city practice globally has shown a rather dynamic nature, especially in the marketing of the city and its sustainability. However, just adopting the smart city brand, almost overnight without significant improvements in the city's ecological sustainability enhancing systems and procedures, will surely not result in the formation of a smart city. Undoubtedly, just developing limited services, e.g. smart water supply, and maintaining the various promised smart environmental management services would not qualify newly developing South East Asian and Middle Eastern cities as truly smart cities, especially as some of the claimed smart titles are built on inherent contradictions. For example, Incheon and Songdo smart cities were built following the destruction of precious wetlands, home to some of the rarest species on the planet (Shwayri 2013). Similarly, regardless of continuous efforts, the smart cities initiatives in Amsterdam were not successful enough to decrease CO_2 emissions generated in the city; emissions are still increasing by about 1 per cent annually (Townsend 2013).

Second, it is also noteworthy to state that sustainable urban development is indeed an oxymoron (see Rees 1997). Realisation of this resulted in Masdar smart city downgrading its title from 'zero carbon emission city' to 'low carbon emission city'. Therefore, the limited measures employed in all of the investigated smart cities initiatives to provide sustainable urban development, such as efficient energy use and recycling waste unfortunately will not reverse the damage done to the environment. In order to achieve sustainable urban futures, comprehensive sustainable urban development and ecological planning perspectives should be incorporated in all stages of development of smart cities, especially at the construction stage.

Last, in terms of built environments, the quality of life and place has been the main motto of many of the smart cities. Perhaps this is an area where these cities are most successful, providing world-class built environment and physical infrastructures and, thereby, an increased quality of life and place perception. For example, Incheon, Songdo and Seoul smart cities have provided pedestrian safety services through a smart curb to maximise the reduction rate of traffic accidents involving pedestrians. Auckland, Barcelona and San Francisco introduced smart parking applications to decrease the time spent while searching for a parking space. Perhaps soon we will see cities designing their smart urban squares as interactive spaces to be used by citizens and visitors. However, as questioned by Yigitcanlar and Lee (2014), we wonder whether cities can actually provide a sustained quality of life and place by mainly focusing on the built environment and mostly neglecting the natural environment.

Institutional development in smart cities

We need to equip our cities with highly dynamic mechanisms to better plan their growth and manage their day-to-day operational challenges. This in turn helps in performing appropriate planning, development and management practices that are core elements of smart cities.

First of all, accumulative advancements in science, technology and innovation have provided sufficient confidence and foundation for pursuing the development of smart cities (Hwang 2008). Even though smart city is not the only internationally recognised brand for smart and sustainable cities, e.g. eco-city, sustainable city, intelligent city, ubiquitous city, knowledge city and creative city among others, it is the one that is rapidly gaining wider acceptance as a potential role model city type. However, despite its increasing popularity, the smart city development process needs to be a more open, transparent, participatory and collaborative one. This is critical for the planning of the development and also management of amenities, activities and the city as a whole. Even though currently available, smart urban technology tools provide an opportunity for including citizens' voices, but they are not being widely used. Governmental and grassroots campaigns are needed to create awareness both on smart city projects and also in participation channels.

Second and most importantly, mega projects like holistic smart city projects require strong governmental policy and financial support, transparency in the spending of the funds, political stability and continuity of strategies. In particular, in the context of developing countries, these smart city projects may not be immune to political influence and at times even may be subjected to corruption and bribery. We often hear of major corruption allegations related to mega projects in countries that invest heavily in smart cities initiatives, including, but not limited to, Brazil, China, Korea, Malaysia and Turkey. For instance, the controversial mega projects of Istanbul, the 3rd Bridge, the 3rd Airport and the Canal Istanbul projects, are among examples where there are corruption allegations and the continuation of the developments despite court rulings and vast community objections (see Yigitcanlar and Bulu 2015). This brings to mind the question of how changing political climates, bureaucracy and transparency have an impact on the formation efforts and processes of smart cities.

Third, current institutional mechanisms may not be sufficiently adequate to manage smart cities, as today most progressive cities update or amend their city or master plans every five years or so. That is to say, planning mechanisms even in proactive cities are still not dynamic enough to deal with the impacts of a changing climate, urbanisation forces and society's changing needs and lifestyle options. As stated by ARUP (2010), the smart city is so different in essence to the twentieth-century city that the governance models and organisational frameworks themselves must evolve. Forming truly smart cities requires moving away from static visioning and planning practices, as cities are living organisms and they are changing every minute of the day, and adopting a highly dynamic mechanism for planning, development and management.

Fourth, even if 75 per cent of the people will be living in urban areas by the mid-twenty-first century, there will still be a significant proportion of the population living in areas with little access to smart urban technology solutions and services. This will render these groups highly disadvantaged and vulnerable. That is to say, deployment of these 'smart' concepts and applications should have a particular focus on including these remotely located people as well. Although we frequently see the involvement of international technology and national telecommunication companies, e.g. IBM, Cisco, Samsung and LG, and construction companies, e.g. ARUP, in smart city projects, the main actor developing relevant smart cities policies and plans is the public sector. There is, therefore, a need for a novel and effective institutional mechanism to bridge the gap between metropolitan cities and remote regions, and turn these regions into 'smart regions'.

Last, smart technologies should not be seen purely as solutions to urban ills, but rather as a set of tools to help us fix what is going wrong. Therefore, we need to adopt an approach that utilises smart urban technologies for integrating and balancing the economic, societal, environmental and institutional development areas of our cities to secure sustainable urban futures (Yigitcanlar and Lee 2014). In current practice, this is a major challenge and, thus, how to create a balanced development and democratise the very process of making smart cities is a critical question. Perhaps a quadruple helix model partnership, i.e. a partnership of public, private, academic and community or grassroots organisations (Colapinto and Porlezza 2012) might be a direction in which to pursue common goals, and integrated and balanced smart city development.

Summary

Since the start of the twenty-first century, the smart cities concept has become a hot topic and a priority policy agenda for many cities in both the developed and developing country contexts. Even smart cities' technologies are seen as crucial for the survival of our species (see Townsend 2013). In 2016, many of the global cities' administrations see smart urban technology applications and systems as potential vehicles to deal with their current and future developmental challenges, whether they are economic, societal or environmental in nature. Previously, in Chapter 5, a number of these cities and their approaches to smart city formation were placed under the microscope. This investigation revealed many challenges along with some best or good practices. This Chapter, which explored the magnitude of smart technology applications for cities, further elaborated these challenges and also provided some suggestions to better strategise actions to deal with these issues.

As explored in this book, we observe two different streams to smart city practice approaches across the globe. On the one hand, the Western smart city approach (i.e. Europe, North America and Oceania) seems to be less critiqued as it promotes an incremental method mainly targeting retrofitting and allowing trial and error in the relatively unexplored world of smart cities, with a lesser risk of wasting taxpayers' money. Additionally, this approach, which is mostly due to the governance culture, is more open to decisions being made with inter-institutional technical consultation and public participation, and initiatives are mostly driven by local government. However, due to the sceptical or perhaps safer steps taken in forming truly smart cities, the progress of this approach is slower. On the other hand, the Eastern smart city approach (i.e. South East Asia and the Middle East) seems be more criticised as it is a more comprehensive method focusing on developing smart cities from scratch. This approach mostly appears to be engaged with economic development goals rather than actually targeting a process to deal with environmental and societal challenges of cities. Additionally, this approach is potentially more open to corruption due to the less transparent nature of governance in these regions in not providing much opportunity for public participation and the initiatives being mostly top-down and driven by national governments. However, due to more ambitious and bolder steps being taken in forming truly smart cities, this approach's progress is faster. Both approaches have their strengths and weaknesses. Nevertheless, both successful and failed attempts are bringing us a step closer to figuring out how to develop the smart cities of the twenty-first century. The findings of the analysis undertaken in this Chapter suggest that an integrated and balanced approach is needed to construct smart cities or cities for the twenty-first century. That is to say, the focus should not be solely technological. Instead, technology applications and the opportunities generated by them should only be viewed as a means to help in all development domains of our cities, i.e. economic, societal, environmental and governance, in an integrated and well-balanced manner. This requires a comprehensive system of approach (see Carrillo *et al.* 2014) and design thinking (see Stimmel 2016).

References

Anttiroiko, A 2013, 'U-cities reshaping our future: reflections on ubiquitous infrastructure as an enabler of smart urban development', *AI and Society*, vol. 28, no. 1, pp. 131–148.

ARUP 2010, *Smart Cities Transforming the Twenty-First Century City via the Creative Use of Technology*, accessed on 13 October 2015 from file:///C:/Users/yigitcan/Downloads/Smart_City_paper_26November2010_low%20res.pdf

Bohn, J, Coroama, V, Langheinrich, M, Mattern, F, Rohs, M 2005, 'Social, economic and ethical implications of ambient intelligence and ubiquitous computing', in Weber, W, Rabaey, J, Aarts, E (eds) *Ambient Intelligence*, Springer, Berlin, Germany, pp. 5–29.

Carrillo, J, Yigitcanlar, T, Garcia, B, Lonnqvist, A 2014, *Knowledge and the City: Concepts, Applications and Trends of Knowledge-Based Urban Development*, Routledge, New York.

Colapinto, C, Porlezza, C 2012, 'Innovation in creative industries: From the quadruple helix model to the systems theory', *Journal of the Knowledge Economy*, vol. 3, no. 4, pp. 343–353.

Hardoy, JE, Mitlin, D, Satterthwaite, D 2013, *Environmental Problems in an Urbanizing World: Finding Solutions in Cities in Africa, Asia and Latin America*, Routledge, New York.

Hwang, J 2008, 'U-city: The next paradigm of urban development', in Foth, M (ed.) *Urban Informatics: Community Integration and Implementation*, IGI Global, Hershey, PA, pp. 367–378.

IBM 2009, *A Vision of Smarter Cities: How Cities Can Lead the Way into a Prosperous and Sustainable Future*, IBM Global Services, Somers, NY.

Marcuse, P 1989, 'Dual city: A muddy metaphor for a quartered city', *International Journal of Urban and Regional Research*, vol. 13, no. 4, pp. 697–708.

Rees, WE 1997, 'Is "sustainable city" an oxymoron?', *Local Environment*, vol. 2, no. 3, pp. 303–310.

Rotondo, F 2012, 'The u-city-paradigm: Opportunities and risks for e-democracy in collaborative planning', *Future Internet*, vol. 4, no. 1, pp. 563–574.

Shwayri, S 2013, 'A model Korean ubiquitous eco-city? The politics of making Songdo', *Journal of Urban Technology*, vol. 20, no. 1, pp. 39–55.

Stimmel, C 2016, *Building Smart Cities: Analytics, ICT, and Design Thinking*, CRC Press, New York.

Townsend, AM 2013, *Smart Cities: Big Data, Civic Hackers, and the Quest for a New Utopia*, WW Norton and Company, New York.

Yigitcanlar, T 2015, 'Smart cities: An effective urban development and management model?', *Australian Planner*, vol. 52, no. 1, pp. 27–34.

Yigitcanlar, T, Lee, S 2014, 'Korean ubiquitous-eco-city: A smart-sustainable urban form or a branding hoax?', *Technological Forecasting and Social Change*, vol. 89, no. 1, pp. 100–114.

Yigitcanlar, T, Bulu, M 2015, 'Dubaization of Istanbul: Insights from the knowledge-based urban development journey of an emerging local economy', *Environment and Planning A*, vol. 47, no. 1, pp. 89–107.

7 Prospects of smart technology applications for cities

The future influences the present just as much as the past.
(Friedrich Nietzsche, philosopher)

Introduction

Since the start of the twenty-first century, long-term strategic planning has become an important mechanism for cities to position themselves for better dealing with the challenges ahead, along with gaining or strengthening the competitive edge for attracting global investment and talent. Today, many of the world's cities are planning long-term visions and strategies (for 2050 and beyond) by considering various smart city development strategies, e.g. London, Melbourne, Perth, Helsinki, Vienna, Stockholm and Paris. The Planning Institute of Australia (PIA) defines 'planning', also referred to as 'city/urban/town and regional planning', as the process of making decisions to guide future actions (PIA 2015). In order to determine the most suitable actions, policymakers and planners need to know the future state of their cities, including their prospective opportunities and threats. This requires estimating what the future will be like. However, we do not have a crystal ball to precisely see what the future will bring. Moreover, as Van Doren (1992: 375) stated, 'prophecy is a risky business', as it may lead to unnecessary or miscalculated actions and wasting limited resources. In particular, in the era of rapid technological advancements, which is upon us now, even forecasting the 2020s is quite challenging. Visions of the scientists and futurists of the nineteenth and twentieth centuries, and science fiction writers and film directors who based their work on these ideas, were mostly inaccurate. At present, we are still far away from using beaming machines for commuting, setting up a colony on the Moon, having holograms as a common medium for communication, replacing books and notebooks fully with their digital versions, making all movies in 3D, choosing the sex of our children, building flying houses and underwater cities, robots replacing human labour or having androids with artificial intelligence (AI) around us.

Furthermore, there are also unintended consequences of technology development that make correct prediction near impossible. For instance, Albert Einstein (his relativity theory) and Marie Currie (her intuitions about radium) have not foreseen that their ideas would mark the beginning of the nuclear age, and cause devastation in Hiroshima and Nagasaki during WWII. Besides, many inventions are the result of coincidence. For example, the drug called Viagra was initially developed as a medicine for a heart condition, and it is now a remedy for male erectile dysfunction, and the female version will be in the market soon. The list can be extended to include many others, such as Teflon, plastic, radioactivity, pacemaker, microwave, superglue, x-ray, anaesthesia, dynamite and many more. However, despite the risk of getting the future all wrong, there are a few things that can be said about the rest of the century. This prediction is made by projecting past and current technology and city development trends into the future and considering that some of the existing trends will somehow continue, such as globalisation, exponential development nature of technology and innovation, urbanisation, aging population, environmental challenges, hunger for shared experiences (see Watson 2012) and borrowing visions and ideas from scientists and futurists. Therefore, Chapter 7 attempts to speculate on the prospects of smart technology applications for cities, with a medium-term perspective until the mid-twenty-first century, and a long-term perspective until the beginning of the twenty-second century. This Chapter particularly focuses and speculates on the imaginable trends of the: (i) future of life on planet Earth; (ii) future of smart technologies; and (iii) future of smart cities.

Future of life on planet Earth

Renowned physicist and author, Stephen Hawking, stated in his speech at Sydney's Opera House in 2015, delivered via hologram from the UK, that he does not think the human race will survive another 1,000 years without escaping beyond our fragile planet. As the only possible way for survival, he suggested we focus on developing technological capability to colonise another planet (Gerken 2015) as sooner or later, disasters such as an asteroid collision or a nuclear war could wipe us all out, or climate change could make life on Earth impossible. Several months after this speech, Stephen Hawking launched a $100 million search for alien life beyond our solar system, funded by a Russian entrepreneur, venture capitalist and physicist, Yuri Milner, which will allow telescopes to eavesdrop on planets that orbit the one million stars and the one hundred galaxies closest to Earth (Sample 2015). Moreover, Kaku (2012: 294) believes that, 'by 2100, it is likely that we will have sent astronauts to Mars and the asteroid belt, explored the moons of Jupiter, and begun the first steps to send a probe to the stars'.

While the search is on looking for life beyond planet Earth, Brunn (2013) recommends the writings of noteworthy nineteenth- and twentieth-century science fiction writers who inspired later generations to think about planetary travel, time-space issues, technological breakthroughs, environmental change, politics, social order and the human condition for us to picture life on Earth and beyond in the next decades to come. These include H. G. Wells's (1895) *The Time Machine* and (1898) *War of the Worlds*; Jules Verne's (1864) *Journey to the Centre of the*

Earth, (1870) *20,000 Leagues Under the Sea* and (1873) *Around the World in 80 Days*; George Orwell's (1949) *Nineteen Eighty-Four*; and Arthur C. Clark's (1951) *The Sands of Mars* and (1968) *2001: A Space Odyssey* novels.

Watson (2012) predicts that life on planet Earth in the late twenty-first century will have the following features: (i) globalisation, localisation, polarisation, anxiety and search for meaning will be the main trends to transform the 'societal domain'; (ii) nanotechnology, biotechnology, emotionally aware machines, ethics and robotics will be the main trends to transform the 'science and technology domain'; (iii) city states, tribalism, happiness, climate change and the environment, and e-action will be the main trends to transform the 'political domain'; (iv) time-starved, shifting, infinite content, user-generated content and personalisation and physicalisation will be the main trends to transform the 'media domain'; (v) mobile, pre-pay and contactless payment, intermediaries, debt, regulation and foreign and non-bank competition will be the main trends to transform the 'financial services' domain; (vi) embedded intelligence, remote monitoring, driverless cars, the environment and the reinvention of public transport will be the main trends to transform the 'mobility domain'; (vii) convenience, portability and speed, seasonal, regional and slow, health versus indulgence, nostalgia, and food science and technology will be the main trends to transform the 'nourishment domain'; (viii) luxury versus low cost, speed and simplicity, changes in household consumption, sustainability, storytelling, authenticity and trust will be the main trends to transform the 'retail domain'; (ix) aging, telemedicine, sleep science, medical tourism, and memory recovery and removal will be the main trends to transform the 'healthcare domain'; (x) growth in tourist numbers, climate change, resource shortages, staying home and time versus money will be the main trends to transform the 'tourism domain'; and (xi) globalisation and connectivity, accelerating technological change, corporate social responsibility and governance, demographic shifts and work-life balance will be the main trends to transform the 'work domain'. Additionally, Watson (2012) insists that there are also some trends that will stand the test of the time and remain unchanged, at least into the 2060s or so. These trends include: an interest in the future and a yearning for the past; a desire for recognition and respect; the need for physical objects, actual encounters and live experiences; anxiety and fear; and a search for meaning.

Future of smart technologies

The digital revolution fulfilled the visions of many scientists and innovators, such as Ada Lovelace, Alan Turing, Vannevar Bush, JCR Licklider, Doug Engelbart and Steve Jobs, that computers would augment human intelligence as tools for both creativity and collaboration (Isaacson 2014). Computers have been rapidly evolving since the 1940s, along with technological developments in hardware, software and network solutions. The most significant developments include vacuum tubes in the 1950s, transistors in the 1960s, integrated circuit boards in the 1970s, microchips in the 1980s, the internet in the 1990s, ubiquitous computing in the 2000s and user-generated content in the 2010s.

The first generation of computers were machines that were only capable of counting and tabulating. The second generation involved programmable machines that we needed to tell what to do. These computers revolutionised the way we live. They shaped and are continuously shaping the way we socialise with each other, e.g. internet and social media; study and shop, e.g. e-learning, online shopping; do business, e.g. e-commerce; and plan and build our cities, e.g. smart cities. The third generation of computers will be the systems that do not need programming as they will have the ability to learn. In other words, they will be the computers with AI that can pass a Turing Test, a test of a machine's ability to exhibit intelligent behaviour equivalent to, or indistinguishable from, that of a human (see Turing 1950).

This also brings to mind the moral problem of intelligent machines. Van Doren (1992) rightfully raises some questions if/when we managed to develop intelligent machines that can think as successfully as a human being. Will they have rights? More specifically, will they have the right not to be turned off? Will there be AI rights, similar to human or animal rights? Steven Spielberg's 2001 movie *A.I. Artificial Intelligence*, Neill Blomkamp's 2015 movie *Chappie* and Alex Garland's 2015 movie *Ex Machina* reflect on these issues. There is also a greater possibility that AI may form in a different way, as a so-called 'human–computer symbiosis'. Human and computer intellect might be coupled together very tightly, and the resulting partnership thinks as no human brain has ever thought and processes data in a way not approached by the information handling machines we know of today (Isaacson 2014). According to Kurzweil (2005), this symbiosis is referred as 'singularity' and will happen in the year 2045, at which point progress will be so rapid that it will outstrip man's ability to comprehend it. The movie *Robocop*, the 2014 version directed by José Padilha, demonstrates this symbiosis.

The famous Moore's Law suggests that processor speeds or overall processing power for computers will double every two years (Schaller 1997). This has been correct since the 1970s and a further continuation of this trend will help bring about the third generation of computers, along with other developments including figuring out how to develop computers that can do both digital and analogue computation similar to a human brain. However, the third generation of computers is still at a distant future. Today, developments in second generation computers are quite remarkable and will help to pave the way for smarter cities in the future. For example, we are not that far from using internet glasses or even contact lenses to see the world the way *The Terminator* sees it through its robotic eyes (science fiction franchise created by James Cameron and Gale Anne Hurd). Google Glass Explorer Edition is the first commercially available version of this technology. An optical head is mounted on the glass that displays information in a smartphone-like hands-free format, and users communicate with the internet via voice commands (Google Developers 2015). This technology, when it is developed further and becomes easier to use, will make accessing information far easier and faster than ever.

Autonomous or driverless cars, i.e. the successful convergence of internet, GPS and sensing technologies on the body of a motor vehicle, are already on the streets in test drives, and it is expected they will be available to the general public in 2017 (Tam 2012). Of course, in order to have driverless cars, we also need to build smart road infrastructures and, fortunately, there is already significant progress on this front as well, for instance, the Smart Highway project in the Netherlands (http://www.smarthighway.net). Once all cars become driverless and are running on electric power on smart roads, traffic congestion and accidents and pollution generated by motor vehicles will things of the past.

While computers are getting smaller, their monitors and TV screens, on the contrary, are getting larger. Gigantic digital screens are already located in many city squares, e.g. Tokyo, Seoul, New York and Toronto, and many universities' digital interactive learning and display spaces, e.g. the CUBE in Brisbane (see http://www.thecube.qut.edu.au). Another use of this large screen technology is equipping all office and home walls with digital smart screens. The use of smart glasses along with these digital walls turns teleconferencing experience into a 3D telepresence. Along with 3D holograms, similar to those in the movie *Star Wars*, we will be able to see 3D images in our contact lenses, glasses or screen walls. This technology, for instance, will revolutionise distance learning, especially for people living in remote areas, on the assumption that they can access the technology. It will transform the collaborative work culture in companies and even research institutes by overcoming the tyranny of distance.

The mobile phone trend before smart phones was to make them as small as possible. With increased smart phone capabilities, phones are now becoming larger and also making tablets redundant. In the near future, flexible electronic paper-based displays could be an answer to reverse this trend, with smaller smart phones and foldable screens. Flexible electronic paper is a display using organic light-emitting diode (OLED) technology that mimics the appearance of ordinary ink on paper. Unlike conventional backlit flat panel displays that emit light, flexible electronic paper displays and reflects light like paper. The main issue with large displays is their lack of portability; however, with OLED technology a laptop or tablet could be just a simple sheet that can be folded and put into our wallets. This technology is already available. In 2011, Human Media Lab at Queen's University in Canada introduced PaperPhone, the first flexible smartphone, in partnership with the Arizona State University Flexible Display Centre (Daily Mail 2011). In 2014, Samsung introduced Galaxy Note Edge designing a dual-curved edged screen for the mobile phone and plans to release a big-screened smartphone in 2016 that folds in half to fit into a user's pocket (Mashable 2015). This innovation will help everyone to be able to carry a smart device at anytime and anywhere.

Wider use of sensing and RFID technologies are expected to expand the limits of ubiquitous computing. This will help in the expansion and wider use of smart urban technologies and systems and perhaps down the track, smart cities will become the norm. In those smart cities, we will most likely be living in a mixture of real and virtual reality. In other words, augmented reality will be part of our daily lives, with virtual images superimposed on the real world (Kaku 2012). This augmented reality technology will especially revolutionise tourism, art, shopping and warfare. Nobody will need a tourist guide in the future when visiting a city or sight; all information will be accessed from smart glasses, capturing visual and audio information transmitted in any language we would like. It will also work as a 'universal translator' for an instant translation of any language, much like in *Doctor Who*, *Farscape*, *The Hitchhiker's Guide to the Galaxy*, *Neuromancer*, *Star Control*, *Stargate* and *Star Trek*. Currently, Microsoft, Google, SpechGear, VoxOx and the US Army are investing in developing two-way translation technologies. In 2014, Skype launched 'Skype Translator' available in 4 spoken languages, i.e. English, Spanish, Italian and Mandarin, and 50 instant messaging (IM) languages (see http://blogs.skype.com/2015/05/12/skype-translator-preview-access-just-got-easier).

Another significant development will be seen in the popularity of and advancements in the virtual world. Today, Second Life, an online virtual world developed by Linden Lab that features 3D-based user-generated content, has over a million regular users (http://secondlife.com). Its users create virtual representations of themselves, called 'avatars', and are able to interact with other avatars, places or objects. They can explore the virtual world, meet other residents, socialise, participate in individual and group activities, build, create, shop and trade virtual property and services with one another (Wikipedia 2015). It is projected that by the mid-twenty-first century virtual life will be the biggest market on the planet, which may even be used in space missions (Giurgiu and Barsan 2008), much like in James Cameron's 2009 movie *Avatar*. Another competing development to avatars is to use 'surrogates' in the actual world and see and feel through their bodies. Although there are significant developments in the field of robotics, achieving fully functional surrogates will take a while. In Jonathan Mostow's 2009 movie *Surrogates* humans live in isolation and interact with each other and the rest of the world through their surrogate robots.

Even though the AI mission of scientists does not seem to be actualised in the near future, there is substantial progress in expert systems, which are specialised databases that are designed to mimic the expertise and knowledge of an expert to offer advice or make decisions. Today, a number of smart cities technologies and particularly decision systems are embedded with such expert systems. The emergency and safety response systems mentioned earlier of Istanbul and Rio de Janeiro are among the examples making use of expert systems. They are also used by medical professionals to diagnose patients correctly. Some health services even have websites that allow users to self-diagnose themselves (e.g. http://symptoms.webmd.com). Additionally, expert systems, also in the form of robots, are already around us. As indicated by Kaku (2012):

[t]oday, many people have simple robots in their homes that can vacuum their carpets. There are also robot security guards patrolling buildings at night, robot guides, and robot factory workers. In 2006, it was estimated that there were 950,000 industrial robots and 3,540,000 service robots working in homes and buildings.

(Kaku 2012: 77)

Jake Schreier's 2012 movie *Robot and Frank* examines the friendship between an elderly adult and a companion robot.

The trajectory is for a much wider use of robotic technologies, particularly in the health and defence sectors. For instance, an advanced version of ASIMO (see http://asimo.honda.com), branded as the world's most advanced humanoid robot, can be programmed as a robot nurse to be used in medical centres or in home care. At present, Japanese scientists and engineers are working on projects for the application of robotic technologies in aged care to provide much needed assistance in the areas of manual labour and personal care for the elderly. With Japan being a super-aged country, this has become a priority (Belardi 2014). Besides robotic technologies, the health problems of a rapidly aging world population will also be dealt with by genomic medicine, stem cell technology, gene therapy and, perhaps, by cloning bodies for spare human organs, which was the topic of Michael Bay's 2005 movie *The Island*.

Nanotechnology is another frontier where we may observe developments that could change our lives. Further exploration of the quantum world would help the placement of nano-machines in our bodies, for instance, to zap cancer cells, as in Richard Fleischer's 1966 movie *Fantastic Voyage*. Besides, nanotechnology could be used for building atomic transistors and quantum computers. According to Kaku (2012: 191), silicon chips, which are getting smaller and smaller as predicted by Moore's Law, will eventually fail, 'because wires and layers in chips are going down in size to the atomic scale, then [we will] start all over again and compute on atoms'. This will lead to the building of quantum computers, which accurately compute on individual atoms themselves. Kaku (2012) points out that 'optical computers', 'quantum dot computers' and 'DNA computers' are competing designs and approaches for building the quantum computer. Only then may we see the appearance of third generation computers as, 'the convergence of computing with robotics and nanotechnology (GRIN refers to Genetics, Robotics, Internet and Nanotechnology), which could give rise to self-replicating machines' (Watson 2012: 3).

Future of smart cities

In recent years, a number of scholars have questioned (e.g. Yigitcanlar and Lee 2014; Yigitcanlar 2015), based on current practices, whether the smart cities model is an ideal form on which to build the sustainable cities of the twenty-first century. Additionally, there are a number of influential books published with predictions on how the future might be like in the twenty-first century, some describing early decades, some mid-century and some beyond. These include authored books, such as *Future Shock* by Alvin Toffler (1970), *World Dynamics* by Jay Forrester (1971), *The Limits to Growth* by Donella Meadows *et al.* (1972), *Twenty-Ninth Day* by Lester Brown (1978), *The Third Wave* by Alvin Toffler (1980), *Megatrends* by John Naisbitt and Patricia Aburdene (1990), *Physics of the Future* by Michio Kaku (2012) and edited collections, such as *The Planet in 2050* by Jill Jäger and Sarah Cornell (2012) and *Urban Retrofitting for*

Sustainability by Tim Dixon *et al.* (2014). These writings help us visualise the future conditions, both in terms of prospects and constraints and also envisage what the future holds for bringing together 'technology and the city' and develop smarter cities. Below is an optimistic speculation, based on current technological developments and trends, of what an ideal future smart city might be like by the end of the century:

- We will finally abandon fossil fuel use for our increasing energy demands. Cities will be fully lit by renewable energy, e.g. solar, hydrogen, wind, geothermal, nuclear fission or even fusion power. Continent-wide 'super grids' will provide much of the world's energy needs (see Purvins *et al.* 2011). Today, investment on such green technologies is a national priority in countries including China and EU member states (see RBSC 2010).
- Smart buildings will revolutionise the urban landscape by being seamlessly integrated into a city's power supply, acting as another node in a citywide smart grid by transmitting locally produced energy back into the system. In such a system, there will be no need for cables, as energy will be beamed invisibly between buildings. Presently, there are major developments in wireless power transfer with applications for automotive, industrial, medical and military sectors (see http://witricity.com). For instance, some smart phones now come with wireless power charges, with power being transferred over short distances by magnetic fields.
- Cars will get smaller, safer, energy efficient, autonomous and intelligent. We will also figure out how to develop magnetic cars and trains. Innovators are already committed to replicating the hoverboard from Robert Zemeckis's 1989 movie *Back to the Future II*. A prototype was developed in 2015, i.e. Hendo 2.0 (see http://hendohover.com).
- Homes will be fully automated and self-sufficient. A typical home will include a localised power supply, on-site water production and waste management, a multilayered building envelope, which will provide a variety of dynamic effects, air purification systems, interactive surfaces, intelligent/self-maintaining appliances and be of a modest size (Future Timeline 2015). Current smart home initiatives constitute the pioneering attempts to develop these fully automated and self-sufficient homes.
- Self-reconfiguring modular robots will fix problems of the aging population or faulty urban infrastructure systems of our cities. In 2013, MIT scientists in Boston developed prototypes of such robots, autonomous kinematic machines with the ability to change their geometry according to the given task (Lomas 2013).
- Similar to the logic of self-reconfiguring modular robots, shape-shifting material will give us tools, toys, furniture, cars, buildings and many other possession items that can be transformed into different shapes and uses according to our desires. So-called 'catoms', 'claytronic atoms' or 'programmable matter' that change their density, energy levels, state of being and other characteristics using thought alone, will make this happen. Researchers at Carnegie

Mellon University in Pittsburgh have developed various prototypes of catoms, varying from small cubes to giant helium balloons (see http://www.cs.cmu.edu/~claytronics/hardware/helium.html).

- The global population will be stabilised at between nine and ten billion. Public health will be a critical issue, especially for the aging population. Health systems will be revolutionised by individuals using self-diagnosing technologies including handheld magnetic resonance imaging (MRI), or smart toothbrushes doing daily saliva tests to monitor our health. At present, a biosensor electrical toothbrush has been designed, which has a brush head with a test channel and a renewable biosensor system within the test channel for performing routine saliva tests (see Solanki 2012).
- In the smart cities of the late twenty-first century, crime will be almost non-existent, as surveillance will be everywhere. Such surveillance will also monitor internal biological state, such as neural activity and pulse, thus giving clues as to people's immediate or future intentions. Much like in Steven Spielberg's 2002 movie *Minority Report* police units will be able to arrest criminals before they commit their crimes.
- Roads and pavements will be immaculate as they are made of special smart materials that clean themselves, absorb garbage and could self-repair in the event of damage. Building surfaces, windows and roofs will be completely resistant to dirt, bacteria, weather, graffiti and vandalism. Street lighting will be more discreet, using a combination of self-illuminating walls, floors and surfaces made of self-illuminating fabricated solid material objects. Some building facades will change shape based on the desire of the voyeur, which will be achieved via augmented reality (which only the individual is aware of), claytronic surfaces and holographic projections (which everybody can see), or a combination of the two (Future Timeline 2015).
- Further advancements in the field of programmable matter will add intelligence to them so they remember previous shapes, adapt to new ones and respond to the designer's wishes. For example, instead of ordering a new computer or a bike, we will download the software programs and recycle the old one made of programmable matter to build a new one. According to Kaku (2012), this will significantly cut down on waste disposal. The smart and programmable matter (self-assembling buildings made 100 per cent from nanotech) will form the foundation blocks of the new generation of smart cities and will also revolutionise the way cities are planned and developed.

Despite these positive developments, climate change will still remain the major challenge for the survival of humans on the planet during the rest of the twenty-first century. This will give a spin on space exploration endeavours, and perhaps make possible the development of a large-scale civilian settlement on the Moon or elsewhere. Interstellar travel will most likely become possible in the early twenty-second century. As for the rest of the millennium and beyond, I would like to draw attention to the speculative lyrics of Zager and Evans' 1969 hit song *In the Year 2525* from the album *2525 Exordium and Terminus* (lyrics available at

http://www.lyricsmode.com/lyrics/z/zager_and_evans/in_the_year_2525.html).
In their song, Zager and Evans predict the twenty-sixth century as an era of struggle for survival; the thirty-sixth century as an era when our actions, words and
thoughts are pre-programmed; the forty-sixth century as an era when everyone
lives in a sophisticated virtual hyper-reality; the fifty-sixth century as an era when
our physical functions are replaced by machines; the sixty-sixth century as an era
of genetically enhanced children with no parents; the seventy-sixth century as an
era when our actions throughout the course of history are judged; the eighty-sixth
century as an era when people evolve into pure consciousness; and the ninety-
sixth century as an era when resources on the planet are entirely exhausted. The
song ends with the following stanza:

> *Now it's been 10,000 years*
> *Man has cried a billion tears*
> *For what he never knew*
> *Now man's reign is through*
> *But through eternal night*
> *The twinkling of starlight*
> *So very far away*
> *Maybe it's only yesterday*

Summary

At the beginning of the new millennium, the twenty-first century was labelled as
the 'century of cities', indicating the critical importance of urban agglomerations
that host the majority of the world's population. Along with rapid technological developments, the planning, design, development and management practices
of our cities are evolving. Today, the smart cities concept and movement is a
global phenomenon with many cities across the world adopting appropriate smart
technologies in their urban processes, with these technologies being economic,
societal, environmental and governance offerings. Examples presented and evaluated in earlier Chapters have shown that smart cities practice is still in its infancy,
due to technological hurdles on how to deliver a large-scale smart city together
with a lack of financial commitment and skepticism. This Chapter advocated the
continuing essential role of smart technologies and systems for our cities by projecting an imaginable future into the beginning of the next century. In summary,
we have just experienced a digital revolution that enabled us to generate basic
technology to consider the development of the main infrastructural items of smart
cities and societies. According to Isaacson (2014: 487–488), 'the next phase of
the Digital Revolution will bring even more new methods of marrying technology
with creative industries, such as media, fashion, music, entertainment, education,
literature, and the arts . . . enabling fresh opportunities for individual imagination
and collaborative creativity'. We shall enter this next phase in the mid-2030s.
This way we will be able to add 'character' or 'soul' to our smart cities and turn
them into unique, dynamic and intelligent urban spaces that are the cradles of

science, technology, engineering and mathematics and also arts to nourish our societies. As for the rest of the century and beyond, scientists and futurists have some ideas based on the continuation of existing trends and the appearance of new ones. These views are shared in this Chapter as speculative comments to end the story I started to tell in this book, investigating the interplay between 'technology and the city', which begins with early *homo sapiens* in 200,000 BC, continues with what Smith (2012) refers to as *homo urbanus* and ends in AD 10,000 with *homo luculentus* (smart human).

References

Belardi, L 2014, *Japan Eyes Robotic Future for Aged Care*, accessed on 5 November 2015 from http://www.australianageingagenda.com.au/2014/08/06/japan-eyes-robotic-future-aged-care

Brown, LR 1978, *The Twenty-Ninth Day: Accommodating Human Needs and Numbers to the Earth's Resources*, WW Norton and Company, New York.

Brunn, SD 2013, 'Geographies in 2050', *Progress in Geography*, vol. 32, no. 7, pp. 1006–1019.

Daily Mail 2011, *Flexible Future: Forget the iPhone, Here's the Smartphone Made out of 'Paper' That Will Shape With Your Pocket*, accessed on 4 November 2015 from http://www.dailymail.co.uk/sciencetech/article-1383903/PaperPhone-The-smartphone-paper-shape-pocket.html

Dixon, T, Eames, M, Hunt, M, Lannon, S (eds) 2014, *Urban Retrofitting for Sustainability: Mapping the Transition to 2050*, Routledge, New York.

Forrester, JW 1971, *World Dynamics*, Wright Allen, Cambridge, MA.

Future Timeline 2015, *2070–2079 Timeline Contents*, accessed on 12 November 2015 from http://www.futuretimeline.net/twenty-firstcentury/2070-2079.htm#.VkPXk7crJjU

Gerken J 2015, *Stephen Hawking Predicts Humans Won't Last Another 1,000 Years on Earth*, accessed on 9 November 2015 from http://www.huffingtonpost.com.au/2015/04/28/stephen-hawking-humanity-1000-years_n_7160870.html?ir=Australia

Giurgiu, L, Barsan, G 2008, 'The prosumer–core and consequence of the web 2.0 era', *Journal of Social Informatics*, vol. 9, no. 1, pp. 53–59.

Google Developers 2015, *Principles*, accessed on 4 November 2015 from https://developers.google.com/glass/design/principles

Isaacson, W 2014, *The Innovators*, Simon and Schuster, New York.

Jäger, J, Cornell, S (eds.) 2012, *The Planet in 2050: The Lund Discourse of the Future*, Routledge, New York.

Kaku, M 2012, *Physics of the Future: How Science Will Shape Human Destiny and Our Daily Lives by the Year 2100*, Pelican Books, London, UK.

Kurzweil, R 2005, *The Singularity is Near: When Humans Transcend Biology*, Viking, New York.

Lomas, N 2013, *MIT Scientists Create Modular Robot Blocks That Can Self-Assemble and Reconfigure*, accessed on 10 November 2015 from http://techcrunch.com/2013/10/04/m-blocks

Mashable 2015, *Samsung's Next Big Phone Could Have a Screen That Folds in Half*, accessed on 4 November 2015 from http://mashable.com/2015/09/15/samsung-foldable-display-phone/#J4eL8ciEWiqu

Meadows, DH, Meadows, DL, Randers, J, Behrens, WW 1972, *The Limits to Growth*, Universe Books, New York.

Naisbitt, J, Aburdene, P 1990, *Megatrends 2000*, William Morrow and Co., New York.

PIA (Planning Institute Australia) 2015, *What Is Planning?*, accessed on 14 October 2015 from https://www.planning.org.au/becomeaplanner

Purvins, A, Wilkening, H, Fulli, G, Tzimas, E, Celli, G, Mocci, S, Tedde, S 2011, 'A European supergrid for renewable energy: Local impacts and far-reaching challenges', *Journal of Cleaner Production*, vol. 19, no. 17, pp. 1909–1916.

RBSC (Roland Berger Strategy Consultants) 2010, *Green Growth, Green Profit: How Green Transformation Boosts Business*, Palgrave Macmillan, New York.

Sample, I 2015, *Stephen Hawking Launches $100m Search for Alien Life beyond Solar System*, accessed on 9 November from http://www.theguardian.com/science/2015/jul/20/breakthrough-listen-massive-radio-wave-project-scan-far-regions-for-alien-life

Schaller, RR 1997, 'Moore's law: Past, present and future', *IEEE Spectrum*, vol. 34, no. 6, pp. 52–59.

Smith, PD 2012, *City: A Guidebook for the Urban Age*, Bloomsbury, London.

Solanki, G 2012, 'Salivary glands – an overview', *International Journal of Biomedical and Advance Research*, vol. 3, no. 3, pp. 162–165.

Tam D 2012, *Google's Sergey Brin: You'll Ride in Robot Cars Within 5 Years*, accessed on 4 November from http://www.cnet.com/news/googles-sergey-brin-youll-ride-in-robot-cars-within-5-years

Toffler, A 1970, *Future Shock*, Amereon Ltd., New York.

Toffler, A 1980, *The Third Wave*, William Morrow and Co., New York.

Turing, AM 1950, 'Computing machinery and intelligence', *Mind*, vol. 59, no. 236, 433–460.

Van Doren, C 1992, *A History of Knowledge: Past, Present and Future*, Random House Publishing, Toronto, ON.

Watson R 2012, *Future Files: A Brief History of the Next 50 Years*, Nicholas Brealey Publishing, Boston, MA.

Wikipedia 2015, *Second Life*, accessed on 6 November 2015 from https://en.wikipedia.org/wiki/Second_Life

Yigitcanlar, T 2015, 'Smart cities: An effective urban development and management model?', *Australian Planner*, vol. 52, no. 1, pp. 27–34.

Yigitcanlar, T, Lee, S 2014, 'Korean ubiquitous-eco-city: A smart-sustainable urban form or a branding hoax?', *Technological Forecasting and Social Change*, vol. 89, no. 1, pp. 100–114.

Afterword

Our population and our use of the finite resources of planet Earth are growing exponentially, along with our technical ability to change the environment for good or ill.

(Stephen Hawking, theoretical physicist)

The volatile landscape of smart cities

The smart city, as a city planning model and emerging urban reality, is a paradigm in continuous transformation. In the Age of Intelligent Cities (Komninos 2014) it is identified that three waves of smart city technologies and corresponding solutions have appeared since the mid-1990s. *Wave 1* corresponds to the start of the web and the first commercial browsers, while the first digital cities were mainly static web pages providing information about the urban area through a combination of texts, data, maps, events and information services about commerce, recreation and city accommodation. Such digital cities were described as 'mirror-city metaphors' as their purpose was to represent the urban environment, offering a spatial intelligence based on the advantages of visualisation. *Wave 2* was marked by the rise of content management systems and web 2.0 solutions, which introduced a collaborative approach, enabling users to interact, exchange information and create virtual communities. Web 2.0 cities were based on social media applications that empowered citizens to improve local government responsibility and accountability. This type of solution is closer to the fundamental concept of the city as a social space of collaboration, offering opportunities for outsourcing and crowdsourcing. In *Wave 3*, technologies and smart city solutions turned to embedded systems, sensors and wireless networks, with cities becoming instrumented, interconnected and intelligent. With instrumentation, the working of the city is made measurable by sensors, smart devices and meters; with interconnection, all parts of a city communicate through wired and wireless networks; and intelligence refers to predictive modelling for forecasting and more informed decisions. The road opened towards the internet-of-things and cities started generating spatial intelligence from sensors, large data sets, analytics and real-time information and response.

A similar view on successive waves in the development of smart cities was recently presented by Cohen (2015), who argues that there are three distinct phases in how smart cities have embraced technology and development, moving from technology-driven, to city government-driven and, finally, to citizen-driven. Smart cities 1.0 were characterised by technology providers encouraging the adoption of their solutions to cities that were really not equipped to properly understand the implications of the technology and how they might impact on citizens' quality of life. Smart cities 2.0 were led by forward-thinking mayors and city administrators in the deployment of smart technologies and other innovations to improve the quality of life. In Smart Cities 3.0, the technology-driven approach or citizen co-creation model is where citizens replace the city-driven approach and users become developers or investors of solutions.

This continuous change also marks the priorities and strategic orientations of big smart city suppliers. Navigant Research (2014) points out that the supplier ecosystem for smart cities is continuously expanding, and established suppliers are moving into the market from the energy, transport, buildings and government sectors, while start-ups are addressing a range of emerging opportunities. The market is complex and dynamic, and top vendors include IBM, Cisco, Schneider Electric, Siemens, Microsoft, Hitachi, Huawei, Ericsson, Toshiba and Oracle.

On 21 August 2015, IBM Smarter Trends (see http://smartertrends.co.uk) closed down and will not be updated any more. Smarter Trends was launched in 2012 and within three years had published around 9,000 articles and over 200 videos on smart building, water management, renewable energy and energy efficiency, healthcare, telecommunications and transport. The aim was to be at the forefront of the green revolution and bring articles and discussions from the world's leading authorities. Now it seems that the orientation has changed and Smarter Trends is being replaced by People4Smarter Cities (see http://people 4smartercities.com), with the focus shifting from technologies to people, from administration to users, from city leaders to the common people (who are city lovers) and from digital solutions for cities to integrated physical-digital systems.

A change also took place in the strategic priorities of Cisco. In 2009, the company launched the global 'Intelligent Urbanisation' initiative, which was designed to help cities around the world by using broadband networks as a utility for integrated city management, better quality of life for citizens and economic development. Then, the company moved to the 'Smart + Connected Communities' initiative, and new models for Smart + Connected Communities are shaped within the 'internet-of-everything' (IoE) approach, with high-level IoE architecture, end-to-end city networks and solutions for smart parking, smart mobility, street smart-light management, sensor-based waste management and environment monitoring (Danaraj 2014).

All these changes indicate that the landscape of smart cities and city intelligence is volatile; technologies and architectures evolve quickly; and leading organisations adapt to upcoming trends and possibilities offered by ICTs and innovative business models. On the other hand, the implementation landscape of smart cities is very fragmented. Most cities are implementing pilot rather than large-scale projects, whose maturity stage can be characterised as 'ad hoc' implementation of department-based discrete projects, or 'opportunistic' project deployment (Clarke

2013). Together with the setting of broadband networks, most popular projects are those offering e-services for transportation (e.g. smart parking, real-time traffic information systems), government (e.g. citizen complaints and requests, online administration services), health and social care, e-marketplaces and cost-effective city utilities (e.g. water supply, waste collection, street lighting).

Besides this volatility, it is feasible to outline some key directions of change and speculate, with some certainty, about upcoming trends in the smart city landscape over a medium-term horizon. We will attempt this exercise in foresight, which might be useful in strategic planning and future plans for cities, by taking into account the structure and operation of smart cities; how the actual stack of technologies is evolving; how it modifies the innovation system of cities; and how the major urban sub-systems of production, living, networking and governance adapt to these changes.

The evolving digital space of cities

It is possible to describe the digital space of cities as a structured edifice composed of successive concentric rings. At the centre are broadband networks, wired and wireless infrastructure and access devices enabling communication, data collection and data exchange. A second ring includes web technologies and platforms enabling authentication, data storage, data integration, processing and visualisation. The third ring is composed of digital applications and solutions in many different domains of the city, from entrepreneurship to education, healthcare, transportation, energy, public safety and others. Then comes data that feed applications, provided by people, social media, sensors and the public administration. The outer ring comprises e-services as only a few applications that work with viable business models are offered on a regular basis as e-services.

Key instances of the current technology and data stack that characterise this digital edifice are: (i) 3G and 4G wireless networks and next generation networks (VDSL2, FTTH), i.e. network interoperability enabling internet usage everywhere; (ii) mobile devices enabling ubiquitous access to data and the web; (iii) cloud-based infrastructure, platforms and software for data storage, integration, processing and analytics; (iv) real-world user interfaces, QR codes over buildings, RFID, mesh sensor networks, low energy consumption meters and control devices; (v) applications for smart phones, GPS devices, voice control, augmented reality visualisation, and responsive design or hybrid applications for the web and smart phones; and (vi) the opening of public data over the web, open access to data from sensors, linked data and semantic web with RDF, SPARQL, OWL and μFormats for M2M communication of embedded devices.

With these technologies, smart cities are coming closer to 'future internet' research, offering a large domain of experimentation for the internet-of-things. The spatial intelligence of cities is moving out of web applications and entering into the domain of data: the meaning of data becomes part of data; data are provided just in time; real-time data enable real-time responses.

Looking ahead, the technology hype cycles published by Gartner (2015b) indicate that the internet-of-things and cloud computing are among the most important trends of the current technology shift in smart cities (see Table 8.1). A new group of applications, such as location-aware applications, near field communication, speech recognition, internet micro payment systems and mobile application stores, which are close to mainstream market adoption, are expected to offer a wide range of new e-services via embedded systems. Augmented reality is also becoming a hot topic, enabled by smart phones and eyeglasses, and is creating next generation location-aware information and services projected over the built space of cities (Gartner 2010, 2012a, 2012b, 2015a).

These technologies introduce new promises and expectations in solving problems of the growth, equity and sustainability of cities. In Europe, the digital agenda foresees that by 2020 all Europeans should have access to internet speeds above 30 Mbps, and by 2020, at least 50 per cent of European households should subscribe to internet connections above 100 Mbps; 75 per cent of the population should be using the internet regularly; 50 per cent should be using e-government; and one-third of SMEs should be selling online (DAE 2013). A lot has also been said about cities becoming measurable systems with Big Data provided by sensors. However, we are still far away from the realisation of these targets, while critical reviews highlight the challenges related to sensor-based smart city solutions (Newcombe 2014). Technologies advance more rapidly than the social acceptance of smart city solutions and only a few new business models enable the offer of technology solutions as affordable e-services. Technology push still dominates the smart city landscape, which is expected to be demand-driven. Nevertheless, disruptions are already visible in the way cities change their innovation systems and daily routines, and new solutions are being offered to urban challenges.

Smart cities and digital disruption of innovation systems

Smart urban environments and broadband networks disrupt established innovation ecosystems by introducing significant changes in their building blocks, networks and nodes. A direct outcome is the enrichment of urban systems of innovation with digital 'partners' and the formation of physical-digital (cyber-physical or hybrid) innovation systems. This happens because innovation micro networks at city level meet with global digital networks. Moreover, digital identities enrich innovation processes and commercialisation; crowdsourcing brings in additional capabilities; and passive consumers turn into active producers of services. In a few words, the nodes of the innovation system of cities increase geometrically and the capacity for innovation is substantially improved.

Physical-digital systems of innovation decision making and the governance of urban change evolve towards higher levels of networking, collaboration and efficiency. All components of the urban system of innovation, research, funding, supply chain, production capability and market reach, are digitally augmented: online technology brokers enhance R&D; crowdfunding is added to mainstream funding; global suppliers enrich the supply chains; and digital marketing and online

Table 8.1 Smart city technologies at different stages of Gartner's hype cycles

Technology Trigger	Peak of Inflated Expectations	Trough of Disillusionment	Slope of Enlightenment	Plateau of Productivity
• Cloud security integration • Information semantic services • Wi-Fi positioning systems • Smart government frameworks	• Internet of things • Real-time infrastructure • Big Data management for government • Augmented reality • Information stewardship applications	• Cloud computing • Virtual assistants • Mesh networks • Consumer generated media • Machine-to-machine communication • Advanced metering	• SaaS • Cloud advertisement • Security as a service • Visualisation • Speech recognition • Idea management	• Location-aware technology • Predictive analytics

marketplaces enlarge regional and national markets. Most of these digital actors are already there, offering e-services that add information, capacity for communication, trade and transactions, and delivery of services and products.

Incumbent companies and start-ups have to operate within this physical-digital innovation environment that disrupts established business models and practices of funding, technology acquisition and market making. Looking forward, the balance between the physical and digital components of the innovation system will dramatically change in favour of the digital. Moreover, navigation within the universe of digital assistants will become more complex and demanding.

A special issue of the *Digital Transformation Review* (Capgemini Consulting 2015) and a series of reports on digital business transformation (Networked Society Lab 2015) highlight how digital disruptions make sense for all companies (a trend we have called 'innovation-for-all') and explore the nature and context of the current digital disruption and the most effective strategic response to ongoing disruptions.

Within smart city environments, the 'platform logic' prevails in business models, which is to create products and services that can serve as a basis for other products and services. The more businesses are using a platform, the more the platform becomes a self-sustaining and open business ecosystem. Promotion of business built on top of a platform entails promotion and sustainability of the platform. Where the city has been the platform for business development, now clouds in the smart city offer open platforms for business growth. Instant scalability and pay-per-use allow for the hosting of any size of digital identities, business transactions, data and analytics. Instead of being an agglomeration of individual businesses, the city is becoming a swarm of business platforms, and hybrid business ecosystems and clusters.

Distributed forms of organisation arise within smart city environments offering high connectivity and opportunities for collaboration. United by a common purpose and mission, a team of digitally connected workers can collaborate and innovate from anywhere. Even small companies can adopt distributed forms of organisation using existing platforms: Facebook for intranet; Dropbox as document repository; Amazon as a cloud; Google docs for collaboration; Salesforce and LinkedIn for product promotion. Distributed organisations attract talented personnel, engineers, programmers and marketers from everywhere and anywhere; user-experience design and user-driven innovation replace packaging and store design. With an open innovation approach, technologies can be retrieved from local university research repositories or global technology brokers, such as yet2com and Innocentive. Crowdsourcing platforms allow for citizen participation in innovation and support the entire cycle of innovation, from funding (e.g. crowdfunding), ideas generation (e.g. idea platforms, prediction markets, content markets and content rating), collaborative product development (e.g. distributed innovation, innovation prizes and competition platforms) and product launch (e.g. crowdsourcing aggregators, micro-tasks and service marketplaces). With extended outsourcing and crowdsourcing, city production complexes evolve towards user-driven communities of practice.

Within smart city environments, demand, customers and users rather than suppliers drive innovations. With the spread of augmented reality solutions and the internet-of-things, all products become hybrid, combining a physical and a virtual identity. The generation of a sea of digital identities is redefining markets and marketing. Using the web, companies and advertisers attempt to insert themselves into the flow of interactions by understanding and practising digital marketing. 'Intention markets' are created, where buyers notify the market of the intent to buy, and sellers compete for the buyers' attention. Such markets grow around buyers, not around sellers. Potential sellers, even those that are not on the market, can capture these signs and contract production before it is being produced. The market-push logic changes to a demand-driven logic. The rise of open marketplaces, content-driven marketing, social media marketing and on-demand manufacturing highlight the priority given to consumers and the transition towards the economy of intention and attention (Bauwens *et al.* 2012).

The disruption of urban systems

Smart city technologies, applications, open data and smart environments, and innovation-for-all modes describe the domain of capabilities and possibilities. But, they are having a tangible impact on the modification of routines that make the urban systems of production, living, networking and governance work.

Cities and communities rest upon routines, established sets of activities by which organisations are engaged in the provision of products or services over extended periods of time. Routines are patterns of production, but also patterns of consumption, lifestyle, mobility and government. Some routines, be they static or dynamic, change bottom-up, as companies, public organisations and institutions adopt smart technologies and smart city business models. Others change top-down, as local and regional authorities launch smart city planning initiatives that revitalise sectors of the economy, districts and the services that cities offer. Smart cities emerge from this convergence of bottom-up and top-down modification of routines, introduced by the market, city stakeholders and city authorities.

It is possible to identify how city routines actually change by observing a small group of cities that lead the experimentation towards smart cities (e.g. Amsterdam, Barcelona, Santander, New York and Singapore); the solutions offered by smart city technology suppliers; and the European research and experimentation related to 'future internet' and the Smart Cities and Communities lighthouse initiatives. These data highlight three high-impact trends.

The first trend is smart growth. It is the disruption of urban economy sectors one after the other, due to the diffusion of smart city technologies and collaborative business models. Uber is disrupting the transportation market by turning citizens into transport service providers. Airbnb is disrupting the hospitality and real estate markets by bringing in unutilised fixed capital investments in housing. These companies are black swans that use the internet to innovate radically in their sector. Some city authorities encourage these disruptions, but others try to delay them. In vain though, because both disruptions are rooted in market imbalances that smart environments reveal and help adjust. Where market imbalances or brokerage business models prevail, smart growth disruption is underway. Financial and insurance services, commerce and healthcare will probably follow. In the sphere of smart growth, the real challenge is to 'discover' how smart city technologies and business models (based on access rather than ownership) will affect key sectors of the urban economy and the specialised districts of cities (e.g. ports, campuses, CBD and industrial and science zones) and prepare business clusters and individual companies to operate within smart urban environments.

The second is the rise of the zero culture systems. This is the pursuit of a better quality of life and place through practices leading to zero CO_2 emissions, zero waste, zero fatal traffic accidents, zero aggression in the public space of cities and other improvements in city life. Zero vision action plans are multidepartmental and multidimensional. They combine institutional rules and ethics, responsibility by all city actors, policymakers and citizens, law enforcement, minimising errors with technology, real-time alert and intervention, sensor networks and detection equipment, as well as new infrastructure design. Such action plans can be achieved through distributed systems that connect urban infrastructure, citizen practice and smart city technologies under the umbrella of common goals and measurable targets to achieve sustainable urban development.

The third trend is the deployment of platforms that integrate distributed capabilities and resources in the domains of energy and mobility in particular. Take, for instance, the energy sector. Deploying smart grids or micro-grids, city districts can introduce a decentralised model of energy production that combines the supply of renewable energy from local resources (e.g. solar, wind, waste), refurbishment of existing buildings to reduce energy spending, smart systems for energy optimisation, building management systems, the active participation of citizens in energy saving with smart metering and solutions enabling improved management, control and maintenance, visualisation, data sharing and analysis. Moreover, the connection of smart power and mobility becomes feasible through the integration, over the micro-grid, of fuelling infrastructure for vehicle fleets using alternative energy fuels, and transport sharing solutions and collaboration logistics. Distributed energy districts offer an alternative future to conventional centralised energy production based on high-polluting coal or high-risk nuclear plants, with enormous environmental advantages.

Towards smart urban futures

Aforementioned trends in the urban economy, quality of life and urban utilities are ongoing and the scale-up is expected to profoundly affect the immediate future of cities. City authorities and the management boards of semi-autonomous city districts should focus on these systemic changes rather than on individual smart city applications and projects. There is a need for strategy and leadership, strategic policies and plans that will integrate bottom-up initiatives at company

⌣ or organisation level with planned projects by various stakeholders, not just the public administration, under a coherent vision for the future of the ecosystems that make up each city. The critical question is not about implementing on-the-shelf smart city solutions, but learning to innovate with smart environments, capabilities distributed among organisations, people and machines, and collaborative business models. This approach will better support the success of the smart cities movement and also create desired smart urban futures.

Professor Nicos Komninos
Aristotle University of Thessaloniki, Greece

References

Bauwens, M, Iacomella F, Mendoza, N, Burke, J, Pinchen, C, Léonard, A, Mootoosamy, E 2012, *Synthetic Overview of the Collaborative Economy, Chiang Mai: P2P Foundation*, accessed on 1 September 2015 from http://p2pfoundation.net/Synthetic_Overview_of_ the_Collaborative_Economy

Capgemini Consulting 2015, 'Strategies for the age of digital disruption', *Digital Transformation Review*, vol. 7, no. 1, pp. 1–90.

Clarke, RY 2013, *Smart Cities and the Internet Of Everything: The Foundation for Delivering Next-Generation Citizen Services. IDC Government Insights*, accessed on 1 September 2015 from http://www.cisco.com/web/strategy/docs/scc/ioe_citizen_ svcs_white_paper_idc_2013.pdf

Cohen, B 2015, *Three Generations of Smart Cities: Inside the Development of the Technology Driven City*, accessed on 1 September 2015 from http://www.fastcoexist. com/3047795/the-3-generations-of-smart-cities

DAE (Digital Agenda for Europe) 2013, *Scoreboard*, accessed on 1 September 2015 from https://ec.europa.eu/digital-agenda/sites/digital-agenda/files/Digital%20Agenda%20 Targets%20Overall%202013%20v10%20with%20scale_2.jpg

Danaraj, J 2014, *The Internet of Everything for Cities: Towards New Models for Smart + Connected Communities*, accessed on 1 September 2015 from http://www.cisco.com/ web/AP/IoEWebinarSeries/docs/smart_connected_communties.pdf

Gartner 2010, *Gartner's 2010 Hype Cycle. Special Report Evaluates Maturity of 1,800 Technologies*, accessed on 1 September 2015 from http://www.gartner.com/newsroom/ id/1447613

Gartner 2012a, *Gartner's 2012 Hype Cycle for Emerging Technologies*, accessed on 1 September 2015 from http://www.gartner.com/newsroom/id/2124315

Gartner 2012b, *Hype Cycle for Smart City Technologies and Solutions 2012*, accessed on 1 September 2015 from https://www.gartner.com/doc/2098315

Gartner 2015a, *Gartner's Hype Cycles for 2015: Five Megatrends Shift the Computing Landscape*, accessed on 7 September 2015 from https://www.gartner.com/doc/3111522? srcId=1-3132930191

Gartner 2015b, *Internet of Things*, accessed on 17 November 2015 from http://www. gartner.com/technology/research/internet-of-things

Komninos, N 2014, *The Age of Intelligent Cities*, Routledge, New York.

Navigant Research 2014, *Leaderboard Report: Smart City Suppliers – Assessment of Strategy and Execution for 16 Smart City Suppliers*, accessed on 1 September 2015 from https://www.reportbuyer.com/product/2480916/navigant-research-leaderboard-report-smart-city-suppliers-assessment-of-strategy-and-execution-for-16-smart-city-suppliers.html

Networked Society Lab 2015, *Digital Disruptors: Models of Digital Operations. Ericsson*, accessed on 1 September 2015 from http://www.ericsson.com/res/docs/2014/digital-disruptors.pdf

Newcombe, T 2014, *Can We Trust Smart Cities?*, accessed on 1 September 2015 from http://www.govtech.com/data/Can-We-Trust-Smart-Cities.html

Index